AMERICAN WALL STENCILING, 1790–1840

American Wall Stenciling, 1790–1840

Ann Eckert Brown

UNIVERSITY PRESS OF NEW ENGLAND   HANOVER AND LONDON

University Press of New England, 37 Lafayette St., Lebanon, NH 03766

© 2003 by University Press of New England

Printed and bound in Spain by Bookprint S.L., Barcelona

5 4 3 2 1

LIBRARY OF CONGRESS CATALOGING-IN-PUBLICATION DATA

Brown, Ann Eckert.

American wall stenciling, 1790–1840 / Ann Eckert Brown.

p.   cm.

Includes bibliographical references and index.

ISBN 1–58465–194–6 (alk. paper)

1. Stencil work—United States. 2. Decoration and ornament, Early
American. 3. Mural painting and decoration, American—18th century.
4. Mural painting and decoration, American—19th century. 5. Decoration
and ornament, Architectural—United States. I. Title: Wall stenciling.
II. Title.

NK8662 . B76 2003

745.7'3'09730903—dc21   2002010580

Throughout the book, photographs and facsimilies without credits are by the author.

This project received support from Furthermore, the publication program of The J. M. Kaplan Fund.

FRONTISPIECE: Panel of original stenciling, circa 1810, from an eighteenth-century house in
Loudon, New Hampshire. The panel is 32 inches wide by 44 inches high, in distemper and
pigmented white wash on original horsehair plaster. It was found in 2001 in a second-floor
bed chamber under numerous layers of wall paper. The name of the artist isn't known.

Dedicated with love and appreciation

to my husband, Henry A. L. Brown,

historian, author,

and

"chauffeur extraordinaire"

❦

In memory of

Janet McLellan Phillips

June 11, 1949–March 26, 2000

Contents

Foreword

Except for severe bouts of twentieth-century minimalism, which, like drought, can drain life of color and refreshment, an expanse of bare white wall is anathema. It begs to be ornamented, designed upon, even made splendid. Instinctively, our eyes follow pattern: forced to look at an acoustic tile ceiling, staring at a wood-grained door, we see rhythms, patterns, and designs even if they aren't there. How much better, then, if they really are, executed in color, embellishing rooms, and enriching those who live in them. No wonder enterprising American painters sought clients for their work, advertised their skills, exploited the fashion for wallpaper and freehand ornament by copying them and beating the price for thrifty homeowners. Before the Revolution they painted walls for their living, if not their fortune, and the stencil, a technique as ancient as prehistory, was the expedient way to decorate a roomful, a houseful of walls. That there were more of these rooms and houses than we knew is just part of Ann Eckert Brown's achievement in this book.

My first impression of early American stenciling came from the black-and-white pictures in Janet Waring's seminal 1937 book, *Early American Stencils on Walls and Furniture*. It was a discovery for me, a way to identify a lost reality—until then, I had seen only 1970s efforts by homeowners with more zeal than information. Because of the innately grim quality of the halftone photographs, the pictures were even more convincing: they looked like old, decaying plaster.

The first (and last) time I ever attempted stenciling was in order to write about it for *Early American Life* magazine. I believe in experiencing something before you can expect others to read about it; so I cut stencils from file-folder cardboard, and outside my office, near the ladies' room, along an industrial buff and Necco Wafer–green back wall where surely no one would care, I traced the design with colored pencils in lieu of paint. But when I encountered a corner and wondered "now what?" I understood on a practical level the sure-handed inventiveness of the old guys, the motif makers, reassemblers, elaborators, and the innovative design wizards named Eaton, and Stimpson, Leroy, and Gleason, "Birdman" of Loudon, and the ubiquitous great "Unknown." I quit at the corner; the illustrations you hold in your hands will show you what they did.

That was twenty years ago. Since then I have learned about stenciled walls by being in a dozen old houses and taverns that still have them, most of them described in this book. I have been in a room decorated with Masonic symbols for nineteenth-century Masons; awakened in a pink-walled room bordered with gray, black, and crimson stencils older than the towering old maple outside the bedroom window; stopped at the threshold of an elaborately stenciled floor as old as the original floorboards, unwilling to add my wear to their slowly vanishing surface. For today's owner of an antique house, the discovery of an early stenciled wall—even a fragment, a shadow of one—is revelation, a shard of the tangible past. Engaging a restorer (often excitedly calling the magazine to get references), the owner frames part of the phantom under glass for future reference. Surrounded by the re-created stenciled room, it becomes the ancestor portrait of a design. Sometimes, the discovery is loose pieces of plaster, the reference for the restorer, carefully stored in a drawer like pieces of a puzzle, or a section of wall still vivid, not having been exposed to light since a cupboards was placed in front of it more than a century ago. This is what was here, the ephemeral evidence says. Behold the restoration of its former glory.

And glorious it was. Many portraits of early Americans in their homes are *of* their homes, for we see walls and furniture, ornament, carpet, pets, teacups. Portraits that show stenciled walls are persuasive as well as charming. Looking at the rooms in perspective in Joseph Leavitt's 1824 painting of the interior of the Moses Morse house in Loudon, New Hampshire, or Jacob Maentel's elderly Rebekah Jacquess in her Indiana parlor, is as good as being there. Pictures so vivid, so literal, both convince and welcome us, for they are warm rather than elegant. It is not untoward to think of staying for dinner. Maentel was a wonderful observer, integrating the setting with the sitter. consider, for example, his portrait of General Schumacker's daughter (page 156), holding her book away from her body as an icon of her learning and, therefore, her status, standing before a window bordered with a pattern of latticework and festooned with painted pink roses. The wainscoting is faux painted to imitate bird's-eye maple. This is a feminine painting: swags of roses echo other curves—the bowback Windsor chair, Miss Schumacker's fashionable empire dress with a modest scarf tucked into the bosom, and her undeniable double chin. It is a genre scene we trust and understand to be the way it must have looked in Pennsylvania in 1812.

Discovering original material in an antique house involves carefully peeling away layers of modernization that "freshened up" and therefore disguised its early decoration. Brown notes the irony of finding early stenciling after removing generations of "the very thing it had been intended to replace"—wallpaper. But the history of wallpaper and stenciling chase each other through the centuries. Stenciling, preferable to wallpaper for "not harboring vermin," nonetheless freely borrowed wallpaper motifs and crossbred them. Successive generations of wallpaper, which became increasingly more affordable after the Industrial Revolution, covered stenciled walls, hiding them, obliterating some and preserving others. Brown notes of a Connecticut house in which the layer of wallpaper covering the stencil design retained its outline: "there was, then, no need to trace the stenciling inside the house, in poor light and amid thirty years' accumulation of dust and mod." Instead, she removed "large sections of the stencil-backed paper to study . . . and to preserve."

Ann Brown continues a trail blazed by early decorative historians such as Janet Waring, Esther Stevens Brazer, and Nina Fletcher Little, as well as others (there is an excellent appendix of these important individuals). They, like Brown, were and often still are members of the Historical Society of Early American Decoration (HSEAD), but she has extended the territory. Many years of concentrated study have enabled the extension of her research to new regions or insufficiently explored ones and allowed her to make fresh stylistic connections between designs, artists, regions, and houses. Her approach, dividing stenciling into folk art and classically inspired, makes social sense, the classical patterns being urban,

more refined in scale, and earlier in execution, echoing the images of Federal style (indeed, the vocabulary of fine furniture inlay—bellflowers, urns, swags, fans, reeded columns, shields—is identical). Folk-art stenciling, by contrast, is boisterous, rural, uses naturalistic, sometimes primitive, sometimes ethnically derived motifs; it's often larger than life. It's more fiddle than violin, more earthenware than china.

Research into American stenciling is relatively recent, and the beginnings were esoteric. Only aficionados of painted design knew about the body of work established by Esther Brazer; the meticulous scholarship of Nina Fletcher Little was published twenty-five years after Janet Waring's 1937 book, and Little's account of new discoveries added a chapter to the second edition of her book in 1972. It seems to me Ann Brown's contribution adds to our sense of the diversity of this domestic decorative art: there are more designs than we knew, they have a greater geographical penetration than we suspected, and they were more prevalent.

Stenciled walls were a product of prosperity. Besides being primarily about design, the entries in this book are populated. Here are American houses and taverns and inns, all occupied over nearly three centuries by families, descendants, artists and *their* descendants, by rescuers, restorers. Preservationists—and visitors like us, enjoying what remains. The result is a book that fairly hums with life and purpose.

Moreover, the designs, like their artists, were itinerant. The progress of wall stenciling followed the progress of roads, rivers, canals, and coastal trading ships; America's burgeoning commercial routes were traveled by decorative artists as well as peddlers and settlers. Like a vigorous vine, these routes grew the beginnings of communities in the hinterlands of a growing nation. Following the wall decorators who must have taken them, Brown brings us, too, along roads and byways long gone. For stencil artists, they linked New England to western Connecticut and New York. they reached into Canada and into southeastern Ohio and the Western Reserve, into Pennsylvania, even well below the Mason-Dixon line for what are so far only a few surviving, but striking, examples. For us, the vanished routes get us into houses that were new in 1800 or 1820, or refurbished for a new republic in a new century. As if we were on a house tour for time travelers, we visit taverns with stenciled ballrooms, climb stairways with risers stenciled in imitation of carpet, walk hallways brilliant with painted designs in imitation of wallpaper. In remote hamlets recently settled, we admire classical urns and eagles in rural New Hampshire, bells and tassels suspended from festoons in New York. We can't help but realize, with a sense of immediacy, the cultural astonishment of the discoveries at Pompeii in the late eighteenth century. The profound influence of that ancient buried color and ornament shows up in, of all places, remote corners of early America.

Stencil sleuths are intrepid adventurers into derelict buildings. Brown writes with satisfaction of a house she couldn't get into on her first try; years later advanced decay made it "possible to gain entrance through a hole in the front door." It revealed gorgeous discoveries amidst the ruins—swags and reeded columns, vines, Greek-key borders. On a basic level, it isn't easy to explore a derelict house unless, perhaps, you are an eleven-year-old. Floors sag and crumble underfoot, rooms can be dark, filthy, and in all ways unpleasant. For all but the most dedicated and purposeful old-house buff, there's nothing to be gained but a sigh of relief on emerging. The knowledge of what they once were makes such houses even more difficult to endure. I saw the vast Rider Tavern in Charlton, Massachusetts, before the wonderful preservation efforts took hold. It had been divided into apartments and fallen into sorry shape, and the empty, dusty, stenciled ballroom on the upper floor was as poignant as an accident victim in the soiled rags of a formal gown.

The dedicated antiquarian has, as well, a single-minded way of restructuring history, tracing a woven coverlet design, the carving on a Queen Anne chair, the shape of a table leg, or the framing details of a building, from one time and place—and human hand—to another. From these fragmentary bits of evidence, tales can be told—and substantiated. The chronicler of design history is no different and, like these other historians of material culture, has an archive of stylistic references to draw upon. They—and I count Ann Brown among them—have the archives at their fingertips and in their head. In the truest sense, they have it by heart, and we are the beneficiaries. Brown gives us a genealogy of design relationships and similarities in shapes—leaves, festoons, flowers and fans—as well as the more abstract record of their juxtapositions, density, size, and spacing. Her absolute familiarity with the myriad variations of folk and classical designs as well as their migrations, her ability to place them in context, is a great advantage to those of us who are glad to know about what remains of these bright, lively images from the quickly receding American past.

Mimi Handler

Acknowledgments

The accumulation of names of persons and institutions that have helped an author on a project that has been ongoing for more than a quarter century is considerable.

However, those private homeowners who are on the front line in the preservation of Federal-period American wall stenciling are the primary source for this book, and deserving of the highest accolades. They warmly welcomed the author into their homes and generously and enthusiastically shared their stenciled walls and knowledge, making the gathering of information and images not just possible but extremely gratifying and enjoyable.

Listed by states (and Canada) in the order they appear in the book, starting with Rhode Island, they are: Jeffrey and Linda Booker, Mr. and Mrs. Vasanth Rao, Mr. and Mrs. Walter R. Hohler, Jr., Norman Saute, Mr. and Mrs. Max King, Erica Gregg and Joseph Tamburini, Marjorie P. MacDonald, Dr. and Mrs. Kuppenburg, Lucille and Dale Harter, Robert and Jan Francher, Robert and Viola Lynch, Lombard John Pozzi, Daniel and Kirsten Romani, Pamela T. Dumas, Mr. and Mrs. Thomas Steere, Martha Grossel and Marilyn Weigner.

Massachusetts: John D. Murphy, Mr. and Mrs. David Kmetz, Thurston Twigg-Smith, Joseph Bosworth.

Connecticut: Edd and Karan Oberg, R. Joe Green, Douglas and Linda Marshall, Eugene and Gemma Baker, Robert and Stacey duBell Mileti, Mr. and Mrs. Adam Williams, Mr. and Mrs. Dennis Scranton.

Maine: Mr. and Mrs. William C. Thomas, Mr. and Mrs. Terry Nadeau, Mr. and Mrs. Peter Blatchford, Jeffery and Mary Parsons.

New Hampshire: Mr. and Mrs. T. Holmes Moore, Mr. and Mrs. Peter Doyle, Jeanne and Peter Jeffries, Dutchie Perron, Esther T. Howard, Mr. and Mrs. John Harris, Jacob Atwood, Mr. and Mrs. Edward Robinson.

Vermont: Barbara Green, John Hausenstein.

New York: Ted A. McDowell, Ronald and Jane Towner, Edward and Carol Pfeffer, Daniel M. Barber.

Canada: Jon Jouppien, James and Arlene Harrison, Nicholas Traynor.

Pennsylvania: Ralph and Karen Artuso, Jane L. Murphy, Wesley T. Sessa, Ray G. Hearne.

Maryland: Barbara Davidson, Mr. and Mrs. Stuart B. Abraham.

Virginia: Roberta Hamlin, Mrs. Virginia Cadden, Mr. and Mrs. Robert Tate, Mr. and Mrs. Roy C. Burner.

South Carolina: Frank and Lisa Wideman.

Ohio: Richard and Diane Oberle, Mr. and Mrs. James Eppley, Dr. Ann Grooms.

Kentucky: Mr. and Mrs. Charles Newkirk, John and Jane Diehl, Mrs. Anne Richmond.

Tennessee: Tracey Parks.

Special thanks to: Robert Hunt Rhodes, Walpole, New Hampshire; Polly Forcier, Quechee, Vermont; Mimi Handler, former editor of *Early American Life* magazine; Ed Hood, research historian, Old Sturbridge Village, Massachusetts; Nancy and Abe Roan, Bechtelsville, Pennsylvania; the late Clay Lancaster, Warwick, Kentucky; Phillip Parr, Caledonia, New York; Jon Joupien, St. Catherines, Ontario; Phyllis Deutsch, University Press of New England.

Historical and preservation organizations: Rhode Island Historic Preservation Commission; Rhode Island Historical Society; Historical Society of Smithfield, Rhode Island; Patricia Lucas, Blandford Historical Society, Massachusetts; Sarah Griswald, former curator of the Gunn Memorial Library and Museum, Washington, Connecticut; William W. Jenney, Calvin Coolidge Historic Site, Plymouth, Vermont; Kevin E. Jordan, Roger Williams University Historic Preservation Program, Bristol, Rhode Island; Robert E. Smith, Palatine Settlement Society, St. Johnsville, New York; Rochester Museum and

Science Center, New York; Catherine Eckert, Historic Shaefferstown, Inc., Pennsylvania; Mr. Hubbard, Commonwealth of Virginia, Department of Historical Resources; Joe Williams, curator, Appomattox Court House National Historical Park, Virginia; Tracey Parks, Historic Cragfont, Inc., Castalian Springs, Tennessee; Claudette Stager, Tennessee Historical Commission; Charlton Historical Society, Massachusetts; James A. Marvin, the Franklin Pierce Homestead, Hillsborough, New Hampshire; Barbara Rowlette, Giles County Historical Society, Pearisburg, Virginia; Farmers' Museum, Cooperstown, New York; Rosalind Magnuson, Brick Store Museum, Kennebunk, Maine; Stephen W. Skelton, South Carolina Archive & History Center; Martha Rowe and Jennifer Bean, Museum of Early Southern Decorative Arts, Winston-Salem, North Carolina; Cathy Grosfile, Colonial Williamsburg, Virginia; Jean Graham Lee, curator, Historic New Harmony, Indiana; Hale Farm and Village, Bath, Ohio; Foundation for Historic Christ Church, Irvington, Virginia; Dianne M. Cram, Peter Wentz Farmstead, Worcester, Pennsylvania; Preservation Society of Newport County, Rhode Island; Kirk F. Mohney, Maine Historic Preservation Commission, Augusta, Maine; Greater Portland Landmarks Commission, Maine.

Spring Green Studio   A.E.B.
Warwick, R.I.
January 2002

Introduction

Folk art is wonderfully uncensored—you can appreciate the aesthetics, but if you look behind it, you also find a way of catching American history.

—Nancy Druckman, *American Folk Art*, Sotheby's

American Wall Stenciling, an illustrated history of Federal-period American wall stenciling, represents more than a quarter century of avidly seeking, researching, and documenting early American wall stenciling executed during the 1790–1840 period.

It begins with examples of painted interiors from America's colonial period, before this type of stenciling began in America. Examples range from a 1712 cottage in southeastern Massachusetts to a 1737 cross-shaped church located on the lower Northern Neck of Virginia.

The body of the text is divided into two parts: Part I focuses on the "Folk Group" of stenciling, so named by the author because many of the design influences were derived from the folk art of the artists' ancestors. Part II concerns the "Classical Group" inspired by the neoclassical craze, which originated in the eighteenth-century Europe that spawned our Federal-style architecture and ornamentation.

To help the reader understand the artistic and historical place of stenciling in our country's developmental period, a history of each stenciled structure is linked to an analysis of its ornamental painting, providing a concise familial and social history of that period, as well as an overview of this early American folk art. Included is information concerning the family responsible for building the structure or commissioning the stencil artist; the history of the surrounding area and its road systems; and, of course, biographical material about the original artists, if known. Data about the twentieth-century artists who restored or re-created the stenciled walls are also included, if applicable.

Numerous photographs of original stenciling are included, but since many extant examples of late-eighteenth- and early-nineteenth-century stencil work are in a deteriorated state of preservation, very faint and fragmented, the author/artist has created facsimiles to illustrate the original stenciled walls, with great consideration for the original artists' intent. These re-creations utilize full-size stencil designs cut by the author. They are arranged and spaced to look as nearly identical to the original as possible. Many were traced with great reverence by the author from walls soon to celebrate their two hundredth birthday. Colors are based on numerous years of viewing early stenciled walls in various states of preservation, as well as research into pigments used originally and the effects of aging on these pigments due to nearly two centuries of wear.

Hopefully this extensive survey will raise recognition of the fact that wall stenciling in America was significantly more prevalent than previously thought by the general public and preservation experts. It was also considerably more widespread, with examples in the Niagara section of Canada, as far west as Indiana, and in southern Tennessee. In addition, it was considerably more diverse, with its practitioners reflecting widespread ethnic and vernacular design influences stylistically and geographically well beyond the wall stenciling found in the New England states.

It is hoped that this vastly expanded view of American wall stenciling will emphasize its importance to architectural history, benefiting the design and preservation communities in several ways. By offering a history and analysis of methods and materials, this survey provides information vital to restoration artists, preservation consultants, architectural historians, and most important, the homeowner, who most often discovers the stenciling. It thus encourages greater authenticity in the restoration of early wall painting and in the re-creation of these same walls when that is the only option.

This often overlooked American folk art, which developed simultaneously with and as a by-product of a new form of government called democracy, deserves to be thoroughly researched, recorded, and meticulously preserved, either in its original location or in museum settings. Without doubt there are still numerous examples of wall stenciling from the 1790–1840 period buried alive under multiple layers of paper and/or paint, waiting to be discovered by unsuspecting homeowners. Let us not allow more of this important and appealing part of America's past to be unwittingly destroyed, thereby losing even more of this nation's material history!

AMERICAN WALL STENCILING, 1790–1840

Chapter 1

English Influence
on Colonial
Painted Decoration

Detail of hand-painted swag found in completely paneled room in early-eighteenth-century southeastern Massachusetts dwelling. Measuring at least 30 inches in depth, it is embellished with intricate fringe and twin tassels suspended from a delicate vermilion bow-tied ribbon.

The art of decorative painting was very much a part of colonial America, predating Federal-period wall stenciling—the subject of this book—by almost a century. Since so many of the founders of America were of English descent, the techniques and materials employed by British artisans had a great influence on American ornamental painting.

Paint had been used in England for centuries to decorate and protect the interiors and exteriors of all manner of dwellings, from humble cottages to grand castles, as well as churches and other public edifices. Paint decoration, applied either freehand or with the aid of a stencil, was the earliest form of English interior wall decoration, preceding walls hung with patterned textiles and later covered with painted paper.[1] (Even today, when patterned walls are desired, paint—often applied through a stencil—is still the first choice of many contemporary British interior designers.)

America's English heritage was a result of the "Great Migration," in which almost 80,000 men, women, and children, or 2 percent of the total population, left Britain between 1620 and 1642.[2] Nearly three-fourths of these emigrants, about 58,000, came to North America, first to Virginia and later to New England. The rest settled in the Caribbean islands and in Europe, mainly Holland and the Palatinate region of Germany.

This great exodus was spawned by a number of unsettling conditions facing the English between 1590 and 1640: economic depressions, epidemics, wars, the failure of the Church of England to provide spiritual satisfaction for many of its people, and its unwillingness to tolerate dissent.[3] Rural farmers and urban artisans were among the most susceptible to these adversities and the most likely to emigrate.

These early settlers, in spite of very harsh initial conditions in the New World, were able to stabilize their lives within a quarter century. Letters were sent back to England describing their satisfaction with their new lives and praising the agricultural conditions. Competing promotional literature, printed by shipping entrepreneurs eager to fill their ships headed for the New World, was circulated throughout the depressed areas of England. By the late 1630s, thousands of English settlers were flooding into Massachusetts.

Farmers were the single largest occupational group, though most of those on the passenger list in 1637 were urban craftsmen who gave up their trades to try farming in the New World.[4] Among the many craft occupations listed in the 1630s in London, the preeminent center of craftsmanship at the time, were "payntor-staynors,"[5] cloth makers, dyers, rope makers, tailors, coopers, joiners, leather workers and metalworkers, shoemakers, brewers, candle makers, thimblesmiths, and pin makers.[6] All of these and more were represented among those who made their way to America.

Within a decade or two, most of these immigrants had secured for themselves a house, land of their own, a productive garden, and some livestock. The artisans, at first forced by necessity to become full-time farmers, were now able to practice their original trades. Usually the return to their craft was on a part-time basis and only if and where there was a demand for their services. In short, they became farmer/artisans.

Farmers in the colonies cultivated flax and hemp almost from the beginning, in order to provide linen for clothing and produce for commerce.[7] In 1718 a mill to press out linseed oil, a by-product of flax, was opened in New Haven;[8] others soon followed in Hatfield, Massachusetts, and Derby, Connecticut. Since linseed oil is used in the preparation of paint, this may have signaled the growing interest in the use of paint to preserve and brighten the wooden exteriors and interiors of colonial homes, which had been mostly free of paint until the end of the 1600s.

A small number of paint pigments were being imported early in the 1700s, but by midcentury more than three dozen pigments were regularly arriving from Europe. Others were of local origin. Some earth colors, such as the umbers and ochers, were mined here; lampblack was a by-product of the New England fishing industry; and indigo was grown in the Carolinas by 1750—second only in local importance to their tobacco crop.[9]

The end of the seventeenth century thus coincides with the first appearance of paint in colonial America. By the turn of the eighteenth century, the simple one-room dwellings of the first settlers had grown into multiroom structures, and new house starts were numerous.[10] This created a fertile ground for second- or third-generation settlers, or new arrivals from England, who had a way with a paintbrush. Many ornamental painters learned their craft from their fathers or grandfathers, who may have trained with one of the English guilds.[11] Others trained through the apprentice system, which had existed in the Old World for centuries. Young men, sometimes fourteen or younger, would apprentice themselves to a master craftsman for seven to ten years to learn the secrets of ornamental painting, a very respectable profession.

By the middle of the colonial period, American decorative painters were numerous and versatile, like their counterparts in the old country. They could grain your woodwork, marbleize your floor to look like imported marble tiles, pinstripe your carriage, make and gild frames, design a tavern sign, ornament your overmantel or fireboard, and even paint a likeness of your favorite aunt, sometimes posthumously! Two well-known immigrant artisans of that era were Thomas Child and John Gibbs, both of whom learned their craft through an apprenticeship with the Painter-Stainers Guild of London.[12] Child immigrated to Massachusetts by 1689 and was established in Boston as a portrait painter and maker and seller of paint by 1701. Gibbs arrived in Boston around 1703 and accepted both common (plain painting) and ornamental commissions.

Simple freehand decoration, such as dots swirled on with a brush or dabbed on with a sponge, painted comma-shaped brush strokes, and simple graining and marbling, began to appear on American walls, woodwork, and sometimes floors and ceilings in the early 1700s. There is documentation of this type of painted decoration, some of which may date to the late 1600s, in many parts of eastern Massachusetts.[13] The early color schemes were simple, most often combining black, white, and red. Walls were usually whitewashed before receiving their decoration in distemper paint. Woodwork was usually done in oil-based paint, with linseed oil as the binder of choice. Medium blues, most often made from Prussian blue pigment, were favorite woodwork colors in the 1700s, along with gray, green, and red.

Faux bois and marbre finishes were very popular in both fine and humble homes, starting early in the eighteenth century. This technique, known as "imitation painting"—very realistic examples of which could be called trompe l'oeil—had been used in England and on the

Continent for many years. In this country it was practiced up and down the East Coast from Maine to South Carolina. For example, in 1736 an advertisement appeared in a Charleston, South Carolina, newspaper informing the public that Richard Marten did imitation marble, walnut, oak, cedar, and so on, at five shillings a yard.[14] In 1743, in the same newspaper, John Sisener, painter from London, advertised that he made "wood into artificial stone."

The large wooden overmantel panels in colonial American homes were favorite areas to receive the services of these early artisans. In England the decorations on chimney boards, overmantels, and overdoors were known in the trade as "furnishing pictures."[15] They continued in use in England until the late eighteenth century, and a bit longer here. Their demise was due to a new style that emphasized plastered walls rather than wooden paneling, which paved the way for the advent of stenciling.

A particularly widespread style borrowed from the English could be called faux textile painting. Textile motifs, especially the draped fabric swag, are often seen on early American overmantels, used as a wall frieze, in portraits both primitive and refined, and on paint-decorated room accessories. Such motifs were probably inspired by the "drapery painters," English artists who were commissioned to paint only the textile elements in portraits executed by academic painters.[16] This practice was still common here in the late 1700s, judging by a contemporary advertisement in a Philadelphia paper, which states, "One of the artists will circumscribe his whole care to the head; and the other who excels in draperies, will confine himself to that department."[17]

Yet another English-inspired ornamentation for the home was the painted floor cloth. These painted canvases (sometimes called oilcloths) evolved in England as an outgrowth of sixteenth-century painted wall tapestries.[18] The earliest examples were stenciled or painted freehand. Later examples were block printed in a manner similar to that used in the manufacture of early wallpaper. They arrived at our colonial seaports in great numbers early in the eighteenth century. By the second half of the century, local artists were creating their own versions of these popular floor coverings. For example, an advertisement appeared in the *South Carolina Gazette* in 1768 for "Wayne & Ruger, Painters & Glaziers," offering to paint "signs and floor cloths, painted as neat as any from London."[19]

A number of early-eighteenth-century American homes have been documented as having rooms hung with textiles. For example, a house advertised for sale in Boston in 1735 had, among other attractions, "two chambers decorated with textile hung walls—one hung with Scotch Tapestry and the other with Green Cheny."[20]

After 1710, wallpaper could also be readily had by those who could afford it. It was first imported from England and France, but even before 1750, locally made paper was available. During this pre-Revolutionary period, walls were sometimes painted freehand with overall designs that resembled textile or wallpaper patterns. When stenciling developed during the Federal period as a popular alternative to cloth and paper wallcoverings, it was from these same design sources that artists borrowed most freely.

Illustrated in the following section are examples of ornamental painting techniques popular during the pre-Revolutionary period.

---

1. Christ Church, 1732
Irvington, Virginia
Artist: Unknown, 1740

ONE OF A HANDFUL of colonial churches, especially in the southern states, to have escaped the ravages of war, natural disaster, and human "improvement," Christ Church in Irvington is considered one of the very finest and best preserved of colonial Virginia churches, a superb example of its particular architectural style and period.

Located on the east bank of the Rappahannock River where it flows into Chesapeake Bay, it is built on the site of an earlier church erected in 1669 by John Carter, founder of the noted Virginian clan. His son Robert "King" Carter, a famous Virginian entrepreneur, built the present Christ Church in his father's honor in 1732.

Its Latin cruciform plan is not unusual for Virginia's Georgian-style churches, but its fine craftsmanship and sophisticated details are quite exceptional.

Most of the finely crafted interior woodwork is of natural black walnut, with the exception of the extraordinary three-tiered pulpit with curved staircase and hexagonal sounding board above. This seems to be grain-painted to resemble black walnut, utilizing a dark black-red graining mixture over a medium purple-red base coat. One of the many horizontal bands of the faux-painted sounding board, an eight-inch-wide convex one, is ornamented with a rather naively executed border of undulating entwined lines with oval medallions in the similarly shaped center. This motif, called a guilloche, was very common in ancient cultures and reappeared in Renaissance-period decorative arts. This border is very worn and faint but still identifiable as painted decoration more of the freehand type than stenciled.

This beautifully preserved colonial church with its rare extant example of southern colonial decorative painting and unique architectural detailing is maintained in excellent condition by the Foundation for Historic Christ Church, Inc. Services are held in the church during the summer months, at which time visitors are very welcome.

(Top) Exterior view of Christ Church. *Courtesy Foundation for Historic Christ Church.*

(Bottom) Interior view showing three-tiered pulpit, which is grained in faux black walnut with a guilloche border hand-painted on sounding board, below the dentil molding. *Courtesy Foundation for Historic Christ Church. From collections of Museum of Early Southern Decorative Arts.*

Peter Wentz Farmstead. *Photo by Philip Nord. Courtesy Department of History and Cultural Arts, Montgomery County, Pennsylvania.*

---

2. Peter Wentz Farmstead, 1758
Montgomery County, Pennsylvania

View of original and re-created sponge painting in kitchen area. *Courtesy Department of History and Cultural Arts, Montgomery County, Pennsylvania.*

THE HOUSE BUILT BY Peter Wentz, Jr., in 1758, is a wonderful combination of German and Georgian architectural styles. Located in Worcester, Pennsylvania, it is historically significant for having served as George Washington's headquarters around the time of the Battle of Germantown. It is now owned and operated as a historic park and farm museum by Montgomery County.

Simple sponged-on dots and brush-painted comma-shaped strokes, as seen in this rural farmhouse, are among the earliest and simplest forms of colonial decoration. Numerous references to this type of ornamentation have been recorded in the New England area.[21] This house also features painted black bands at the baseboard level, another treatment often seen in New England. The popularity of dark-painted baseboards declined after 1800, and by 1815 the style was probably passé in most areas.

The original colors include lampblack, yellow ocher, Prussian blue, and red lead pigments popular in the mid–eighteenth century. The painted decoration in distemper was applied to whitewashed walls. All woodwork and baseboards were covered with paint ground in oil.[22]

The re-creation of the exterior and interior paint finishes was completed in 1976 by Frank S. Welsh of Bryn Mawr, Pennsylvania.

View of decorative scheme between chair rail and baseboard (dado) of "George Washington" bedchamber. *Courtesy Department of History and Cultural Arts, Montgomery County, Pennsylvania.*

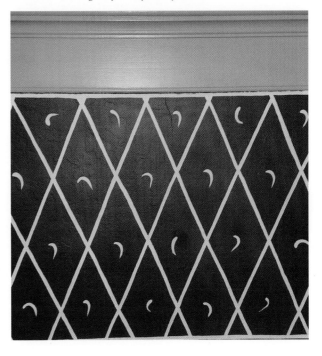

Nicholas-Wanton-Hunter house. *Photo by Richard Cheek. Courtesy Preservation Society of Newport County.*

---

3. Nichols-Wanton-Hunter house,

circa 1750

Newport, Rhode Island

AN URBAN RHODE ISLAND residence containing fine examples of eighteenth-century faux bois and marbre finishes, the Nichols-Wanton-Hunter house was built between 1748 and 1754 by Deputy Governor Jonathan Nichols. After his death, it was owned by Colonel Joseph Wanton, a Loyalist, who moved to New York after his Rhode Island properties were confiscated at the time of the Revolution. During the war, the French Admiral de Ternay was headquartered (and died) in this house. It was purchased at auction in 1805 by William Hunter, United States senator and first minister to Brazil.

In 1945 the Preservation Society of Newport County purchased the house and began a careful restoration. As later coats of paint were removed, mid-eighteenth-century graining and marbling was revealed in four rooms. Two rooms are grained to look like cedar (a treatment known as "rose cedar" graining), one to resemble walnut, and the last has black-on-white faux marbre pilasters and baseboards to complement the putty color of the room's paneling. Nick Durante of Yonkers, New York, re-created this early paint finish in the 1950s. One

Nicholas-Wanton-Hunter house parlor painted in treatment known as "rose cedar" graining. *Photo by Richard Cheek. Courtesy Preservation Society of Newport.*

or two panels of original finish were retained in each room.[23] Across Narragansett Bay, in Wickford, Rhode Island, three marbleized and grained rooms similar to those in the Hunter house were found in untouched condition in the 1950s and are now installed in a private residence in New York.[24]

Newport, one of the five earliest and most populous colonial cities (along with Boston, New York, Philadelphia, and Charleston, South Carolina), was devastated in the Revolutionary War during a long and difficult occupation by the British. In December 1776 the British fleet, comprising four frigates, a number of transports, and five thousand troops, took Newport in the name of George III. They did not evacuate until October 1778, almost two years later. After the war, Newport was superseded by Providence as the commercial and shipping capital of Rhode Island.

---

4. Kit Matteson Tavern, circa 1740
West Greenwich, Rhode Island

THE KIT MATTESON TAVERN was originally built by Silas Matteson as a farmhouse around 1740, about the time West Greenwich separated from East Greenwich. It is named after Christopher "Kit" Matteson, who inherited it from his father and began operating it as a tavern in the early 1780s. Located on the Old New London Turnpike, it became a local gathering spot and site of town meetings.

Over the years it fell into major disrepair until purchased in 1974 by the Harter family, who embarked on a twenty-year restoration of this colonial-era farmhouse. While removing plaster, they discovered that both the keeping room and the meeting room above were entirely paneled with hand-painted beveled pine paneling, decorated with whimsical elements of faux graining, fish, and a flower-filled vase over the mantel, all painted in black. The black paint appears to be oil-based, but no paint analysis has been done. In addition, one fireplace lintel was painted to match the fireplace brick surround.

Now carefully restored by the owners, these two rooms are a fine example of eighteenth-century painted interior decoration in rural Rhode Island.

Exterior of Kit Matteson Tavern.

View of fireplace surround in second-floor meeting room of Matteson Tavern, with primitive flower-filled vase in center panel and three fish above. Notice the stone lintel painted to resemble brick.

5. Sproat-Ward house, 1712
Lakeville, Massachusetts

THE SMALL, one-and-a-half-story Sproat-Ward house, built in 1712 by James Sproat and inherited by his son Robert in 1737, contains unusual late colonial (ca. 1760–70) painted decoration, located in a small, fifteen-by-fifteen-foot upper chamber that is completely paneled in wood. Three walls and the ceiling are of random-size horizontal sheathing, and the fireplace wall is of raised panels. The dado area is painted with a dark wood finish. The rest of the room, including the ceiling, is done in a light maple finish. The frieze decoration features large, bold, freehand drapery swags in blue-gray, with red and black fringes. Tassels in the same red and black hang from vermilion bows and streamers.

The overmantel features two similar flower-filled classical urns on a blue-gray ground. It is framed with black-over-white marbleized bolection molding. It is said that prior to this treatment, a portrait of King George III occupied this prominent place.[25] His demotion was perhaps an indication of diminished loyalty to the Crown and growing patriotism during the latter part of our colonial period.

The floor is stenciled in white and dark blue-green on a wood-colored background. Several border designs are used, the most prominent being a tulip motif, popular with floor stencilers well into the Federal period.[26]

All the paints used in this ornamentation appear to be ground in oil, with very little touch-up or inpainting to early decoration that was never covered with paper or paint.

The early part of this house had features such as twelve-inch oak planks spiked onto the sills and beams as protection from Indian raids, and a secret room. Extensive additions were made to the house over the years, making it all the more fortunate that its original late-colonial-period decorative interior painting survived intact.

Late-colonial-period decoration in completely paneled, 15-foot-square room on second floor of the Sproat-Ward house, featuring hand-painted swags and overmantel, stenciled secondary border, and a stenciled floor.

Chapter 2

Wall Stenciling
in Federal America

By 1790 the war with England had been won and American independence gained. The Constitution had been written by fifty-five delegates, known as Federalists (from twelve states), to the 1787 Philadelphia convention, and had been ratified by conventions in the thirteen original states (the last was Rhode Island in 1790). George Washington had been sworn in as the first president and had, without a model to follow, organized a new form of government called democracy. Thus began America's Federal period.

This new nation was a land of vast empty spaces. Less than half of its 800,000 square miles was within the boundaries of the original thirteen states, where more than nine out of ten citizens still lived. Of the four million people counted in the 1790 census, 90 percent were farmers who had settled within a few hundred miles of the Atlantic seaboard. They were hardworking and self-sufficient, and lived better with less labor than their European counterparts.[1]

After the war these rural husbandmen, home from service in the military and feeling expansive about the future, decided the time was fortuitous to renovate their farmhouses. Some added rooms to the ground floor; some built upward by enlarging the second floor or adding a third story; some moved whole houses and joined them to their existing house; and, of course, many built new homesteads. This building activity provided much employment for local craftsmen and commissions for artisans, both settled and itinerant.

Five percent of Americans lived in the ten largest cities in 1790.[2] These urban centers were comfortable and fairly prosperous. Although trade was a bit shaky during the early years of nationhood, the merchant class was financially stable enough to build numerous new homes or update existing ones in the newest style, known as the Federal style. This had its roots in the classical revival that swept Europe after the discovery of the Pompeiian ruins early in the eighteenth century, a revival shaped by the Adams brothers in England and their disciples, Hepplewhite and Sheraton, the famous English

Eagle motif from the Farmersville Tavern (I.38). Wing span is fourteen inches. Depth from highest star to tail is ten inches.

cabinetmakers and authors of stylebooks. These books did much to define American architecture and decorative arts during the Federal period.

Postwar expansiveness took other forms as well. Between 1790 and 1800 the first great wave of migration to the western frontier began, stimulated by land sales at auction and by the certificates for frontier land that many war veterans received as payment for military service.[3] By the beginning of the nineteenth century there were thirty thousand pioneers in Kentucky and Tennessee, and thousands more were moving each year into the fertile valleys of Ohio.

The westward movement created a need for better roads. Beginning in the 1790s, states made extensive improvements to their roads, which by the first quarter of the nineteenth century could be described as adequate in the East and less so, but still passable, over the routes leading to the western frontier. New towns sprang up like mushrooms along these new roads, providing an ever expanding market for woodworkers and painters to ply their trades.

There was no shortage of artisans available to decorate these new homes—both established artists in the urban areas and fresh arrivals from Europe. Moreover, many former artisans-turned-farmers, recently home from the war, were looking for ways to supplement their farming activities—either by returning to their original trade or taking up a new one, perhaps as an apprentice to an established artist.

With new and renovated houses in urban, rural, and frontier areas, expanded road systems linking these areas, and an ample supply of artists willing to travel in search of commissions, conditions were right for the stencil technique to be rediscovered as a serious competitor to the practice of ornamenting walls with paper, which had outlasted the earlier fashion for textile-hung walls.

Wall stenciling began to appear in America shortly after the conclusion of the Revolutionary War. It quickly became a popular alternative to wallpaper, for a number of practical reasons. First, it was considered cleaner than wallpaper, which tended to attract or conceal insects and other household pests. For example, an advertisement appeared in a South Carolina newspaper in 1762 for "paper hung with a paste that has a peculiar quality of destroying all vermin in walls."[4] Such pastes could not have been very effective, for the problem persisted well into the nineteenth century. Rufus Porter, who traveled up and down the East Coast painting murals during the

1824–45 period, said about wallpaper, "It is apt to get torn off, and often affords behind it a resting place for various kinds of insects." De Witt Clinton, who served several terms as governor of New York between 1817 and 1828, noted in his travels around that state that "by and by, in the best private houses, you frequently see papered rooms, which serve as an asylum for bugs and other vermin, instead of painted or stained apartments, which never admit them."[5]

The second advantage was that stenciling could be applied directly to new, uncured plaster walls, whereas a waiting period of six months to a year was required for the application of wallpaper, which promptly peeled off if applied to fresh plaster. Third, it was many times faster to stencil your walls than to have them paper-hung—and it was much cheaper as well. An ornamental painter by the name of William Priest advertised in a Baltimore newspaper in 1796 that he worked "in imitation of paper-hangings, by a mechanical process, which, from its facility, enables the artist to paint a room—upon lower terms than it is possible to hang with paper of equal beauty."[6] Stenciling was a kind of modern fresco treatment that not only expedited the decoration of new dwellings but also minimized the cost.

As stenciling caught on, two major and distinctly American styles evolved almost simultaneously. The first, the more widespread (and thus more familiar to us), started at the end of the eighteenth century in eastern Massachusetts and expanded steadily westward, perhaps as far as Texas. Its earliest practitioners were descendants of the original settlers of the Boston area. I have dubbed it the "Folk Group," since many designs used by these artists appear to derive from the folk art of their ancestors. These designs were combined with motifs borrowed from locally made wallpaper, which was manufactured in the Boston area as early as 1750–60.

The second type, much less prominent than the first, I call the "Classical Group." It was inspired by the same neoclassical craze that gave birth to Federal-style architecture. Its practitioners, probably part of the large influx of artists from Britain and Europe who arrived in America after the Revolution, traveled up and down the eastern seaboard from Kennebunk, Maine, to Charleston, South Carolina, by packet ship and inland over the early road systems. This type of stenciling stayed mostly in New England and tended to be preferred by a more urban, affluent clientele, whereas the folk style, which was more vernacular and less self-consciously sophisticated, was more likely to be found in rural areas and in unpretentious homes, although there were plenty of exceptions to this general rule.

A surprisingly large, varied, and interesting body of work was produced over a period of fifty to sixty years by artists working in these two styles, which indicates that stencil-decorated walls were much more popular and widespread during the Federal period than is generally recognized today. One of the ironies in the history of stenciling is that it often ended up, many years later, covered over by multiple layers of the very thing it had been intended to replace—wallpaper. Although stripping off the paper invariably removes some of the stenciling, in most cases the paper has (albeit unintentionally) preserved important remnants of a unique and quintessentially American art form.

PART I

The Folk Group of American Wall Stenciling

"Folk Group" is the name given by the author to a style of wall stenciling that developed in rural eastern Massachusetts, perhaps as early as 1790, to fill a need for painted wall decoration that did not sacrifice efficiency and frugality for beauty.

Of the two genres of wall stenciling examined in this book, the folk style is the more democratic. It first appeared in remodeled early farmhouses, some of which started as one-room seventeenth-century stone-enders, and was later found in farmhouses and taverns along the roads leading westward to the frontier.

The principal design sources for the folk style seem to be the motifs found in the seventeenth- and eighteenth-century decorative arts of early English settlers as well as patterns of wallpaper, both imported and locally made. Many variations of early designs moved westward with the artists as they sought new markets for their handiwork. The use of similar, but not necessarily identical, motifs can be explained by the ease with which designs could be copied, either directly or from memory. The sharing of designs by master and apprentice during the fifty- to sixty-year period of stenciling's heyday also contributed to the repetition of motifs. (It has been suggested from time to time that stencil designs may have been disseminated by being published, but no evidence for this exists.)

The most popular layout was very similar to the typical wallpaper layout of the time. The elements included horizontal borders at the ceiling (frieze), baseboard, and chair rail, if there was one, with the frieze being the largest and most important. Vertical borders divided the wall into panels, between twelve and twenty inches wide, which were filled with alternating floral and geometric designs known as fillers.

A second design scheme called the open layout was used less often. The narrow vertical borders, instead of dividing the wall into panels, were used around all the architectural elements of the room (doors, windows, and mantels) and to define the four corners. The framed wall spaces were then filled with the same alternating filler motifs without the interruption of vertical borders. Some artists gave the overmantel area a special treatment, such as flower-filled baskets, vases, or urns. It is interesting to note that as the height of ceilings increased, from low-ceilinged early farmhouses to Federal-style high ceilings, the earlier frieze motifs were enlarged accordingly—and the original frieze designs were sometimes used as baseboard decoration.

The most common color scheme was red and green stenciling on white or light gray walls. Yellow, blue, and off-black were occasionally used for the designs; other background colors were yellow and light red, with blue appearing later in the period. Most often, dried pigments were mixed with hide glue dissolved in boiling water to make a stencil paint called distemper. Oil-based paint was always used on the woodwork, and less often for stenciling. Background colors were created with plain or tinted whitewash.[1]

The body of work produced by artists working in the folk style appears to be considerable, suggesting that a large number of artists, often working with a second craftsman or apprentice, were needed to produce this volume of work. But as of now, only about ten names have come to the fore, many of whom are impossible to document.[2]

The obscurity of these early stencil artists can be attributed to several factors. First, being mostly farmer/artisans living in rural areas, many did not advertise; their commissions were gained primarily by word of mouth. Their work was considered purely functional, and thus they were not credited by name for their services; a simple "paid for painting" might be noted in household ledgers or diaries. By the same token, very few artisans felt the need to sign or date their work. Indeed, the list of extant signed walls is extremely short, representing only a small fraction of the total number of recorded stenciled houses.

(Facing page) Portrait of Rebeckah Jaquess (Mrs. Jonathan Jaquess) of Poseyville, Indiana, posed in front of typical "Folk Group" wall stenciling. Painted by Jacob Maentel in 1841. *Courtesy Abby Aldrich Rockefeller Folk Art Museum, Williamsburg, Virginia.*

Chapter 3

The Southern New England States of Rhode Island, Massachusetts, and Connecticut

Rhode island was settled in 1636 by Roger Williams (1603–83), a Puritan clergyman educated in England, who was exiled from Salem, Massachusetts, with a small group of followers. He founded the city now known as Providence, which later became the capital of the State of Rhode Island and Providence Plantations, one of the original thirteen colonies.

Early settlers were each granted home lots in Providence and farmland in an area then known as West Providence. By 1650, fifty-two five-acre homesteads had been allotted along the Providence River waterfront. Several generations passed before the farms in the northwestern section were developed, but by 1731 this rural area had grown large enough to warrant a separation from urban Providence. Glocester, Smithfield, and Scituate became towns at this time, followed by Burrillville, Cumberland, Johnston, North Providence, and Cranston, and in 1781 Foster was added (where signed stenciling has been found).

The area developed quickly for several reasons. The growing maritime and fishing ventures of Rhode Island ports created a demand for wood for shipbuilding and farm staples to outfit the fleet; increased road construction provided a link to the coast; and a shortage of open land elsewhere in the colony drew settlers to the outlying areas. This growth culminated in a local building boom during the first quarter of the nineteenth century, which generated plenty of commissions for wall stencilers.

Five of the six artists working in the folk style in Rhode Island left samples of their handiwork in houses in the northwestern section of the state, many of which were built by descendants of Rhode Island's first families. Preeminent among these artists is J. Gleason, whose name was found stenciled on a wall in Foster by the Rhode Island Historical Preservation Commission while surveying the town for the *Statewide Historical Preservation Report*, published in 1982.[1] This section of Rhode

Detail of stenciled "large daisy," 12 inches in diameter, from David Dudley house (I.12) of Douglas, Massachusetts, believed to be the work of J. Gleason.

Island converges with south-central Massachusetts and northeastern Connecticut to form a three-state area where a great deal of stenciling was done during the early 1800s (and possibly the late 1700s). The commission's report also credits J. Gleason with numerous other Rhode Island stenciled walls that date to the building boom in the area that occurred between 1800 and 1830.

I.1. Deacon Daniel Hopkins house,
circa 1800
Foster, Rhode Island
Artist: J. Gleason (signed), circa 1800

THE BUILDER OF the Federal-style farmhouse depicted here, Daniel Hopkins (1758–1844), a descendant of Governor Stephen Hopkins, was a colonel in the local militia and a deacon of Elder Hammon's Second Baptist Meeting House in Foster. The southwest parlor has exquisitely carved woodwork, which has never been painted, and choice wall stenciling in shades of red, green, yellow, and dark gray on a whitewashed ground. An adjoining small room also had stenciling at one time, which has since been painted over. The woodwork is said to have been carved at sea by the owner's sea-captain brother. The signed stenciling, a bit faded but with minimal overpainting, is the finest extant "Folk Group" stenciling found to date in Rhode Island.

The existence of this signed stenciling, executed sometime between 1790 and 1810, is both a rare treat for wall-stenciling enthusiasts and a mystery of great proportions. First, why did J. Gleason sign this house and not the others that are clearly by his hand; and second, who exactly was J. Gleason?

The first question is the easier. He apparently signed his work in the Hopkins house because it was a very important commission; after all, it was a fine Federal house built by a direct descendant of Stephen Hopkins, governor of Rhode Island for nine years, chief justice of the Superior Court, first chancellor of Brown University, member of the Continental Congress, and signer of the Declaration of Independence. It may also have been Gleason's first commission in the area, since some sources date this house as early as 1790.[2]

The second question is a bit more vexing. John Barber White's Gleason family genealogy indicates that the Gleasons left England in 1640, settling first in Watertown, Massachusetts, just west of Boston. Later generations moved inland, until by the 1750s they were well established in Sudbury, Marlborough, and Oxford, rural

Hopkins house exterior. *Courtesy Rhode Island Preservation Commission.*

Massachusetts towns just north of the Rhode Island border. They had large families with numerous sons, many of whom had first names starting with the letter *J.* Thus far the author has found at least five J. Gleasons of lineal descent who were of the right age and locale to be identified with the stencil artist. Gleasons with possible connections to the Hopkins house include James Gleason,[3] b. 1751 in Oxford, Massachusetts, d. 1839 in South Gore, Massachusetts; his eldest son, also James Gleason,[4] b. 1772, whose second wife was Roxy Cutler, a common surname in northwestern Rhode Island; and younger son, Abiel,[5] b. 1790 in Oxford, Massachusetts, who married Nabby Hammon of Foster, Rhode Island.

Interior view of Hopkins parlor showing still extant stenciling and the now painted-over work in a small ancillary room. *Courtesy Rhode Island Preservation Commission.*

Detail of stenciled signature found in 1978 in a front parlor of Hopkins house.

THE FIRST STEERE to own the Steere house, Elisha, John Appleby's brother-in-law,[6] purchased the farm from Thomas Waterman, who built the house in 1810. Elisha, a captain in the local militia and a Quaker, initially ran a saw- and gristmill, but over the years the farm was converted to dairy farming and later fruit growing. The Steere family played an early and important role in northwestern Rhode Island's history.

Stenciling was discovered in 1996 during extensive renovation by the seventh-generation Steere owner of the farm. When paper was removed from the walls, still discernible stencil designs were revealed, albeit quite faded and with most of the green elements missing, in two first-floor rooms and the front hall stairway.[7]

This was a very important discovery because the designs are identical to ones recorded in the Hopkins house and the Smith-Appleby house, indicating that the same hand, namely J. Gleason, stenciled all three houses. The "bell and swag" frieze and "diagonal leaf" vertical in the left front parlor are identical to those used in the Smith-Appleby house, and the "arch and candle" frieze used in several rooms is identical to that in the signed Hopkins house. (All of these designs will be seen again in subsequent houses in this group.) Also, one of the floors and the front stairway in the Steere house are marbleized in the same grisaille coloration as in the Smith-Appleby house.

There is also a Gleason family connection to this house: Uzziel Gleason,[8] b. 1785, younger brother of James Gleason of Oxford, married Lydia Steere of Burrillville, Rhode Island, in 1815, continuing a pattern of James Gleason's brothers marrying into northwestern Rhode Island families.

View of re-created stenciling in front parlor of Steere house looking through to front-stair-hall stenciling.

I.3. Smith-Appleby house, 1696
Smithfield, Rhode Island
Artist: J. Gleason (attributed), 1809

Marbleized floor extant in the front parlor, exactly like that still retained in corresponding room in Steere house. Remnants were also found in front stair halls of both homes. *Courtesy Historical Society of Smithfield.*

THE FIRST PART of the Smith-Appleby house, one of Smithfield's oldest and most important structures, was erected in 1696 by Elisha Smith, a grandson of John Smith, one of the original party of six men led by Roger Williams who founded the first settlement in Rhode Island. It is believed that Smithfield was named after this family.

The house, originally a one-room stone-ender with loft above, grew over the years. In the early 1700s an entire house was moved from nearby Johnston and carefully joined to the original house; next, a one-story extension was added to the back; and finally, a two-story kitchen ell was added to the right front. The final result was a spacious twelve-room dwelling. The name honors the two families who lived in the house consecutively from 1696 to 1958. The Smithfield Historical Society acquired the property in 1971, and restoration has been ongoing ever since.

Janet Waring visited here in the 1930s when she was doing research for her book on wall stenciling and recorded stenciling in one first-floor room and the attic stairway.[9] The rest of the rooms were wallpapered at that time.

The author visited the house in 1981 just after the wallpaper had been stripped from all the walls, and was able to make out stencil designs in four rooms on the first floor as well as in hallways and stairways from the first floor to the attic. Four of these areas had remnants visible enough to trace and record; the other two required educated guesswork.

The stenciling was probably executed around the time of John Appleby's marriage to Patience Harris on June 18, 1809. A new bride in the house was an excellent reason to spruce up walls with the newest in stenciled decoration.

There are also signs of grained woodwork, a black and white marbleized floor in a front parlor and front stairway, and painted black baseboards throughout the first floor.

Author's facsimile of stenciling that was once in left front parlor, showing designs identical to those in Steere house (I.2).

I.4. *Paine-Mowry Tavern, circa 1790*
Greenville (Smithfield), Rhode Island
Artist: J. Gleason (attributed),
early nineteenth century

THE TWO-AND-A-HALF-STORY, gable-roofed Paine-Mowry Tavern, built during the late eighteenth century, was demolished in the 1970s to make way for the Apple Valley Mall. It was one of two taverns owned by the Mowry family during the nineteenth century located at Mowry's Corner, Greenville. The taverns were later converted to private homes, and Mowrys lived there for many years.

Janet Waring, who visited the tavern in the 1930s, was told by family members that all four rooms and the hall on the ground floor were originally stenciled, but even as early as 1830 the parlor was so worn that its new owner[10] "reluctantly papered it because no one in the neighborhood could be found to re-stencil it." Two small bedrooms escaped papering, and Waring was able to examine and record the stenciling. She found designs, techniques, and colorations that matched what she had seen in the Smith-Appleby house a few miles north.[11]

Mowry descendants also provided insight into the type of paint used by the stenciler. They remembered a warning "not to wash the walls and blur the ornament." This is a clear indication of distemper paint, which was the same type used in the previous three houses.

The designs found in the Paine-Mowry Tavern have all been seen before in the Hopkins, Smith-Appleby, and Steere houses. This is clearly another example of Gleason's handiwork, since his two types of wall layout—paneled and open—are also found in this tavern, as they are in two of the houses discussed earlier in this chapter.

(Top) Early tavern sign from one of several Mowry family taverns in Smithfield area of Rhode Island. *Courtesy Old Sturbridge Village.*

(Bottom) Early photo of original stenciling in a second-floor chamber of Mowry Tavern. *Courtesy Old Sturbridge Village.*

THE WETHERBEE-HILL FARMHOUSE is a typical five-room center-chimney house, with the kitchen located in the front, a layout peculiar to Foster architecture. This house may have started life as a half house, as many in the area did, later to be enlarged or "lengthened," perhaps when Job W. Hill purchased the property around 1850.

During a 1963 renovation, stenciling was found in four rooms, and photographs were taken by the owners before the walls were repapered. Three rooms appear to have Gleason-type work; one in particular, the left back room, is almost identical to the signed room in the Hopkins house, with the same large "arch and candle" frieze, "entwined leaf" vertical, and "small carnation spray" motifs. The stencil colors appear to be the same, but the background, instead of plain white, is pale pink,[12] a commonly used wall color during that period, achieved by adding a bit of red ocher to the whitewash.

However, the remaining room, with one stenciled wall still visible, is very uncharacteristic of Gleason work. The stencils are similar but not identical, and some motifs not seen before in Gleason work appear. The layout is very busy and disjointed, definitely not as balanced as that by Gleason, and the colors seem to be a bit off. The overall impression is that this room was executed by a different hand[13] and probably at a later time.

There is another house in Foster with stenciling similar to this atypical panel: the Welcome Rood Tavern, built in 1789, has stenciling in an 1825 addition.

I.5. Wetherbee-Hill house, circa 1810

Foster, Rhode Island

Artist: J. Gleason (three rooms attributed), early nineteenth century; unknown (one room), after 1825

(Top) Facsimile of stenciling in a parlor of Wetherbee-Hill house with designs and layout almost exactly like those in the signed Hopkins parlor (I.1).

(Right) Detail of the "tulip" motif in parlor stenciling.

THE WESTCOTT HOUSE probably started life as a typical mid-eighteenth-century stone-ender and grew into a much larger house with at least five rooms on the first floor by the end of the eighteenth century. It was extensively renovated between 1823 and 1827 by Josiah Westcott, who acquired the property from his father, the Reverend John Westcott, a Baptist minister in Foster for many years. The renovation included enlargement and refinement of the first-floor rooms, plus a major enlargement of the second story and addition of a third level.

Josiah Westcott (1781–1867) was a direct descendant of Stukely Westcott, one of Roger Williams's associates. A self-educated man, he taught school and did carpentry work during the winter, and engaged in agriculture on his large farm in Scituate during the summer season. He filled various municipal offices in Scituate and Providence as town clerk, representative, and senator. He also commanded the Captain General's Cavaliers for eight years. His brother Artemis, who is said to have owned one-third of the estate, was a carpenter, wood-carver, and painter.[14]

The house contains two types of stenciling. The older, found under wallpaper in two first-floor rooms, was very faint but recognizable Gleason work (probably executed while Reverend John Westcott still lived there). The second type, found on the renovated second floor, is not characteristic of Gleason and seems to be of a later period (after the 1827 renovation). It is not known if brother Artemis's painting skills were advanced enough to execute this complicated later decoration, which combines stenciling with freehand painting—a type of work I call "compose," which will be seen again in subsequent entries.

Facsimile of stenciling original to a parlor of Westcott house.

Elishu Fish Tavern.

I.7. Elihu Fish Tavern, 1759–1783
Scituate, Rhode Island
Artist: Unknown, 1828

THE FISH TAVERN started as a small one-and-a-half-story residence built by James Thornton in 1759; several enlargements to the west side of the structure followed. In 1783 a new owner, Theophiles Blackmar, added a full half-house to the east side of the building consisting of a second-floor ballroom, first-floor dining room, and a cellar kitchen, all necessary ingredients for a tavern with the advantage of being located on the Great North Road from Providence to Plainfield, Connecticut.

The new tavern was purchased in 1801 by Elihu Fish, whose family had resided in Scituate since the 1730s, and was run as a tavern by him for twenty-five years. During this period the old road was improved into the Plainfield Turnpike, accommodating a steady flow of stage lines connecting Hartford (Connecticut), Providence, and Boston.

During its tavern days the original section to the west was reserved as a private residence for the publican's family members. The stenciling was found under wallpaper during a recent renovation in the front hall of this private, family section of the building. It probably dates to the 1828–40 period, when Moses Potter owned and ran the roadhouse, and was part of a renovation to upgrade the private living quarters before settling his family into their new home.

The construction of the Providence to Danielson Railroad brought the demise of the stagecoach lines that traveled this road and the taverns that serviced them.

Another house located nearby in Scituate, the Battey-Barden house, built between 1816 and 1831 by Horace Battey, had at least four rooms of stenciling by the same hand. Only the front hall retains its original stenciling, which was executed by an artist influenced by the Gleason work of an earlier date in this northwestern area of Rhode Island.

Fragment of interesting "duck" frieze found in stair hall inside door to the left.

Early-twentieth-century view of Battey-Barden house. *Courtesy Erica Gregg and Joe Tamburini.*

I.8. Battey-Barden house, circa 1825

Scituate, Rhode Island

Artist: Unknown, circa 1825

THE BATTEY-BARDEN HOUSE is an excellent example of a Federal-style farmhouse built by prosperous residents of a rural area. It was built between 1816 and 1831 by Horace Battey (1793–1881), who was a deacon in the Baptist church, justice of the peace, and storekeeper. The Batteys settled in Scituate in the mid–eighteenth century. They were involved in civic and religious affairs and were among the town's early industrialists. In 1860 the farm sold at auction to Job W. Barden and remained in the Barden family until 1962. When the new owners found stenciling under wallpaper, they invited the Providence Preservation Society to record the stenciling before they repapered. A subsequent owner rediscovered the stenciling, now badly faded, under wallpaper and re-created some of it. The only original stenciling still in place is that which decorates the front entranceway.

This circa 1825 stenciling was executed by an artist influenced by the Gleason style.

Facsimile of stenciling with "duck" frieze originally in a first-floor parlor of Battey-Barden house. *Courtesy Erica Gregg and Joe Tamburini.*

Original stenciling still extant in front stair hall. *Courtesy Erica Gregg and Joe Tamburini.*

I.9. Wemacs farm, mid–eighteenth century
Exeter, Rhode Island
Artist: Unknown, circa 1800

THE WEMACS FARMHOUSE, located in west-central Rhode Island, was probably built in the eighteenth century as a tiny one-room structure that grew into its present configuration over many years of additions and renovations. The stenciling is the simplest and least professional seen thus far. Possibly earlier than the previous examples, it could have been executed by the owner of the house. Its designs suggest those found on early carved wooden furniture and gravestones. The red ocher motif is a simple six-petal daisy; the yellow ocher motif could be described as a "compass work roundel," commonly found on room furnishings and cemetery markers, and even carved into ceiling beams.[15] These basic designs were executed in distemper paint.

The house's current owners kindly alerted the author when they removed paper prior to applying fresh wallpaper, allowing the stencil work to be photographed and traced before being hidden again.

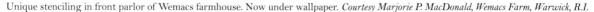

Unique stenciling in front parlor of Wemacs farmhouse. Now under wallpaper. *Courtesy Marjorie P. MacDonald, Wemacs Farm, Warwick, R.I.*

Stenciling from first floor of Cutler Tavern or Stand, once located in Glocester, Rhode Island. *Courtesy of The Rhode Island Historical Society.*

I.10. Farnum-Cutler Tavern, 1827–34
Glocester, Rhode Island
Artist: Unknown, 1827–34

CYRUS FARNUM (1809–1893), the original owner and operator of this nineteenth-century tavern, was active in politics, serving both as state representative and state senator. In 1846 he sold the estate to Thomas Cutler of Killingly, Connecticut.

The tavern contained wall decoration very different from the stencil designs seen thus far and somewhat atypical of the folk style. A freehand painted blue swag at the frieze area is combined with large vine-and-flower vertical borders stenciled thirty-four inches apart, covering the space between ceiling and dado (there is paneling below the dado). There is no evidence of a secondary horizontal border at the chair rail or dado area.

This most interesting design, found in a first-floor waiting room, was recorded by the Rhode Island Historical Society before the dismantling of the tavern in 1968. A sample of the original stenciling on plaster is in the collections of the society.

The realistically painted swag frieze was a popular motif of the early decorative painters, as noted in the introductory essay on colonial painting techniques; it reappears in subsequent entries.

❧

I.11. Tillinghast farm, circa 1750
Foster, Rhode Island
Artist: Unknown, circa 1830

THE LENGTHENED, single-story Tillinghast farmhouse contains four rooms of lightly restored stenciling by the same hand as the Cutler Tavern (I.10), making it a wonderful example of this unusual stenciling.

One room is almost identical to the Cutler Tavern in style and coloration; the next is a reversal of the coloration, with yellow stenciling on a blue-green ground, embellished by painted accents. The next is a very elaborate variation of the same designs, but with a new, flamboyant frieze of large stylized leaves and dots with copious freehand accents.

Compared with the anteroom of the Cutler Tavern, the last room is definitely a more sophisticated example of this painter's "compose" style. This elaborate room was restored by Connecticut artist Helen Howard in the late 1970s. The fourth decorated area, the front hall, has more motifs executed in the compose manner. This area and the first two rooms were restored by Providence artist Ida Schmulowitz about 1987.

The use of hand-painted accents to embellish stenciled motifs has a long history. Such accents were reportedly used in France and England as early as the fifteenth century and no doubt occurred in the decoration of early French and later American wallpaper—perhaps an inspiration for the talented Tillinghast farm artist.

Some elements of this work are reminiscent of the (later) decoration seen in the Westcott house (I.6), namely the swag, the saw-toothed horizontal border below the swag, and a small vertical border, although the work in the Westcott house is much more complicated, just as the Tillinghast work is more complicated than the stenciling in the Cutler Tavern. This suggests a remote possibility that Artemis Westcott was the artist responsible for all three.

Stenciled room in Tillinghast house using same designs as in Cutler Tavern but in reverse coloration.
Courtesy Tillinghast house, Foster, R.I.

Massachusetts

The Massachusetts Bay Company was granted a royal charter from the English King Charles I in 1629, making Massachusetts the second-oldest colony in America, after Virginia, which became a Crown colony five years earlier in 1624. Settled mostly by Puritans seeking religious freedom, the Massachusetts Bay Colony grew rapidly, with its port city of Boston soon becoming one of the five largest colonial seaports. The early Puritans were not given to aesthetic indulgence, believing as they did that the human mind should devote itself solely to matters of religion, but by the eighteenth century their tastes for plain, unadorned homes had begun to waver. Color and pattern were becoming acceptable, with painted floor canvases, woven carpets, papers, and simple painted designs used to brighten walls, floors, and furniture.

Paint materials, wallpaper, and the latest in decorating styles, along with artists ready to apply them, started arriving in Boston from Europe on a regular basis as the eighteenth century progressed, making Massachusetts an area of early and vigorous decorative painting activity. Nina Fletcher Little's 1952 book, *American Decorative Wall Painting*, records numerous examples of colonial Massachusetts painted interiors. Surviving examples of Federal-period wall and floor stenciling are very early, if not the earliest in the original thirteen colonies; highly diverse, indicating many different hands; and evenly scattered throughout the state, with examples located in the eastern sections tending to be earlier than the western work.

Wallpaper, a major source of designs used by wall stencilers, was being manufactured in the Boston area by the mid-1700s, and decorative wallpaper borders were widely used in eastern Massachusetts. Two borders in particular had a great influence on the state's stencil artists: made around 1790, they are known as the "cone and leaf" and the "feather and ribbon." They were popular in both homes and taverns, such as the Red Horse Tavern in Sudbury, where they served as a convenient source of inspiration for traveling artists. Motifs from these two borders appear on walls from eastern Massachusetts to western New York State.

Stenciling by the early Massachusetts artists is of great importance to any understanding of this American art form, because it was the primary source from which decorative stenciling spread north, west, and south into the frontiers of the rapidly expanding new nation. However, since Massachusetts stenciling was extensively researched and published starting in the 1920s by such experts as Edward Allen,[16] Janet Waring,[17] Esther Stevens Brazer,[18] and Nina Fletcher Little, the following section, along with sections on the remaining four New England states (Connecticut, New Hampshire, Maine, and Vermont), which were also well documented by these authors, is considerably shorter than the previous section on Rhode Island.

For reasons still unclear, only a handful of Rhode Island stenciled houses appeared in these earlier groundbreaking books. Thus, very little was known about wall and floor stenciling in Rhode Island until the author initiated her research in the 1970s, producing much previously undiscovered and unpublished material. Since the Rhode Island discoveries contain a very high proportion of new material, they are considered significant enough to publish in their entirety in this volume. The sections on Massachusetts and the other New England states are limited to the most important, varied, and interesting examples of known work, along with any new discoveries that have come to light recently. (These sections include notations as to the location of additional information on the abundance of stenciling in the region.)[19] The same approach has been used for New York State, much of whose wall and floor stenciling, which was greatly influenced by New England work, has already been discovered and published.

Exterior of David Dudley house.

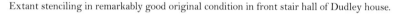

I.12. David Dudley house, 1813

Douglas, Massachusetts

Artist: J. Gleason and/or Moses Eaton

THE STENCILED David Dudley house is located on the village green of an eighteenth-century hilltop town in an agriculturally based inland area, just over the border from northwestern Rhode Island. It was established at a time of initial colonial settlement along an early east-west trail. By the early 1800s the area was connected by busy toll roads from Boston to the east, Hartford to the west, and Providence to the south.

An early traveler through this area, John Brown Francis of Providence, wrote in his diary in November of 1818, "There is a rage throughout the country [Massachusetts] for new meeting houses and for building costly dwelling houses. The mania of New England, the manners of the people, and the appearances of all the villages indicate cultivation and wealth."[20]

The Dudley family, descendants of an early governor of Massachusetts, built or owned many of the fine Federal houses in Douglas Center and ran the tavern on the green from 1770 to 1899. This house was built in 1813 by Paul Dudley, local housewright and publican, for his brother David.

Well-preserved stenciling was found under wallpaper in the front hall and left front parlor. The initial viewing

Extant stenciling in remarkably good original condition in front stair hall of Dudley house.

Early-nineteenth-century extant stenciling in front left parlor of Dudley house.

by the author was very evocative since, without a doubt, the parlor was stenciled by J. Gleason. However, the two-tiered hallway featured designs commonly associated with another artist, namely Moses Eaton. Thanks to Janet Waring, Eaton is a very well-known artist credited with a large percentage of the known folk-style wall stenciling (due partially to the lack of other candidates).

All the designs on the parlor walls match those from Rhode Island walls previously attributed to J. Gleason. The two-color, large daisy motif in particular bears a striking resemblance to that in the Westcott house of Scituate, Rhode Island (I.6).

The hall features two filler motifs and a vertical, yet to be seen by the author on a wall by Gleason. They can be seen on numerous walls attributed to the Eatons (p. 54) in New Hampshire and Maine; however, close examination shows slight differences between designs on this wall and stencils found in a paint box belonging to the Eatons in collections of the Society for the Preservation of New England Antiquities. Perhaps these minute inconsistencies are due to the necessity to recut stencils many times during the forty- to fifty-year span of Eaton's work,

or perhaps they reflect personal style preferences or techniques incorporated when an artist borrows from another or copies from a mutual source. An early collaboration of some sort by J. Gleason and the Eatons cold also account for this puzzling sharing of designs.

The beautifully manicured Douglas cemetery, which dates to the mid–eighteenth century and is just across the green from the David Dudley house, provides a very bizarre location for wall stenciling. A small family tomb contains stenciling at the top and base of its cement walls. The designs are unfamiliar and seem to be of a later date (about 1830) than the Dudley house stenciling. The tomb, entered by descending five or six steps, is now empty, but outlines of three plaques containing the names of those who once rested here can be clearly seen on the main wall. People of wealth and culture, possibly leading citizens of this early Massachusetts village, must have built this uniquely ornamented tomb—perhaps members of the Dudley family?

Goodale farmhouse. *Courtesy Persis Corporation, Honolulu.*

I.13. Goodale farm, 1703
Hudson (Marlborough), Massachusetts
Artist: Unknown, circa 1800–1810

THE MOST ANCIENT section of the interesting and important Goodale stenciled house was built by John Goodale, grandson of the emigrant and the first settler of Marlborough, in 1703. Over the years the two-story, one-room-per-floor house grew into a stately sixteen-room home with numerous outbuildings. It remained in the same family for seven generations, until in 1926 a disastrous fire and changing farm economics forced its sale to a nonrelation, Edna Little Greenwood, an early and avid collector of American decorative arts.[21] With the aid of her friend George Francis Dow,[22] a well-known antiquarian and historian, she restored and filled the house and outbuildings with her vast collections.[23] Following her death in 1975, the house was purchased by a distant relative of the Goodale clan, Asa Thurston Twigg-Smith of Hawaii,[24] who commissioned the Society for the Preservation of New England Antiquities (SPNEA) to restore the property, thereby preserving this remarkable piece of history for posterity.

During the Greenwood-Dow restoration, stenciling was found under wallpaper in five second-floor rooms, enlarged about 1800 by Abner Goodale to accommodate a growing family and perhaps the additional workers

Stenciling in a second-floor chamber. Section to the right is original and that to the left is re-created. *Courtesy Persis Corporation, Honolulu.*

needed to run a thriving farm. He raised the rear of the house to two full stories, making the entire building a full two-room depth and two-story height, then built a new roof. Some of these rooms were partitioned, creating numerous new sleeping chambers. New sections and old received new plaster walls in some areas at that time. Although early stenciling is very difficult to date, since there is usually no definite proof of age, the author believes that the stenciling was applied shortly after the completion of this renovation, dating the work to 1800–1810. Both artists and designs were locally available: Abner's wife was the daughter of the proprietor of the Red Horse Tavern (Wayside Inn) in neighboring Sudbury, which sported two circa 1790 stenciled floors painted by an unknown artist, along with early wallpaper for inspiration. However, other possible stencil dates have been proposed. Alexander J. Wall, in a 1936 article,[25] and Janet Waring's 1937 book both give 1778 as the date of the stenciling. In addition, Waring (who undoubtedly discovered and saw firsthand more stenciling than most in the field) groups the Goodale stenciling with similar designs in two Rhode Island houses stenciled by J. Gleason (I.2 and I.4) and two unattributed houses in Massachusetts, and concludes that they were all executed before 1800. SPNEA, on the other hand, as part of their 1990 *Historic Structure Report on the Goodale Farm*, concludes that the stenciling dates from 1840–41, believing it to be part of a major renovation to the house in the Greek Revival style by David Goodale between 1840 and 1841.[26]

Considering that the plaster in the stenciled rooms has been dated to the 1800 period[27] and that family oral history attributes the stenciling to a period during Abner's ownership (1780–1823), the author is comfortable with 1800–1810 as the most probable stenciling date. A thorough study of the Goodale Collection, housed at the Sturbridge Village Library, has revealed no conclusive information to substantiate the 1840–41 date, or to challenge the circa 1800 date. By 1840 the stenciled areas would have been worn, soiled, and out of fashion, in need of a fresh coat of paint or even wallpaper in the newest Grecian style. In the 1840s an increasing number of books and magazines were promoting the use of wallpaper in the new classical revival styles, either hand-blocked or made by the new machine method.[28]

As to the artist or pair of artists responsible for these wonderful colorful designs, there are several possibilities. We know that the Gleason family settled early in this part of eastern Massachusetts and indeed were neighbors and relatives of the Goodales.[29] However, the ancestors of another well-documented stencil artist also helped to settle this region. The Eaton family arrived from England in the seventeenth century and settled in the Watertown area. Moses Eaton, Sr., was born in Needham, just twenty miles east of Hudson, in 1753, and lived there until 1793, when at age forty he moved to Hancock, New Hampshire. His son Moses Jr., probably the best-documented stencil artist, was born in Hancock in 1796. Several unanswered questions remain about Moses Eaton, Sr., including whether he learned the art of wall stenciling (perhaps as an apprentice) before moving to New Hampshire; if so, from whom; and how much work he did before leaving Massachusetts. We will probably never know conclusively whether Gleason, one of the Eatons, a combination of both, or neither actually worked on the Goodale house. Abner Goodale himself has also been suggested as a possible artist. Whoever was responsible, it is very clear that the Goodale stenciling, which could be the earliest extant example of this genre, greatly influenced both J. Gleason and the Eatons, and indeed many other artists working during the Federal period.

Original panel of stenciling from a second bedchamber. *Courtesy Persis Corporation, Honolulu.*

Only two small sections of the original, nearly two-hundred-year-old stenciling remain intact, with the rest re-created at various times and with varying degrees of authenticity. Considering the very vulnerable materials used in the original execution and the many assaults on its existence over the years, it is amazing that any has survived at all. Following is a brief summary of its history, both known and surmised:

1. Stenciling was applied about 1800 using distemper paint for the stencil designs on a pigmented whitewashed background. Both types of paint are water soluble and thus could easily have been washed off with plain water.

2. During the next century or so, overpainting was done, possibly with water-soluble paint in the front rooms and oil paint in two small back rooms.

3. Numerous layers of wallpaper were applied except to two small areas, one in each front bedroom. One was behind a large cabinet and the other was intentionally left exposed by the family.

4. The house was purchased by Edna Little Greenwood in 1926 and restored under the direction of George Francis Dow. Paper was removed, taking whitewash with it and revealing stenciling in five areas. The stenciling was re-created by William Houck, a Boston artist, at this time. In the front rooms where original stenciling survived, he was able to re-create it in a very authentic manner. The three small back rooms, however, due to the loss of original work and overpainting with nonsoluble paint in several rooms, presented little evidence as to the original layout or design, forcing the artist to improvise. A lack of knowledge about early stenciling at the time resulted in some design choices that were somewhat inappropriate according to today's standards. Distemper, which was still commonly used in the 1920s, was used for the re-creations.

5. After Edna Greenwood's death in 1975, the house was purchased by Asa Thurston Twigg-Smith and restored by the SPNEA. The stenciling was cleaned and stabilized, and missing sections inpainted with distemper and pigmented whitewash. Thus examples of important early-nineteenth-century work, along with 1920s work by pioneers in the field of paint restoration, have been preserved side by side to be studied and enjoyed by future architectural paint historians.

I.14. Unknown house
Probably Hudson, Massachusetts
Artist: J. Gleason

Facsimile of stenciling from an anonymous house in Hudson, Massachusetts.

THIS RE-CREATION OF stenciling in an unknown house was inspired by pictures found in the Historical Society of Early American Decoration collections at the Museum of American Folk Art Library in New York City. All of the designs, already in the author's collection, were recorded either at the Goodale farm in Hudson or in houses in northwestern Rhode Island stenciled by J. Gleason. This particular stenciling is important because this is the first time the author has seen the "kaleidoscope" design, used so profusely by Gleason in Rhode Island, on a wall that could be in the Hudson, Massachusetts, area.

The re-creation is based on three different views of a room with these designs, found in a file of photographs collected by Esther Brazer while researching early American painting techniques in the 1930s and 1940s. The photographs were identified on the back, in Mrs. Brazer's hand, as simply "Mr. & Mrs. B. K. Little, Hudson, Mass." Their location in the file came immediately after pictures of the Goodale farm stenciling, which were marked "Edna Little Greenwood, Time Stone Farm, Marlborough," on the back and were taken after the 1926 restoration.

A check with Jane Nylander, head of the Society for the Preservation of New England Antiquities and an expert on the history and collections of the Littles, indicates no references to stenciling in the Littles' early home in Hudson, called Little Acres. It is also interesting to note that these pictures did not appear in Mrs. Little's 1952 book on wall painting. It looks as if the house containing this important stenciling will remain a great mystery, one of many in the study of early wall stenciling.

(These mystery pictures are very intriguing to the author because they show J. Gleason designs commingling with those from the Goodale farm, on a wall possibly located in Hudson, Massachusetts, reinforcing the probability of Gleason's participation in the execution of the Goodale stenciling.)

Israel Gibbs House. Photo circa 1910 by Sumner Gilbert Wood. *Courtesy Blandford Historical Society.*

I.15. Israel Gibbs house, circa 1800
Blandford, Massachusetts
Artist: S. E. Betts and L. W. Langdon

Overmantel in a second-floor bedchamber of Gibbs house, with artists' names clearly stenciled in center of panel. Photo circa 1910 by Sumner Gilbert Wood. *Courtesy Blandford Historical Society.*

A PHOTOGRAPH TAKEN early in the twentieth century, by pioneer photo-historian Sumner G. Wood, might prove to be the only surviving image of the work of two early stencil artists. Wood visually recorded the homes, highways, and artifacts of Blandford to be used as illustrations for his three books: *Taverns and Turnpikes of Blandford,* which he published in 1908; *Ulster Scots and Blandford Scouts,* 1928; and *The Homes and Habits of Ancient Blandford,* published posthumously by the Blandford Historical Society in 1985.

Among Wood's unpublished photographs in the collections of the Blandford Historical Society is a most interesting photo of a stenciled overmantel complete with a pair of rare stenciled signatures of the two artists responsible for the decoration. It is identified by Wood as "frescoes, bedroom in the house of Mrs. Gibbs." Also included is an exterior view of the house containing the stenciling identified as the Hannah A. Gibbs house on Chester Road.

The Gibbs family came to Blandford, an early Scottish settlement, in the 1730s and settled in the north end along what is now Chester Road. They were, in fact, of English descent, but Israel Gibbs's marriage to Mary Hamilton made him the progenitor of Scotch-Irish stock. Later Gibbses followed his lead and married into Scotch clans.

Blandford was crisscrossed by numerous important early road systems and, until the railroad left it isolated, was listed in the almanacs of the day as an important stop for post and stage routes, with numerous taverns to provide food and entertainment for travelers and locals alike. It is hard to imagine this now serene town as the bustling cosmopolitan center that it undoubtedly once was.

Originally called Glasgow, Blandford was settled primarily by Scotch-Irish Presbyterians from Ulster Ireland, who fled from their homeland to Ireland and from there to America due to political and religious oppression starting in 1719. Wood describes them as men of sterling qualities who were resourceful pioneers and who became substantial citizens and ardent patriots. The "Presbyterian circuit" soon developed with much intercourse between their settlements in New England, New York, and Pennsylvania, with like social, religious, and racial interests. Scots traveling for social reasons such as courtship or business would carry verbal and written news and messages from one settlement to the other. Thus, it is not surprising to find the same Scottish surnames in most of the early settlements.

The Scots seem to have a deep-seated affinity for orna-mentation. After all, numerous artists were bred in the ancient painters' academies and artists' guilds found in the cultural centers of Scotland such as Edinburgh and Glasgow. The author has found many Scottish towns with paint-decorated walls, such as Loudon in New Hampshire, Argyle, New York, and Stewartstown, Penn-sylvania. The "Presbyterian circuit" could have been a convenient way for itinerant artists to announce their arrival in the next town along the route or even secure future commissions through family referrals.

The stenciled house depicted here, built around 1800 perhaps by Israel Gibbs, Jr., remained in the family until the 1950s, when they sold it to the Coons family, who then sold it in 1981, at which time it was dismantled and either sold piece by piece or rebuilt in New York State. In either case the survival of the stenciled walls seems doubtful. This early Wood photograph seems to be the only remaining image of this most important stenciling. Fortunately, history-conscious neighbors traced some of the designs and have clear memories of all the rooms on the first floor, and at least two on the second floor, as hav-ing stenciling.

There is also a picture of the name "Betts" peeking through wallpaper on another Gibbs house. Recently, there have been reports of stenciling having been in a house in the center of town and in one on Otis Stage Road, both in Blandford. Also, Sumner Wood states that the Taggart Tavern had "frescoed walls,"[30] a description he used for the stenciling in the Gibbs house. In addition to these five possible stenciled houses, the Washington Tavern in Westfield, just east of Blandford, is pictured in *Ulster Scots* showing scroll-type painted decoration[31] on either side of a fireplace in an upper front room. Bland-ford obviously was visited by more than one traveling artisan.

I.16. Josiah Sage house, 1803
South Sandisfield, Massachusetts
Artist: S. E. Betts and L. W. Langdon
and/or Stimp, 1824

VERY FINE STENCILING ornamented at least five rooms of the Josiah Sage house, built in the southern Berkshire region of Massachusetts close to the old Sandy Brook Turnpike, which runs south to Hartford, Connecticut. Its designs were carefully recorded by Gina Martin in the 1970s,[32] which is fortunate for historians of early stencil-ing since the Sage house burned to the ground not long after.

Once a prosperous area, Sandisfield was the financial center of the county, with its rich farmers acting as moneylenders for the local businessmen. Josiah Sage, the builder of this house and one of the wealthiest men in the area, was at one time believed to be a partner in Hitch-cock, Alford & Co., the famous chair manufactory in Riverton, Connecticut. However, recent information sug-gests that another Josiah Sage, one of five in the Sandis-field area at that time, was the actual partner.

Many of the motifs seen on the walls of the Stratton Tavern (I.17) were found on an attic wall of the Sage house as a sort of sampler of the artist's portfolio, with the date 1824 scratched in the plaster above. However, the designs actually used to ornament the first- and second-floor rooms are much more elaborate and bear a striking resemblance to those in the Israel Gibbs house (I.15).

Since this house has traditionally been attributed to

Stimp, one wonders about the relationship among the three—Stimp, S. E. Betts, and L. W. Langdon.

A set of twenty-eight stencils that match those seen in the Sage house and the Gibbs house was found before 1970 in a house attic in northern New York State, quite near the Vermont border. According to the stencils' owner, Jessica Bond of Dorset, Vermont, they appear to be quite old, are expertly cut from high-grade paper, and still retain layers of old paint as well as color notations on the back.[33] Unfortunately, they are not labeled with the name of the artist!

Facsimile of stencil decoration in a second-floor chamber of Sage house, showing a pineapple frieze that is similar to, but not exactly like, that in Gibbs house (I.15).

I.17. Hezekiah Stratton, Jr., Tavern, 1760
Northfield Arms, Massachusetts
Artist: Stimp (attributed), after 1810

BUILT ABOUT 1760 for Hezekiah Stratton, Jr., whose father, Hezekiah Sr., moved west from Concord, Massachusetts, in the early eighteenth century, this house is one of the northernmost examples of the high-style architecture preferred by the Connecticut Valley elite of the period. These were the first large dwellings in the area to incorporate design elements from English pattern books.

An enormous ell, larger than the original house, was added about 1810, an indication of the rapid growth and prosperity enjoyed along the Connecticut River at that time. Not long after its completion, several artists, perhaps traveling on the river, applied stenciled and freehand scroll-type decoration to four of the new upstairs chambers.[34] The freehand-painted flowers and lozenges are attributed to Noah Graves,[35] and the stencil work is thought to be by an artist known only as "Stimp." This may be a short form of Stimpson or a misspelling of Stemp, a common surname in the Surrey area of England.

Stimp's work is found up and down the banks of the Connecticut River and westward into New York State. He was described as middle-aged in 1834 when he worked in

(Left) Early view of one of two stenciled bedchambers in Stratton Tavern. *Courtesy Old Sturbridge Village.*

(Below) Early image of one of two freehand-painted chambers in Stratton Tavern. *Courtesy Old Sturbridge Village.*

Washington, Connecticut, which would place him in his mid-twenties when the addition to the Stratton Tavern was completed. Perhaps he was at the beginning of his career after an apprenticeship with another (unknown) artist. A possible indication of early work is the noticeably smaller scale of this stenciling compared to later work attributed to him—which suggests either that Stimp enlarged his designs to accommodate later, higher-celinged houses or that other artists were using adaptations of Stimp's designs, just as he was using adaptations of some Gleason-Eaton designs.

The decoration in this tavern is the second of two examples of Stimp-attributed stenciling in Massachusetts to be included here. (For more information on work by this artist in Massachusetts, see Janet Waring's book.) This Massachusetts group includes walls with predominantly Stimp motifs side by side with a few recognizable Gleason-Eaton designs, another indication that these early artisans readily borrowed from one another, either by tracing directly from a wall or by using, as apprentices, their teachers' designs when starting out on their own.

The Stratton house and its decoration fell on hard times in the twentieth century. Old Sturbridge Village came to the rescue, providing much preservation expertise in order to save the old house, which also had served as a tavern. Finally it was sold to a private party, who moved it east to Concord, the original seat of the Stratton family.

Two panels of stenciling, one from each room, two panels of scroll painting, and a stenciled floor survived the move from Northfield to Concord. One example of each type of wall decoration and the floor are installed in the main part of the house. The other two painted plaster examples are carefully stored in a nearby barn.

Connecticut

The settlement of Connecticut in the 1630s was the beginning of the westward movement of the mostly English colonists in the New World. When news of the great fertility of the Connecticut River Valley reached eastern Massachusetts communities, many land-hungry settlers who had grown restive under strict Puritan laws began to migrate westward. Slightly before this English migration, the Dutch had established a short-lived trading post and fort near the site of the present state capital, Hartford.

Despite the fact that Connecticut did not have a particularly large or impressive colonial port or city, numerous artisans were attracted to the area, as proven by the impressive amount of colonial and Federal-period decorative painting that has been recorded in the state. The direction of travel for settlers as well as artists was not only the overland east-to-west movement from coastal Rhode Island and Massachusetts but also south to north utilizing the much more convenient water route that serviced the early urban centers developing along the banks of the Connecticut River. This southern approach could have introduced the talents of artists from the mid-Atlantic and southern states to this southernmost New England colony.

Travel on the Connecticut River was crucial to the development of the entire valley. Sailing vessels connected the lower Connecticut or tidewater towns with other eastern seaport towns. Farther up the river, the chief locomotion was provided by sturdy "polemen" who muscled their raftlike boats through rapids and narrows. By the first quarter of the nineteenth century, canals were in place that skirted the trickiest spots, making travel on the river much faster and more comfortable than traveling by overland routes.[36]

There are myriad and diverse examples of wall stenciling in Connecticut. Some are by artists seen before in Rhode Island and Massachusetts; some will be completely new to readers. In addition we will see, again, work most assuredly by the elusive J. Gleason of northwestern Rhode Island fame.

THE HIGH-STYLE Federal house of Abner Richmond, with a grand two-story front entrance and overdoor fanlight featuring inlaid "lace glass" tea saucers, was built on ninety-four acres of land purchased in 1802 by Abner Richmond, who was born in Woodstock, Connecticut, in 1761. He represented the fifth generation of Richmonds to reside in America. His earliest ancestor, John, arrived in Massachusetts in 1635 and was one of the original purchasers of Taunton, Massachusetts, in 1637.

In 1812 Abner received compensation from the town of Ashford for land taken to build a new road through Richmond—land quite close to his "new dwelling house." This development might have been the inspiration to reconfigure his home to include a tavern. A public room and second kitchen were added to the first floor and public sleeping quarters to the second. The remaining areas were slightly renovated to serve as the private quarters for the Richmond family. The new tavern soon was located on what is now called the old Hartford and Boston Turnpike, the last part of which (called the Center Turnpike)[37] was charted in 1826 to connect the northwestern corner of Thompson, Connecticut, to Tolland, Connecticut—thus completing a pike from Boston to Hartford whose earlier parts had been in operation since about 1800. This connection would have made Westford a very desirable location for a tavern.

Remnants of beautifully designed and executed stenciling were found in the 1970s under much wallpaper in one of the back second-floor chambers.[38] Perhaps this

I.18. Abner Richmond house, 1803–12
Westford, Windham County, Connecticut
Artist: J. Gleason, circa 1820

(Top) Abner Richmond house, with superb Federal two-tiered front entrance and classical palladian window at second level. *Courtesy Abner Richmond House, Ashford, Conn. Owners: Edd and Karan Oberg.*

(Bottom) Beautifully designed overmantel in same chamber of Richmond house. *Courtesy Abner Richmond House, Ashford, Conn. Owners: Edd and Karan Oberg.*

View of stenciling in a second-floor bedchamber or sitting room of Richmond house. *Courtesy Abner Richmond House, Ashford, Conn. Owners: Edd and Karan Oberg.*

room was a special sitting area for family use or the master sleeping chamber. Many motifs used to ornament this fine room are identical to ones used by J. Gleason on Rhode Island walls, including two designs found in the signed Hopkins house in Foster, Rhode Island. This stenciling seems to be the work of a more mature and inventive Gleason with a large portfolio of stencil motifs who is now ornamenting overmantels with an eye-catching arrangement of twinned vases filled profusely with red carnations, elements of which bear a striking similarity to work by Stimp, particularly the twinned flower-filled vases similar to those found in the Sage house[39] of Sandisfield, Massachusetts. The twinned large, oval motifs above the vases also were used by Stimp, as seen in the Nathaniel Holcomb house in northwestern Connecticut, whose stenciling was recently restored by expert John Canning.[40] Each nineteenth-century artist created a new design by reversing one repeat of his "arch and candle" frieze stencil design. When one compares the two, differences are readily obvious, reflecting the slight variations in the borders. What is not obvious is which artist was influenced by the other. The date of the Stimp work, reportedly after 1835, seems to be later than the Gleason version, according to the architectural history of these two houses.

Gleason did not limit his work to this northeastern section of Connecticut, since a fragment of wall plaster with the signature "diamond and petal" vertical border he used recurrently is in the collections of the New Haven Colony Historical Society and is identified as being from the New Haven area, which is southern coastal Connecticut.

At the time the Richmond house stenciling was executed, Gleasons resided just east of Westford in Thompson, Connecticut. John Gleason[41]—brother of James, who was mentioned in connection with the signed Hopkins house (I.1)—was born in Oxford, Massachusetts, in 1745 but removed to Thompson after his marriage in 1780. Their son, John Jr., was born in Thompson about 1800. Thus we have two more possible candidates for the real J. Gleason!

I.19. Hamilton house, circa 1820

Ellington, Connecticut

Artist: J. Gleason (attributed)

RECENT RESEARCH CONFIRMS that a good number of Federal homes were stencil-decorated, but only a small percentage of this work has survived into the twenty-first century. The walls that have, remarkably, survived are valuable artifacts of America's materials-culture history.

An example is the once-handsome Hamilton house of Ellington, Connecticut, whose current status is not known. It had been abandoned for close to thirty years before being purchased in early 2000 by a Willington, Connecticut, dealer in antique-restoration materials. A condition of the sale was that the house be removed from the lot as soon as possible.

Before the move commenced, the house's new owner spotted stenciling peeking out from under a thick layer of wallpaper and paint in the left front parlor. He called the author, who visited in June 2000. At that time the house was observed to be in a sad state of neglect. Many of its original architectural features, including the front door enframement, had been removed by previous owners or by scavengers. What remained of the outline indicated that the original door surround was of the Federal triangular pedimented type, probably with a half-fan skylight,

Stenciling in Hamilton house photographed shortly after being discovered under multiple layers of wallpaper.

wide pilasters on either side, and dentil trim complementing the trim still visible at the roof line. In addition, the front interior stairway had been removed.

In spite of lying entombed for over a century beneath six layers of paper, red oil-based paint, and a layer of thick water-based plaster, a good portion of the stenciling clung tenaciously to the walls. The rest came off with its covering. The water-based stencil paint had partially bonded with the water-based plaster overcoat, leaving a clear impression of the stencil designs in a portable form on back of wallpaper. There was, then, no need to trace the stenciling inside the house, in poor light and amid thirty years' accumulation of dust and mold. Instead, the author removed large sections of the stencil-backed paper to be studied in the studio and preserved as a material record of the Hamilton house wall stenciling.

All of the motifs found in the Hamilton house were already in the author's collection, filed under J. Gleason. Many had only recently been viewed in the Abner Richmond house, located a short distance east of the Hamilton house.

Unfortunately, the story of the Hamilton house and its Gleason stenciling will not have as happy an ending as that of the Richmond house. Even if the Hamilton house is reconstructed at a new location, the stenciled plaster cannot survive the dismantling process. The fate of the Hamilton stenciling is shared by a lamentably large percentage of original stenciled walls. A careful recording of their designs is an essential step for ensuring their preservation and re-creation.

❧

I.20. Joshua LaSalle house
Windham, Connecticut
Artist: Unknown, circa 1820

ONE WALL OF STENCILED, wooden paneling was removed from the Joshua LaSalle house in the 1950s and installed in the American Museum located in the outskirts of Bath, England. This fine museum, with its extensive collection of early American decorative art, was the brainchild of two Americans, John Judkyn, an art collector and quarry owner, and Dr. Dallas Pratt, a New York–born physician. Opened in the 1960s, it is housed in Claverton Manor, a lovely old Georgian mansion surrounded by sweeping lawns and a memorable view of the River Avon. For three years Judkyn and Pratt toured the states gathering treasures to be shipped to England and installed in their new museum.

The LaSalle house wall, sheathed with feather-edged

View of stenciled sheathing from Joshua LaSalle house, which once stood in Windham, Connecticut. *Reproduced by permission of the American Museum in Britain, Bath,* ©.

boards ornamented with stenciling, was installed in the museum's "stenciled bedroom," which also features stenciled American furniture and stenciled room accessories of wood and tin, plus a wonderful stenciled counterpane as an example of stenciling on textiles.

The stencil layout of the panel depicted here is unusual: it has no horizontal borders at ceiling or floor, just two alternating vertical border designs. A layout scheme like this was used by William Houck, who in 1926 recreated the early-nineteenth-century stenciling in a back room of the Goodale farm, Hudson, Massachusetts (I.13).

The artist attribution is not clear: the broad-leaf design was frequently used by Gleason, but the more delicate second design in the alternation is more closely asso-

ciated with Moses Eaton. This second design was found on the back of a small fragment of wallpaper from the William Slater house in Mansfield, Connecticut, by Sandra Tarbox. It was also used on the walls of the Daniel Kingfield house of Brookfield, Vermont.

It is interesting to note that Windham County is accommodated with several early turnpike roads, two of which intersect each other at right angles at the town of Windham, the seat of the county—one from Boston to New London and the other leading from Hartford to Providence. There is also a turnpike leading from this apex to Middletown, Connecticut—a very convenient route for early traveling artists seeking commissions in Connecticut. This is undoubtedly the reason for the great concentration of all types of stenciling in northeastern Connecticut.

Stimp in Litchfield County, Connecticut

Recent research by the Gunn Museum of Washington, Connecticut, which staged a most interesting and informative exhibit on Litchfield County wall painting in September 1998, has given a possible name to the artist known only as "Stimp"—who was first introduced to us by Janet Waring in her 1937 book. She wrote that a man by that name "drifted into the village [Washington Center] when he was past middle age" and "that his background was obscure." Local verbal history relates that in 1834 this same artist, "crazed with drink, came to the house of his chief benefactor [Isaac Hartwell] and attempted to kill him." Stimp was overpowered, led to the village whipping post, and eventually carted off to the Litchfield jail.

A recent study of the jail records provided no information as to the full name of Stimp; however, a study of local tax records by Sarah Griswald, past director of the Gunn Museum, has found numerous references to a Caleb H. Stimpson, paying taxes between 1837 and 1846 to towns in Litchfield County where Stimp-stenciled walls have been found. There is also information suggesting that earlier generations of Stimpsons lived in the Litchfield area and, according to the 1840 Connecticut census, were still living in the area. This information indicates, first, that Stimp was a traveling artist who lived and worked in an area long enough to show up on tax rolls and, second, that he in all likelihood had family roots in Connecticut.

The largest number of written references to Caleb H. Stimpson, and perhaps some of the most interesting, were found in the town of Washington. In an 1839 ledger kept by Daniel Hartwell[42] is a notation saying that Stimpson paid the sum of $1.22 for 17½ pounds of veal, which is interesting in content but also because of the distinct possibility that Daniel was related to Isaac, the focus of Stimp's wrath according to Waring. In addition, in 1840 he paid a tax bill of $20 to Washington, and in the 1840 Connecticut census a Caleb B. Stinson appears as a head of family in Washington (perhaps another example of the notoriously bad spelling often exhibited by early census takers).

A few samples of the numerous houses in Washington, Connecticut, stenciled by Stimp, a.k.a. Caleb H. Stimpson:

The Isaac Hartwell house, built in the first quarter of the nineteenth century, was the home of Stimp's benefactor, whom he reportedly tried to murder. Stenciling was found in a parlor under multiple layers of wallpaper prior to 1937. Its deteriorated condition required its complete repainting by a local artist, according to Waring.[43]

The Samuel Clark house, built in the first quarter of the nineteenth century, was restored in the 1930s, at which time stenciling found in a second-floor chamber was in good enough condition to require only light retouching. This house probably contained more stenciled rooms.[44]

The Titus house, built in 1760, has three or four rooms of stenciling under later hardened whitewash.[45]

The Logan house, built in 1820, has one room of re-created stenciling with a single panel of original work retained. It probably contained more Stimp work originally.

Bethlehem was another Litchfield County town where Stimp lived and worked. Several references to Caleb Stimpson in Bethlehem tax records have been found. In 1842 he paid a $20 tax on unspecified property, and in 1845 he paid a $12 tax on a cow and a clock.

The Martin house, which was built in Bethlehem in the first quarter of the nineteenth century, had numerous rooms of Stimp stenciling, which was recorded and covered with a protective covering of Sheetrock in the 1970s. It is now owned by the Antiquarian and Landmarks Society.

Woodbury is another Litchfield County town where Stimp apparently lived and worked long enough to appear on a tax roll. In 1846 he paid a $10 tax bill to this town. It is interesting to note that his property tax payments decreased from $20 in 1840 to $10 in 1846.

The Peet house, built in New Milford, also Litchfield County, contains at least four areas of Stimp stenciling including a flower-filled vase with vermilion birds and hearts, which was retrieved and recorded by Sandra Tarbox in the late 1970s. No tax records were found here containing the name Caleb Stimpson, but there was a Solomen Stinson listed directly after Caleb Stinson in the 1840 Connecticut census for the town of New Milford. The early-nineteenth-century Peet house is currently under extensive restoration by restoration architect Chandler Saint.

It is interesting to note that just north of Litchfield County, in the Berkshire area of Massachusetts, there was another Peet house with rooms decorated by Stimp. Waring mentioned a house on the outskirts of New Marlborough, Massachusetts, that was built by Edmund Peet, a minister who died in 1828. Stimp is credited with much stenciling in this southwestern area of Massachusetts.

Caleb H. Stimpson's body of work in Connecticut seems to reflect the work habits of a very prolific, perhaps travel-weary, older artist, who if he learned his craft as a teenager could have been putting brush to wall for over forty years. It seems reasonable to imagine him thus in his later years: his main concern seems to be filling walls in the most expedient manner possible. Therefore, he uses larger motifs in order to fill the wall space faster, and he all but gives up the use of the paneled layout (dividing the wall into vertical panels using narrow, intricate vertical borders spaced about twelve inches apart before filling with alternating geometric and floral motifs). He opts for the faster method, which is simply to fill the space with alternating large and easy-to-stencil motifs. His work in Connecticut, though very charming, is not as ambitious artistically as his earlier work.

His signature designs, the pinwheel and acorn border, traveled with settlers into northern New England and New York State. They can be found in numerous homes and taverns leading west, some stenciled by his hand, probably prior to his lengthy stay in Connecticut, and some by Stimp protégés and/or copyists.

It is interesting to note that Stimp stenciling shares many designs with that of J. Gleason, suggesting a possible earlier connection with the older artist who left his signature in Foster, Rhode Island.

I.21. Hubbard house, 1794
Cromwell, Connecticut
Artist: Stimp (attributed) circa 1825

THE SUBSTANTIAL two-story Hubbard house, located just south of Hartford on the old Hartford Turnpike, was built in 1794 and operated as a tavern from 1808 to 1833.

Typical Stimp stencil decoration was found before 1926 on the walls of its ballroom. His large "arch and candle" frieze motif (a variation of one used by J. Gleason) was found, along with many other designs previously seen on Stimp walls in Massachusetts and Connecticut.

In another room, on the opposite side of the house, is an overmantel with a stenciled Masonic symbol over a large stenciled urn filled with drooping leaves and berries, quite similar to ones to be seen in western New York State (I.40). Perhaps because of the anti-Masonic movement of 1826–27, this tavern provided a less conspicuous gathering place for Masons than their suburban temple. The 1826–27 date could suggest a date for the Masonic panel but not for the ballroom work, which seems to be by a different hand, namely Stimp.

Hearsay has it that one of the artists came from Hartford or New Haven, but his name has long since been forgotten![46]

Wall stenciling thought to be from Hubbard house. *Courtesy Susan Hibbett.*

Exterior of Sereno Holcomb house.

I.22. Sereno Holcomb house,
first section, 1803; second, circa 1820
Granby, Connecticut
Artist: Unknown, second quarter nineteenth century

THE FIRST SECTION of the Sereno Holcomb house, located at the corner of the early North Hartland and Granville Highways, was built in 1803 by a Jesse Munson, Jr. Unusual stenciling was found in a fine Adamesque addition to the street side of the dwelling built by Sereno Holcomb (1785–1863) early in his fifty-three-year residence in this charming farmhouse.

The stencil artist commissioned by Holcomb to ornament at least four rooms utilized designs used by earlier artists such as Gleason, Eaton, and Stimp, ones of his own design that are completely new to this study, plus ones seen only once before, in the front hall of the Carr house (II.9) of Wickford, Rhode Island.

The Granby front hall, partially cleared of its wallpaper covering, shares a color scheme, a stylized swag frieze, and a twelve-petal-daisy filler motif with decoration in the front hall of the Wickford house.

In the Granby parlor, recently re-created by John Canning & Co. of Southington, Connecticut, a spandrel-type design is incorporated into a very strong vertical border used at twenty-two-inch intervals entirely surrounding the rooms. This identical motif was seen in the Wickford front hall as a spandrel joining at the corners a Pompeiian-type freeform foliate vine that frames various wall panels.

Other areas with stenciling include a bedchamber, which has recently been painted over but in a way that allows the stenciling to be easily retrievable when desired, and a second parlor that will be re-created by Canning, probably before the publication of this book.

The origins of this artist, whether in the Connecticut River Valley or the East Coast of New England, the amount of work executed by him between northern Connecticut and coastal Rhode Island, and of course his name will undoubtedly remain a mystery—one of many in the study of American wall stenciling.

Stenciling re-created by John Canning Co. in a front parlor of Holcomb House.

I.23. Nathaniel Holcomb house, 1719

Granby, Connecticut

Artist: Probably Stimp, after 1835

Stenciling re-created by John Canning in a first-floor room of Nathaniel Holcomb house. *Courtesy The Nathaniel Holcomb III house (1719), Granby, Conn.*

THE NATHANIEL HOLCOMB house, a meticulously re-stored, early eighteenth-century house said to be the oldest in Granby, was placed on the National Register of Historic Places in 1982. Built by Nathaniel Holcomb III, who was just one generation removed from the original settlers of Granby, the house has been owned and altered by numerous families over its long history. Consider Morgan, a successful surgeon, who purchased it in 1835 and renovated the original "borning room" into his new place of business. The final touch of his transformation was commissioning a stencil artist to ornament the newly plastered walls with cheery green and red stenciling on a lively yellow ocher ground.[47]

The stenciling, recently re-created by John Canning & Co., contains many motifs suggesting those used by Stimp, but similar stenciling has also been seen on walls decorated early in the nineteenth century by Gleason and Eaton. A round element made by arranging one repeat of the "arch and candle" motif with one semicircular unit up and one down to form a circle was seen before in the Richmond house (I.18) of Westford, Connecticut. Since the Holcomb stenciling dates to after 1835, and that in the Richmond house to the first quarter of the nineteenth century, the Holcomb house artist (probably Stimp) must be the copyist.

Reportedly, the name L. W. Langdon was stenciled on a panel of the Hall-Thompson house in East Granby.[48] Langdon also signed the Gibbs house (I.15) in Blandford, Massachusetts, which is just east of Granby on the early road connecting Stockbridge, Massachusetts, to Hartford, Connecticut. His work in Blandford showed a possible Stimp influence, as does the work in the two Holcomb houses.

Chapter 4

The Northern New England States of Maine, New Hampshire, and Vermont

The ornamentation of their house interiors with painted decoration must have been far from the minds of early settlers in New Hampshire, Maine, and Vermont, with the daily struggle for survival their prime concern. Northern New England, with vast uncivilized areas between small pockets of primitive, fortlike homes that developed along the rustic early road systems, was extremely vulnerable during the French and Indian Wars. The exceptions were a few seaport towns such as Portsmouth, New Hampshire, which by 1700 was a thriving deepwater port with strong cultural and financial ties to Boston.

Not until 1763, the end of the French and Indian conflict, did conditions improve enough for safe and financially rewarding settlement of this wild and dangerous area. Farmers, craftsmen, and entrepreneurs—mostly from crowded sections of the three southern New England states—started to slowly move northward into the area, with the rate greatly increasing after the end of the Revolution. Some came in single-family units, others as whole groups from a particular area, regularly naming the newly settled towns after the ones they had recently exited.

Meet the Eatons

The story of the Eaton family presents a picture typical of many immigrants to northern New England during the post-Revolutionary era. Moses Eaton's ancestors arrived in Watertown, Massachusetts, from England in about 1635, and became the original settlers of Dedham, Massachusetts. The direct line of Moses (1753–1833), a fifth-generation Eaton, stayed close to the eastern shore of Massachusetts for most of the eighteenth century, engaging in farming. Other branches of the family, however, removed to Windham County, Connecticut, and another migrated into New York State.

Flower-spray motif found in a bedchamber of John Durkee house, stenciled around 1820 by Erastus Gates, an ancestor of President Calvin Coolidge. *Courtesy Old Hotel Antiques.*

Moses Easton's military service during the Revolution included being picked by Colonel Benedict Arnold to participate in Arnold's famous march to Canada,[1] for which Eaton was paid the grand sum of seven pounds. Arnold selected only soldiers who were under thirty (Eaton was twenty-two at the time) and were above average height (very advantageous for a future wall stenciler).

In 1793, at the age of forty, Moses moved with his wife, two children, and three brothers from Needham, Massachusetts, to Hancock, New Hampshire, where he was a farmer for many years and his descendants became prominent citizens of the community, according to an Eaton family genealogy written in 1884.[2] It is amazing that a history of the Eaton family, written only fifty years after Eaton's death, did not mention the fact that he had talents other than farming. He, in fact, was a practicing wall stenciler, perhaps the earliest of his group, and taught his son Moses Eaton, Jr. (1796–1886) the art of wall stenciling. Junior became the most documented stencil artist to date and, along with his father, can take credit for the lion's share of the folk-genre wall stenciling found in New Hampshire and Maine.

Moses Jr. probably learned his craft at a very early age from his father, for by the age of eighteen he is said to have been an accomplished stencil artist. By twenty-seven, when his dad was seventy and perhaps retired, he worked for a time with a well-documented folk muralist, Rufus Porter[3] (1792–1884), who was very close in age to Eaton. They reportedly worked together decorating homes mostly in southern New Hampshire and Maine. Moses stenciled the walls, and Rufus painted murals and grained woodwork and fireboards. His association with a renaissance man such as Porter might have inspired Eaton to enlarge the number of painting techniques he could offer to his clients by adding faux graining and marbling for woodwork and perhaps even furniture. He may even have contemplated painting a mural or two. In 1824, almost simultaneous with his partnership with Eaton, Porter wrote and published a book on painting techniques and other interesting words of wisdom titled, *A Select Collection of Approved, Genuine, Secret and Modern Receipts, for the Preparation and Execution of Various Valuable and Curious Arts.* The first edition, published in Concord, Massachusetts, subsequently was published in four more editions in Concord, New Hampshire.

An interesting possibility is that just about the time Porter began painting murals in 1822,[4] he also learned the latest methods of wall stenciling from the Eatons, and

later passed these techniques and designs on to his assistants. The Eatons in turn passed their newly gained information on graining and mural painting along to their assistants. This, combined with the publication of the Porter books in 1824–1826, could account for the wide and rapid dissemination of similar techniques and designs found in homes with painted decoration dating to the second quarter of the nineteenth century.

Perhaps inspired by the much-traveled Rufus Porter, a very active itinerant from 1814 to 1840 (including a two-year voyage to the Northwest Coast and Hawaii), Moses Jr. reportedly embarked on an extensive trip west in the 1830s. This most likely occurred after his father's death in 1833. Later in this book we will see examples of wall stenciling from Tennessee and Indiana that bear a striking resemblance to Eaton work in New England. They are the work either of a meticulous Eaton copyist or of Eaton himself.

Several artifacts attributed to the Eatons have found their way into museum collections. A stencil artist's box used by Moses Jr., and probably by his father before, came into Janet Waring's possession while she researched her 1937 book. Its contents make a statement about the work habits of the artist. It contained eight large, round, very worn brushes, with bits of paint stuck in the bristles, and seventy-eight stencils—component parts for forty complete designs—still edged with thick green, red, and yellow distemper paint. There were no register marks (marks cut into stencils to guide the placement of the second color, usually red, on the already stenciled green part of the motif), indicating the work ethic of a very self-assured and experienced craftsman, working in a very free, spontaneous, and, above all expeditious manner. Stencils were made of oiled heavy brown paper, similar to contemporary oak tag. A rather surprising find was a collection of small carved pine blocks from a much earlier time of a type used to stamp designs on textiles or even wallpaper, perhaps indicating a link between the Eatons and the stamping or printing trades. Waring also tells of seeing a small lump of vermilion paint in a corner of the same attic that yielded the stencil box. Vermilion was a very dear pigment in the time of the Eatons; perhaps the lump could have been minium or red lead (see appendix A on paints). After Janet Waring's death in 1942 at age seventy, the box was donated to the Society for the Preservation of New England Antiquities by her sister, Susan Waring of Yonkers, New York.

More recently, in 1987, a beautifully grained pine box

(approximately 9 × 15 × 3 inches) containing nine samples of faux graining and one sample of bright yellow ground color was acquired by the Museum of American Folk Art (MAFA) in New York City.[5] Reportedly it had been in the Eaton family for many years and was perhaps used by the stencil artists. It is not clear whether this box with its samples was executed by one of the Eatons or simply acquired by them as a sort of learning aid to their study of a new type of graining. The box illustrated the "wet" method of graining, which was introduced in Britain about 1800, probably by way of France.[6] Wet graining involved applying a semitransparent dark to medium oil-based glaze over a lighter base coat. When wet, the glaze was manipulated with many different tools, exposing the lighter base color to create the desired configuration. This method proved to be more subtle than the earlier "sponging" method—where paint was applied in a graining configuration on a dry surface with a brush, then dabbed at with some kind of tool. Tools used for the wet method included brushes of various types, combs, sponges, feathers, etc.

American country painters developed a unique variation of the "wet" graining method. They used a glaze of vinegar and dry pigments, which they manipulated mostly with a putty made of whiting and linseed oil (glazier's putty.) This type of graining can be seen on many pieces of furniture and small room accessories made in the New England area in the first half of the nineteenth century.[7] Under close examination of the graining samples in the MAFA grained box, numerous bubbles appear in the unworked glazed areas, suggesting that the glaze was not totally compatible with the base coat, a reaction that occurs when a vinegar glaze is applied over oil paint. The unpredictable nature of this technique was further heightened as the oil in the putty acted with the vinegar during drying time, creating a great variety of tonal gradations between the light undercoat and the dark glaze above. Another sample in the box, however, the leaf motif in green glaze, suggests a tool much firmer and more durable than a putty stamp, which tends to break down gradually during use and is incapable of creating the exact repetitions seen on the sample. A rigid, durable stamp such as a carved wooden textile stamp, cleaned between each stamping, would be a viable tool for this configuration.

It would seem that Moses Eaton, Jr., in addition to stenciling walls in a beauteous and expedient manner, could also perhaps grain your furniture and woodwork, and adorn your walls and overmantels with scenic murals featuring bright vermilion or minium birds and pears. He certainly seems to be a Yankee itinerant artist who used old-fashioned thrift and creativity to make his name synonymous with the best of early American wall stenciling.

Maine

The northern Maine wilderness was very slow to settle; therefore it did not provide many commissions for traveling artists. Southern Maine, which shared economic and cultural ties with New Hampshire (since mostly emigrants from Massachusetts settled both areas at about the same time), has a large concentration of stenciled walls mostly executed during the second quarter of the nineteenth century.

Margaret Fabian's stencil survey (appendix B) recorded at least forty homes in Maine with stenciling, the greater percentage displaying the Eaton type—much of which will be familiar, but a few indications of change will be evident. The greatest of these is perhaps the work of a more artistically mature craftsman seeking variety through new combinations of color and design.

Exterior of Reverend Perley house. *Courtesy Mr. and Mrs. William C. Thomas.*

I.24. Reverend Samuel Perley house, 1798
Gray, Maine
Artist: Moses Eaton, Jr. and/or Sr., 1825–30

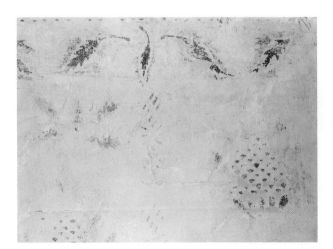

Extant stencil decoration in front stair hall. *Courtesy Mr. and Mrs. William C. Thomas.*

SAMUEL PERLEY, born in 1742 in Ipswich, Massachusetts, was a Harvard-educated minister, lawyer, and physician and a lifelong intimate of President John Adams. He built this house in the Maine wilderness around 1798.

In 1803, at age sixty-one, he gave his estate to his sons, Abraham and Isaac, on the condition that they support him, his wife, and a daughter "until life shall expire." It was to be a very comfortable retirement, since part of this agreement stipulated that Samuel "shall always have hansome velvet jacket and britches" and "one quart of good West India Rum weekly," in addition to more prosaic necessities.

Apparently son Isaac and his family lived on the right side of the house, and his father (Samuel), mother, and sister lived on the other, or left, side of the house. This large residence with its front and back stairways would have provided ample space and privacy for all three generations of the Perley family.

Most likely it was Isaac who commissioned the Eatons to ornament the walls of the Perley family's fine estate. The only two areas of original Eaton work found to date are in the front stair hall and the left front chamber; however, it is likely that more rooms were originally stencil-decorated.

Although the original distemper paint is quite faded, these walls—especially those in the chamber—show the work of a very gifted, experienced, and creative artist who mixed many new designs with old favorites. The overmantel decoration, unfortunately quite worn, seems to have been a large flowering tree with birds perched on top. The tree probably was created by positioning the large carnation-spray stencil repeatedly in different directions. This technique was used often by stencil artisans to decorate the overmantel or the focal point of a room. More birds are perched whimsically on stenciled flower baskets and floral sprays throughout the room, including on a narrow panel between two front windows.

The work in the Perley house displays a fine balance of design and color, and careful attention to the placement and symmetry of the room's layout. All in all, in spite of its fading, these decorations comprise a fine example of Moses Eaton's talents as a stencil virtuoso.

Moses Eaton–attributed stenciling still extant in a bedchanber of Perley house. *Courtesy Mr. and Mrs. William C. Thomas.*

I.25. David Thompson house, 1750
West Kennebunk, Maine
Artist: Moses Eaton, Jr., 1825

View of a wall stenciling from Thompson house parlor before it was demolished prior to 1937. *Courtesy The Brick Store Museum, Kennebunk, Maine.*

BUILT IN ALEWIVE, MAINE, in 1750, on land acquired by Richard Thompson in 1714 as part of a first grant, this house was sadly dismantled in the 1930s. Fortunately, two panels were rescued, albeit with great difficulty, since the plaster was said to have been made of lime ground from baked clamshells, a type of plaster that is "hard as flint." The panels from second-floor rooms are now safely installed at the Brick Store Museum on Kennebunk's Main Street, founded in 1936 by Edith Cleaves Barry, widow of William F. Barry, who was responsible for saving the stenciled panels.

Some of the motifs seen on these sturdy plaster walls are identical to those seen before, but the rich coloration is refreshingly new. Instead of just red and green stenciling on pink or yellow walls, we have the addition of a rich, dark mulberry color, perhaps an indication of the use of cochineal pigment to color the distemper, since this color seems more vibrant than Spanish brown. The combination of dark, rich mulberry, lively orange-red, probably minium (red lead), and dull gray-green stenciled units is very distinctive, especially on a ground of deep, warm gray. Walls in a neighboring house with the same coloration and designs were said to have been painted with milk-based paint. This is quite possible since recipes for paint made by mixing powdered pigments with skim milk arrived in America early in the nineteenth century from England by way of France,[8] introduced as an inexpensive substitute for glue distemper and durable enough to substitute for oil-based paint.

New designs, some not in the famous Eaton stencil box, are seen on these walls, such as the single maple leaf, sunflowers, a large red and black bird perched on the usual overmantel basket (not pictured), the pineapple with leaves, and a new variation of the swag-and-double-tassel motif, replacing one of the tassels with a folded leaf. This is an indication that Moses Jr. was constantly designing new stencils or using old ones in a new manner, not content to follow his father's lead indefinitely.

Stenciling from a second-floor chamber of Thompson house. *Courtesy The Brick Store Museum, Kennebunk, Maine.*

I.26. William GoV house, 1810
Gray, Maine
Artist: Unknown, 1830–35

THE ONE-AND-A-HALF-STORY Cape-style house of William Goff, said to have been the home of the village cooper, contains a fine original example of stenciling by one of many Eaton copyists.

All the designs in red and green on a white ground are variations of well-known designs attributed to the Eatons, such as those in the Reverend Perley house a few miles away. Close inspection of the stencils in the Goff house reveals that they are similar to, but not exact copies of, the Eaton motifs. They are executed with a tad too much distemper paint on the brush, and positioned on the wall in a manner atypical of the Eatons, with the pineapples placed on a level horizontally, not alternated horizontally as well as vertically with the five-oak-leaf motif. While the effect is very pleasing, it was not stenciled by an Eaton, but rather by one of the many anonymous artists working in the Eaton mode.

Panel of stenciling from a parlor in Goff house, just a short distance from Perley house (I.24). *Courtesy Terence and Tori Nadeau.*

The stencil decoration was found in the original left front parlor, under thirteen layers of wallpaper and a thin plasterlike coating. Also uncovered in the same room was a Rufus Porter–like overmantel mural depicting tall trees in the foreground and at least three tiers of hills. It is badly worn. Apparently the green paint used for the foreground hills and the foliage of the six large trees and numerous small trees may have been removed with the wallpaper. What is left is a stark winter scene of skeletal trees and alternating white and gray hills. (The white seems to be bare plaster.)

The condition of the mural and stenciling was examined closely, as were the materials used; neither proved conclusively that the two areas of decoration were created by the same hand, at the same time.

This onetime home of the village maker of barrels and casks—an essential occupation in the early nineteenth century—is nicely restored and features important examples of in situ early wall stenciling and mural painting.

New Hampshire, the earliest northern New England state to be settled, was the adopted home of both Moses Eatons, Sr. and Jr. Perhaps that is one reason why it was an area of vigorous wall-stenciling activity, by numerous artists. Numerous New Hampshire walls were stenciled by the Eatons between 1800 and 1840, according to a survey conducted by the late Margaret Fabian of Lebanon, New Hampshire. In 1988 she completed a survey inventory project that took her to 460 homes and taverns throughout New England. In seven years she recorded nearly 130 stenciled structures in her home state of New Hampshire, about half of which she attributed to the Eatons. She also found a goodly amount of stencil work by an artist she called the "Borderman," which is synonymous with my "Classical Group," which I examine in part II of this book.

I.27. Major William Berry house, 1785
Pittsfield, New Hampshire
Artist: Moses Eaton, Sr., circa 1800

THE BERRY HOUSE was built and inhabited by family members from its construction in 1785 until its sale outside the family in 1964. That is just twenty years short of two centuries of continuous family ownership!

An ancestor, William Berry, resided in Portsmouth, New Hampshire, as early as 1631. Four of his descendants emigrated westward to the Pittsfield area after the Revolutionary War. Together with their numerous offspring they built substantial homes, many of which are still standing.

Early twentieth-century photograph of William Berry farm. *From H. A. L. Brown Collection.*

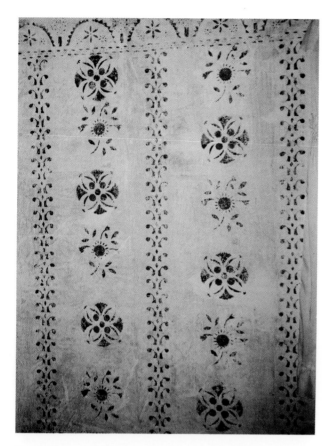

Panel of Eaton stenciling from Berry house bedchamber.

Overmantel from Berry house left front chamber showing typical Eaton "basket of flowers" and "willow tree" motifs.

Major Berry's farmhouse contains our first examples of the famous Eaton stenciling, determined by the age and location to be the work of the older Eaton, Moses Sr. Berry family tradition tells us that the artist boarded with the family for a considerable time while decorating most rooms in this house and perhaps other Berry houses in the neighborhood.

All second-floor rooms reportedly had stenciling, and it was probably seen in all first-floor rooms and the hallway as well. All rooms except one were covered with wallpaper so long ago that the last Berry to live here was completely unaware of the stenciling underneath. Fortunately the left front bedroom retained its stenciling through the years as the "stenciled guest bedroom," accommodating various Berry family members over the years, including the author's mother-in-law, Susanne R. L. Brown of Spring Green, Rhode Island. This choice example of Eaton work remained safe and visible for some 170 years, only to be papered over for a brief period in the 1970s.

Many rooms of stenciling were found under a thick layer of paper by new owners around 1979, at which time it was recorded by Margaret Fabian during a brief and fortuitous window of opportunity. All stenciling is once again under paper, except the "guest bedroom," which was restored by the Wiggins Brothers, David and Gerald, neo-itinerant painters. According to Gerald the stenciling was so pristine that only a small amount of inpainting was required, since the brief wallpaper coverage did little damage.

Images on these walls will seem familiar, and with good reason. The motifs, layout, and scale suggest the work of J. Gleason. Three of the motifs, the small "arch and candle" frieze and two fillers, the "willow tree" and the "small carnation spray," here used without buds, are very similar, but not identical, to those used by Gleason, hinting again at a possible unknown connection between the two early artists.

All of the stencil designs used to ornament this house are contained in the Moses Eaton stencil box in the collections of the Society for the Preservation of New England Antiquities, Boston, Massachusetts.

THE FREESE HOUSE remained in the family until it was dismantled about 1950. Fortunately, Janet Waring visited before 1950 to photograph and record stencil designs found in a first-floor parlor and hall, designs hidden under wallpaper for many years.[9]

The parlor walls were removed professionally prior to dismantling and stored at Old Sturbridge Village for many years until being privately acquired around 1980.

Since many of the motifs used by the Eatons on the Freese house walls are similar to those seen on walls stenciled by J. Gleason and Stimp, a visual comparison of stencil designs shared by the three might shed light on any common design influences. Perhaps this exercise might even help in separating the original motif user from the copyists by producing some insight as to the chronological order of execution. Of the three, J. Gleason has a simplicity in his work, which might be indicative of the original usage of these designs, with Moses Eaton, Sr., having an unknown connection with Gleason and Moses Jr. and Stimp being the later copyists.

View of stenciling in front parlor of Freese house of Deerfield, New Hampshire, before it was dismantled in 1950.

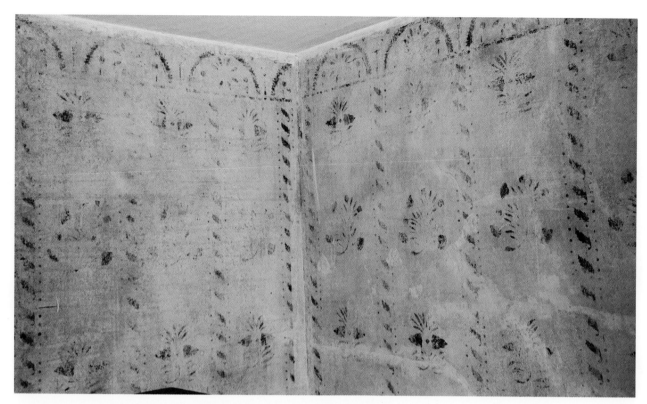

Stenciling found in a back first-floor room of Kilburn house. *Courtesy Esther T. Howard.*

I.29. George Kilburn house, 1825
Walpole, New Hampshire
Artist: Stimp, circa 1830

STENCILING UTILIZING well-known Stimp motifs once adorned at least two rooms of the modest Kilburn cottage in southwestern New Hampshire. Located on the eastern bank of the Connecticut River about twenty-five miles north of the Massachusetts boundary, it is not an unexpected place for this artist to visit.

Dutchie Perron, a Walpole artist, discovered stenciling that apparently had never been covered with paper or paint in a first-floor back room while researching wall stenciling in the Walpole area in the 1970s.

During a 1999 visit by the author, the stenciling in this room was found in very good condition, and the same frieze was seen peeking from behind a flapping wallpaper corner in a front parlor.

This area of New Hampshire is not far from Stratton Tavern (I.17) in Northfield, Massachusetts, although the style and choice of designs on the Kilburn house walls seem to be an example of later work by Stimp, whereas the Stratton stenciling is thought to be an example of his early stenciling.

You will be seeing these designs again when we go west with the settlers as they moved into the New York frontier areas.

INCREASE WARREN, the builder of this house, was born in Hubbardston, Massachusetts, in 1785, and earned his living as a farmer and tanner. He removed to South Village in 1824 and, shortly after, built this house with its seven fireplaces of brick fired right on the property.

The house served as a stopover for drovers taking their cattle and produce to market in Brighton and Boston.

During a 1960s restoration, stenciling was discovered in practically every one of the house's twelve rooms. Stencil patterns in red and green, with an occasional accent in dark green, were applied to horsehair-plastered walls covered with pink or yellow whitewash.

The artist is unknown, just one of the many journeymen artists who traveled along the Connecticut River Valley. This artist also visited the ballroom of the Hall Tavern originally located in Charlemont, Massachusetts, now situated at historic Deerfield Village. Many of the same red and green designs can be seen on the tavern's yellow walls.

I.30. Increase Warren House, 1824
Westmoreland, New Hampshire
Artist: Unknown, second quarter nineteenth century

Warren house of Westmoreland, New Hampshire. *The home of John and Susan Harris.*

Stenciling from a second-floor chamber. *The home of John and Susan Harris.*

Settlers began trickling into Vermont at the end of the French and Indian Wars, with Connecticut to the south the main source for these early pioneers.[10] Therefore Vermont has been called the "Child of Connecticut," with the state's first farmers, tradesmen, and artisans migrating up the Connecticut River Valley to their new homes in Vermont. This northward movement, plus the continuing flow from crowded New England states to the east, produced a dramatic increase in population, which rose from an estimated 30,000 in 1781, to 85,425 in 1790, to 217,985 by 1810.

This northwesternmost area of New England, which did not accept statehood until 1791 when it separated from New York, was the destination for numerous settlers during the final years of the eighteenth century and the first quarter of the next.

I.31. John Durkee house, 1800

Stockbridge, Windsor County, Vermont

Artist: Erastus Gates (attributed), circa 1820

THE TOWN OF STOCKBRIDGE in Windsor County could be a reference to an area in Connecticut as well as in Vermont. The profusion of Connecticut place names in Vermont reflects the origin of many of its earliest settlers.

Ownership of the area around Stockbridge, Vermont, was long disputed by New Hampshire and New York, and the town has the distinction of being granted charters by both of those states[11]—in 1761 by New Hampshire's Governor Wentworth and eleven years later, when Governor Dunmore of New York State followed suit. However, the granting of charters did not mean settlement, for it was not until 1784 that John Durkee became the first permanent settler of the town.

In about 1800 Durkee transformed his original simple cabin into this spacious two-story farmhouse. Sometime later Erastus Gates, who stenciled numerous homes in Windsor County, was commissioned to decorate the walls with colorful stenciling—one room of which, a second-floor chamber, still survives in fairly good condition.

Located on a once busy intersection known as the Four Corners, the house was purchased by James Whitcomb in 1864 to be run as a hotel for about forty years.

In 1906 it was purchased by P. W. Green, who changed its name to the Stockbridge Inn. Now owned by the third generation of the Green family, it has housed an antique shop since 1981.

It is interesting to note that at least one of the designs seen on these Vermont walls, the vermilion cabbage-rose motif, found its way with settlers to the Western Reserve area of Ohio (I.61).

Early twentieth-century photo of Durkee house. *Courtesy Old Hotel Antiques.*

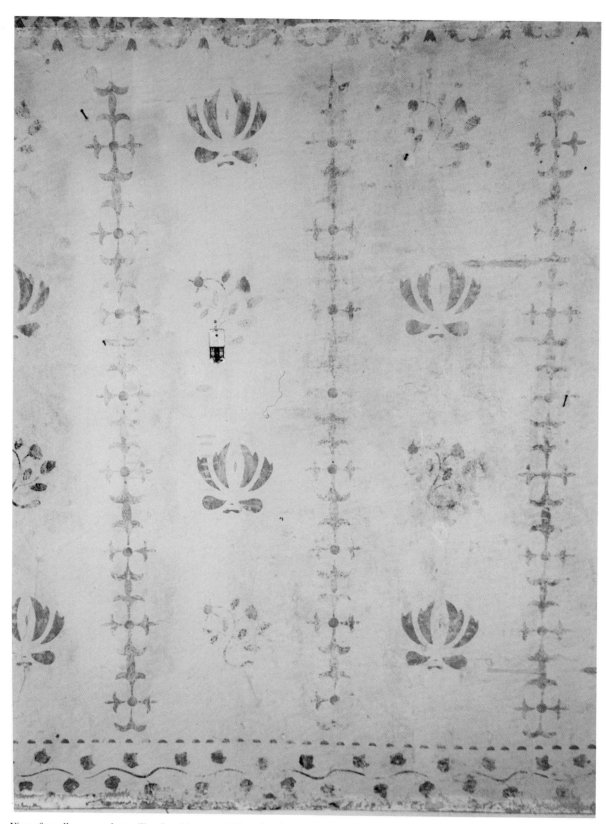

View of a well-preserved stenciling found in a second-floor chamber of Durkee house. *Courtesy Old Hotel Antiques.*

THE PARLOR OF THE Counterpane house, a once-dilapidated center-chimney cape, contains unique stenciling of a type used between 1820 and 1840 to ornament such textile room accessories as bedcovers, bed and window hangings, or table covers. Designs were stenciled in paint or dye on lightweight cotton, often unbleached muslin. These stenciled textiles, sewn and decorated by the lady of the house, are extremely rare today due to their fragile nature, but examples are still to be seen in museum collections (I.20).

The designs on the walls—painted in blue, gray, yellow, and several reds, on natural plaster—strongly suggest walls hung with stenciled counterpanes, and were probably executed by the homeowner.

The derelict house containing this charming stenciling was saved from extinction by restoration expert John Hauenstein[12] of Charlotte, Vermont, who purchased and subsequently moved it thirteen miles to its present bucolic location in Charlotte. Though difficult to move, the stencil-ornamented plaster walls were carefully stabilized, removed, transported, and installed intact in the parlor of Hauenstein's meticulously restored home.

It is encouraging to note that as knowledge of the artistic and monetary value of eighteenth- and nineteenth-century painted interiors grows, homeowners are making the effort to preserve stenciling original to their period homes, adding great beauty and value while preserving an important part of early American architectural history for future generations.

Stenciled muslin apron re-created by the author from a circa 1830 original in collections of Rhode Island School of Design Museum. Designs bear a strong resemblance to those stenciled on wall.

View of unusual stenciling in a front parlor of the Counterpane house, Vermont. *Courtesy Early Preservations.*

I.33. John Coolidge homestead, 1785
Plymouth, Vermont
Artist: Erastus Gates, 1830

Original stenciling in the parlor of Coolidge house. Photo circa 1930.
Courtesy Vermont Division for Historic Preservation, President Calvin
Coolidge State Historic Site.

CAPTAIN COOLIDGE, born about 1756 in Boston, Massachusetts, first set eyes on what was to become the ancestral home of the thirtieth president of the United States, Calvin Coolidge, when he was marching from Massachusetts with his company to reinforce the northern army at Fort Ticonderoga, New York, in 1778. He was so moved by the beauty of the wilderness and the Green Mountains that he vowed to return at the end of the war and adopt Vermont as his home.[13] The first dwelling built by this pioneer was a simple log cabin. A frame house, white-plastered on the outside (as was frequent in Vermont), replaced the first some years later. A third structure, a large clapboard house with eight or more rooms, was later attached to the original structure, the whole becoming an ell (a usual development for houses in the area at that time). The new building was built after Captain John's death in 1822 by his eldest son, Luther (1792–1856).

At least five rooms of the fine new house were stenciled by a young artist, Erastus Gates[14] by name. This attribution is quite positive since Gates became the son-in-law of Luther Coolidge, perhaps after a courtship quite

possibly started when Gates was stenciling this house and others in the area!

The work depicted here, featuring Eaton-type designs in red and green on yellow and pink grounds, is said to have been executed by a very young Gates (most likely after an apprenticeship with an established craftsman), and his stenciling has been found on numerous other walls in the Windsor County area of southern Vermont. Undoubtedly he was under the influence of Eaton, or an Eaton copyist, since Gates's work includes exact copies and variations of Eaton designs, plus designs of his own invention applied to the surface in a very Eatonesque manner.

According to Janet Waring, the house completed by Luther Coolidge was vacant and dilapidated by 1923, and reduced to complete wreckage soon thereafter.

Other homes in Windsor County with Gates's stenciling are the Slack house, which once stood on Slack Hill in Plymouth; the Captain Noah Wood house, which is still extant in South Woodstock; and the Cady house, which once stood in the town of Hartland.

Members of the Coolidge family still remain in the Plymouth area, and reportedly their love of the land has never dimmed. President Coolidge said in 1928, "I could not look upon the peaks of the [Green Mountains] without being moved in a way that no other scene could move me."[15]

An area that includes a later Coolidge homestead where Calvin was born and administered the presidential oath of office by his father in 1923, the country store where the president set up his summer office in 1924, and a cemetery containing six generations of the Coolidge family was placed on the National Register of Historic Places in 1970.

It is sad that the first Coolidge homestead, built three miles up the mountain on land cleared from the wilderness by Captain John (the first Coolidge in Vermont) and improved into a fine house by his son Luther in 1825, along with its fine examples of American folk stenciling by Erastus Gates, could not be part of this tribute to the thirtieth president of the United States and his family.

Chapter 5

The State of New York and Neighboring Canada

Detail of a round motif, 7½ inches in diameter, used by youthful stencil artist Steven Clark in western New York State.

In 1609 Henry Hudson, funded by the Dutch East India Company, sailed up a large river that would later bear his name and claimed the surrounding area for the Netherlands—whose merchants were the greatest global traders in the world at that time. It was to become their center of commerce in the New World. Starting in 1624 at Fort Orange (Albany), settlements, collectively called New Netherland, soon stretched from western Long Island and lower Manhattan, on the south, along the banks of the Hudson River toward Fort Orange on the north. Many French Protestants called Huguenots, fleeing religious persecution in the homeland, immigrated with the Dutch.

Only forty years later, in 1664, James, Duke of York, sailed into New Netherland's harbor and, without firing a shot, claimed the area for England, renaming it New York. In 1709–10 Queen Anne of England settled scores of Palatine German refugees[1] along the Hudson, Mohawk, and Schoharie Rivers, "as a frontier against the French and their Indians."[2]

All diversely different ethnic groups played pivotal roles in the social and economic development of New York, as well as contributing to the decorative arts of colonial and Federal America.

Prior to the signing of a peace treaty with the Indians in 1779, the new state of New York was only seventh in population among the thirteen original states, most residing in lower Manhattan and western Long Island, with others clustered along the banks of the Hudson and a few stragglers (mostly German) along the Mohawk and Susquehanna Rivers.

Ten years later, in 1789, when George Washington was sworn in as the first president of the new nation at New York City's newly renovated Federal Hall, few imagined that the then modest port city of New York, so badly pillaged during occupation by eighty thousand English troops between 1776 and 1783, would soon mature into the commercial and cultural center of the country.

Manhattan Island offered the best harbor on the Atlantic seaboard—a large saltwater harbor, sheltered and deep enough for even the largest of ships to dock wharfside. It was the entrance to a water route from the Atlantic Ocean to inland America by way of the Hudson and Mohawk Rivers, connecting New York City with the western frontier. The water-level banks of these rivers were also used for early road systems, canals to enhance the navigability of the rivers, and after 1835 for railroad beds—all transporting settlers and commerce to and from western New York, northern Pennsylvania, and Ohio. Early in the nineteenth century, the rate of westward movement, much of it from the thin-soiled areas of Connecticut and Massachusetts, increased greatly over the newly built road systems. To accommodate the throngs of travelers, public houses sprang up along the way, which were also frequented by the locals as meeting places for pleasure, business, and occasionally the local Masonic lodges. In eastern New York, by 1815, new arrivals and locals enjoyed sixty-two public houses in the fifty-two miles between Albany and Cherry Valley.[3] In 1818, John Brown Francis, the aforementioned diarist, observes this about a section of road between Amsterdam and Schenectady: "Every third house as a moderate calculation on my route so far, offer's entertainment for man & horse."[4]

Colorful stenciling decorated the interiors of numerous taverns and dwellings built during this period of rapid expansion, much of it similar to that seen in New England by artists such as J. Gleason, Stimp, Moses Eaton, and Erastus Gates, but some strikingly new. It is not clear if documented New England artists traveled west, or if this similar work is that of their apprentices or copyists who enlarged their design portfolios as they moved from one stenciled tavern to the next, dispersing designs as they stenciled their way west.

Early ad for stagecoach route from Albany to Utica. *From H. A. L. Brown collection.*

In addition to the obvious New England influence, that of the early Dutch and German settlers of the area deserves study. While Dutch control of the early colony lasted for only forty years, the descendants of the first Dutch settlers were very much in evidence at the end of the eighteenth century. Many must have continued the use of early Dutch decorative motifs to ornament their homes and furnishings. Their painted and carved furniture, tin-glazed tiles, and textiles (perhaps also the beautiful tooled and painted leather produced in the Netherlands and used on the walls of the finest Dutch homes) share design motifs with colonial and Federal American decorative arts.

The tulip motif, in particular, is omnipresent in American furniture decoration and wall and floor painting. Even though the tulip was originally brought from Turkey to Europe by Busbequius, the Austrian ambassador to Turkey in 1554, it was the Dutch who were responsible for entrepreneurially cultivating and promoting the tulip throughout the world, resulting in the "tulipomania" of 1634–38, with the price of the bulbs more than that of precious metals.

The use of flowering sprays, more often than not tulips, enclosed in a diamond on ceramic tile and on leather wall hangings, is a device seen often on American freehand painted walls (I.17), which in turn inspired at least one wall stenciler (II.27). Freehand wall painting seems to predate wall stenciling by about ten years. Margaret Coffin, in her book on painted walls, lists numerous walls in houses built by Dutch descendants in the Hudson River Valley[5] with scroll-type decoration often featuring a wall panel divided into a diamond grid with a floral design featured in the center.

Similarly the German folk decoration descending from the "first wave" of Germans to settle the Hudson River area must have added their design influences. These could be seen in their fraktur writing, folk art drawing, and painted furniture with stylized symmetrical flower groupings and early folk designs, such as the fylfot or pinwheel, one of the oldest and thought to represent good and evil. The work of one stencil artist in particular seems to have come under the German influence: Stimp (perhaps Caleb H. Stimpson) utilized numerous stylized tulip designs, and the fylfot was practically his signature!

Several studies of New York State wall stenciling have been conducted in the last quarter of the twentieth century. In 1979 Leigh Rehner Jones, while part of the Cooperstown Graduate Program, authored an unpublished

House-blessing fraktur by Henrich Weiss dated 1791, hand-drawn, lettered, and colored on paper, 8¼ inches × 13¼ inches. *Courtesy Schwenkfelder Library, Pennsburg, Pennsylvania.*

thesis on stenciling in four central New York counties—Otsego, Chenango, Cortland, and Tompkins—during the 1800–1840 period.

A 1985 exhibit with catalogue titled *Wall Stenciling in Western New York, 1800–1840* was staged by the Rochester Museum & Science Center (RMSC) with research by Philip Parr, a freelance stencil researcher, and Janice Wass, curator of history, RMSC. The catalogue contains invaluable information on several signed houses, plus written documentation of an interesting new stencil artist.

Most of New York's great abundance of stenciled buildings are located in the Upstate area, with only one example from Manhattan or Long Island, the earliest and most densely populated areas of the state. It has been established that Federal-period wall decoration rarely survives in rapidly evolving inner city areas, such as Manhattan and western Long Island.

Most New York stenciling is of the folk genre, with only three classical examples found thus far. The classical examples are entirely different artistically and scattered from the most southeasterly tip of Long Island to the northwestern area of the state, with the third not quite halfway between.

The author has a sense that New York wall stenciling gets more sophisticated, with a greater variety of designs and a higher level of technique, as one moves westward through the state—seemingly the work of local talent plus numerous experienced artisans, many at the peak of their artistic prowess, who passed through on their way west.

New York State has a wealth of well-preserved, vastly diverse, beautifully executed, and still extant stenciled walls, none of which can be, with any degree of certainty, attributed to the celebrated Moses Eaton Junior!

I.34. Gow-Crawford house, 1815
Argyle, New York
Artist: Unknown, circa 1825

LOCATED IN EASTERN New York not far from the Vermont border, Argyle was granted by patent in 1764 to Scotch immigrants and their descendants who came over with Laughlin Campbell in 1738–40.[6] The Campbells were a very powerful and warlike clan who occupied the country of Argyle, an island off the coast of Scotland.[7] The new town of Argyle was given to eighty-three families, who commenced settling in 1765. The house that contained stenciling depicted here was built about 1815 by Archibald Gow, who came to America from Scotland in 1765.

Around 1984, when the house and its important stenciling was in imminent danger of collapse, Adele Bishop, a well-known stencil artist based in Dorset, Vermont, just across the state line, alerted the Department of Historic Preservation at Roger Williams University in Bristol, Rhode Island. Kevin Jordan, acting department head, and housewright Steve Tyson organized a crew of students from the university to remove one stenciled wall, which is the only surviving part of this house. It was installed in a reconstructed eighteenth-century barn on campus, which houses the university's performing arts center.

The fusion of designs on this well-preserved wall is intriguing, since some strongly suggest the earlier work of J. Gleason in Rhode Island, while others suggest those in the Sage house of Sandisfield, Massachusetts (I.16), and the Gibbs house in Blandford (I.15), while others are entirely new. This is curious because the Sage house[8] has traditionally been attributed to Stimp, and the Gibbs house stenciling is signed by Betts and Langdon. It could be that both the Gow house and the Sage house were indeed decorated by Betts and Langdon, with many motifs borrowed from Gleason and Stimp—all very evocative conjecture! Another New York house, located a bit farther north on the Vermont border, reportedly has the same distinctive frieze as the Gow house but in a different coloration. An 1819 brick house located in Granville has three areas of original stenciling: a bedchamber, stairway, and second-floor hall, with the same frieze design on a wide blue-gray band. Unfortunately the artist either did not sign his work or the signature was lost long ago, perhaps located in one of the first-floor rooms.

As we progress westward into the later years of wall stenciling under the New England influence, artist attribution will become ever more difficult. The sharing of designs will become more prevalent, the same colorations and wall layouts will continue in favor, and the fact will remain that the application of wall stenciling does not leave any distinguishing marks of the artist, as is true with other painting techniques. Of course, all of these characteristics make it virtually impossible to actually assign names to stenciled walls that have not been signed by the artist.

Original stenciling from Gow-Crawford house, which once stood in Argyle, New York, just over Vermont border. *Courtesy Roger Williams University—Historic Preservation Program, Bristol, Rhode Island.*

Bump Tavern, which originally stood in Ashland, New York. *Courtesy New York State Historical Association, Cooperstown, N.Y.*

I.35. Bump Tavern, circa 1800

Ashland, New York

Artist: Stimp (attributed), circa 1830

THE BUMP TAVERN was built in the late eighteenth century on an early road just south of the Catskill Turnpike, which connected the Hudson River to western New York. It was later purchased by the Bump family, who moved to New York from Connecticut around 1810.

It was moved in the 1940s to the Farmers Museum in Cooperstown, New York. In preparation for the seventy-one-mile move, the tavern was cut into seventeen pieces, each of which was transported by truck to be rejoined at the crossroads of the village museum. Carter Burnett, museum engineer at the time, devised this original and very effective method of building removal.[9]

During the ensuing restoration, stenciling was found under wallpaper in three second-floor rooms; a bedchamber, ballroom, and hall. Most of the original plaster was beyond restoration. One section, however, was salvaged and is now preserved under a protective cover of easily raised wallboard for viewing.

Stenciling traditionally attributed to Stimp was also found in the Perry house, Dover Plains, New York,[10] right over the border from Litchfield County, Connecticut, where numerous examples have been found (see I.21).

The history of Greene County, New York, named for Rhode Island's General Nathaniel Greene, is of particular interest, since several Stimpsons, said to be from Connecticut, are credited as being among the first permanent settlers of both Windham and nearby Ashland. According to French's 1860 *Gazetteer* of New York, Elisha Strong and several brothers named Stimpson were the first settlers of Ashland in 1788.[11] Nearby Windham was first settled in 1790 by George Stimpson, Abijah Stone, and Increase Claflin. Also a Reverend Henry Stimpson was the earliest minister in the area.[12] It is interesting that Stimpsons played such a large role in the settlement of the original location of a tavern with stenciling attributed to Stimp (possibly Caleb H. Stimpson).

Stenciling in the historic Bump Tavern was re-created by the late Shirley Spaulding Devoe in the early 1950s. Devoe was a prolific writer and a researcher of the decorative arts of the eighteenth and nineteenth centuries. Insight into the perils of early wall decorators and tavern guests as well was gained by Devoe as she stenciled the north chamber one dark snowy day in March: "the cold wind found its way in through the fireplace and small openings—my mind dwelt upon the old timers working in houses without central heating."[13]

Devoe also re-created two early stenciled floors, one now in the taproom of the Bump Tavern and another in the Lippett house, a red farm cottage diagonally across from the tavern. Both floor designs are from razed local houses. Devoe's straightforward description of the floor-stenciling technique is "the same as for walls—accomplished by crawling around on hands and knees." Sounds like a tedious and physically taxing vocation!

Devoe was a valued member of the Historical Society of Early American Decoration (HSEAD), which was founded after the death of Esther Stevens Brazer in order to continue her work of researching and proliferating early painting techniques. A few years after Devoe re-created the Bump stenciling, the New York Historical Society at Cooperstown became the first repository for the ever-growing HSEAD collections. They remained there until 1980, when they were transported to the Hermanus Bleecher Building, a larger exhibition and storage facility in Albany, New York. Since 1993 the organization's collections have been housed at the American Folk Art Museum in New York City, which has a new spacious facility scheduled to open in 2002, capable of correctly displaying and storing the valuable collections of this fine organization.

View of ballroom stenciling re-created by Shirley Devoe.

I.36. *Stencil house, early nineteenth century*
Columbus, eastern New York
Artist: Unknown, circa 1825

THE "STENCIL HOUSE" was built early in the nineteenth century in Columbus, New York, which is located in eastern New York not far from the original location of the Bump Tavern (I.35). The area was convenient for emigration not only from New England but also from states to the south such as Pennsylvania and New Jersey.

Fortunately the distinctive stenciling found in this house was executed on pine sheathing, which is easily removed compared with stenciled plaster. In 1952 three rooms of stenciled paneling were removed before the house was dismantled and moved to Vermont's Shelburne Museum.

Founded in 1947, the museum was the creation of Electra Havemeyer Webb,[14] an early and avid collector of American folk art. Included in the museum's many early structures are fine examples of wall stenciling, one with folk-style decoration and the other in the classical style.

The wood paneling with stenciling from three first-floor rooms survived the transplant in excellent condition with only minimal conservation required. The late Duncan Monroe skillfully executed the restoration.

Some of the designs in the Stencil house have been found on Connecticut walls; a few are exact copies, and others have variations. Many, however, are of new invention, suggesting the work of an artist new to this publication. The artist was at first thought to be James Morrow, whose name was found stenciled over the parlor mantel. However, later research by Nancie Ravino, of the Shelburne Museum, discovered that James Morrow did not arrive in Columbus until 1850. The proprietor of an apple orchard, he probably bought the house soon after 1850. The stenciled signature on the overmantel, which was probably applied some twenty years after the stenciling, proved to be the mark used to identify his apple crates!

Interior view showing three stenciled front rooms of Shelburne's "Stencil house." © *Shelburne Museum, Shelburne, Vermont.*

I.37. Christian Nellis Tavern, 1747

St. Johnsville, New York

Artist: Unknown, 1815–1820

View of original stenciling in a second-floor chamber of Nellis Tavern.
Courtesy Palatine Settlement Society, St. Johnsville, New York.

THE NELLIS TAVERN was inhabited continuously from 1747 to 1968 by Nellis family members, first as a farmstead and later as a turnpike public house and store. Unfortunately an ensuing period of abandonment soon turned this historic structure into a condemned ruin, inspiring numerous unsuccessful rescue efforts—the most fanciful being the idea to float it down the Mohawk River to the Fort Plain Museum a few miles east on the banks of the Mohawk.

The ultimate rescue, however, occurred in the summer of 1978, when Roger Johnson, a lifelong resident of St. Johnsville, fortuitously spotted a bulldozer belonging to the New York State Department of Transportation parked against the west wall of the structure.[15] The response to his concerned inquiry was that the building would be razed in order to straighten Route 5 as soon as the crew returned from lunch, about one that afternoon. Since it was then eleven in the morning, Johnson spent the ensuing two hours making desperate phone calls to local preservationists, all of whom responded enthusiastically to saving the tavern from the wrecking ball, at least temporarily, in order to record the richly colored stencil-

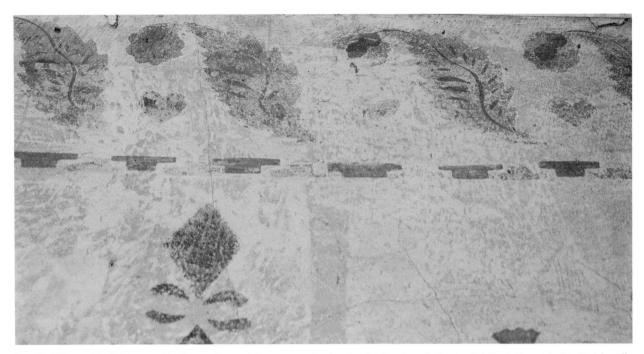

Detail of "diagonal leaf" frieze used in first- and second-floor rooms, showing fine detailing in red. *Courtesy Palatine Settlement Society, St. Johnsville, New York.*

ing just discovered by Johnson behind peeling wallpaper in the easterly first-floor room. What a remarkable twist of fate—that Roger Johnson happened to be passing the tavern at that pivotal time and recognized the importance of the building and its stenciling!

His efforts to save the tavern were successful. It is still standing and enjoying a meticulous restoration by the Palatine Settlement Society, which became its proud owner in 1984. Their long-term aim is to make the Nellis Tavern a fine example of restoring and interpreting 250 years of material from the building's three distinct building periods.

The initial section, a one-and-three-quarters farmstead built by Christian Nellis (1697–1774) in 1747, is an excellent extant example of Palatine German construction techniques. Christian was a French Huguenot who arrived here in 1710 at age thirteen with his widowed mother, an older brother, and younger sister.[16] They came from the Palatine area of Germany by way of St. Catharines,[17] England, with what is called the "first wave" of German migration under the auspices of Queen Anne of England. The farmhouse entrance faced south toward the Mohawk River and the King's Highway, the two dominant means of eighteenth-century travel in the Mohawk region.

The second construction phase occurred around 1800,

when Christian Jr. (1734–1808) raised the roof to extend the building to two and a half stories, incorporating a ballroom on the south side of the second floor as well as additional sleeping quarters, and enlarging the tavern, which had been in operation since about 1783 to accommodate the ever increasing westward migration. Perhaps the store was incorporated into the first floor at this time. It is not clear if the Georgian woodwork and front door were part of the initial construction or added at this time.[18]

The third and final phase was the construction of a two-story addition to the east side around 1810–15, probably by Christian III. A Federal-style entrance facing the newly opened Mohawk Turnpike (Route 5), located north of the tavern, was added. The woodwork in this new addition is predictably of the Federal style. It is in this addition that the stenciling, a fine example of American folk art, was found, well preserved under much wallpaper. This new discovery was visited and recorded by numerous stencil preservationists, including the author, which is fortunate since, once exposed to light, the stenciling quickly deteriorated during the next twenty-year period.

Stenciling found in five areas was executed in distemper paint on white or light gray water-soluble grounds. The first-floor room, which was originally divided into

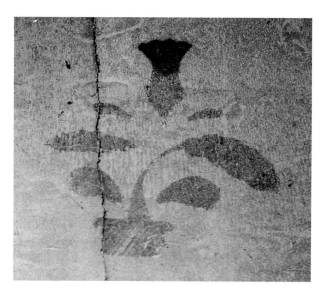

Close-up of "single tulip," which is now nicely potted. Compare to example I.5. *Courtesy Palatine Settlement Society, St. Johnsville, New York.*

three areas, has three distinct stencil schemes in green with red accents. The two rooms on the second level have designs in the same green and red color scheme with the addition of yellow elements.

Most of the designs are variations of those used in New England by Gleason, the Eatons, and/or Stimp, with a few refreshingly new motifs mixed in. Two variations are of particular interest: the single-tulip filler motif, used by all three of the above-mentioned artists, is now firmly planted in a green pot; and the pinwheel or fylfot, Stimp's signature design, has been transformed, by the addition of a stem, from a German folk symbol to something from nature such as a four-leaf clover.

This talented artist's style is characterized by the use of very intricate red veining on the numerous leaflike stencil designs in his vast New England–inspired portfolio.

Undated initials found on plaster in a second-floor closet were optimistically thought to be those of the stencil artist. The plaster section containing the initials was removed and subsequently broken. The author reconstructed the fragments, to discover that what was thought to be CVC was actually CCV and executed freehand in oil-based paint, not consistent with previously recorded stencil artist signatures. Wallpaper hangers, house-painters, and carpenters also commonly signed their work in this manner. However, since stenciling attribution is a very ambiguous science, often based on educated guesswork rather than fact, the possibility that CCV are the initials of the artist responsible for the handsome Nellis Tavern stencil decoration cannot be ruled out entirely.

Much has been accomplished thus far to make the building structurally sound, and great progress has been made developing a procedure for restoring the stenciling and the plaster that it adorns.

Morgan Philips, an internationally known architectural conservation expert, before his untimely death in 1996 devised a plaster restoration plan to conserve the deteriorated areas under and around the stenciling. The anticipated date for this procedure is the year 2000, after which the stenciling can be re-created.

This slow, thoughtful restoration of the Nellis Tavern by the Palatine Settlement Society will hopefully produce a fine example of early Mohawk Valley architecture dating to an important period of American settlement and expansiveness. The stenciling, applied during the height of western turnpike travel, is a vital part of the visual history of this tavern, area, and country.

THE SECOND-FLOOR stenciled ballroom of the Farmersville Tavern, a stagecoach stop between Albany and Buffalo, must have been a visual feast for stencil researcher Annabelle J. Schwab on her initial visit in the 1960s. Originally, the back wall of this large room, encompassing the entire second floor, was divided into three or four small sleeping quarters, each just large enough for a bed, chest, and possibly a chair. The partitions were removed long ago, leaving the wall covered with three unrelated complete stencil layouts with different side-by-side frieze motifs, verticals, and fillers, all highly ornamented but unattached in appearance. Fortunately this uniquely stenciled great room was thoroughly photographed and traced by Mrs. Schwab, Elizabeth Nibbelink, and Norma Annabal[19] before the tavern burned to the ground in 1973.

Many of the designs found in this tavern are identical to those seen previously in the Stencil house (I.36) from eastern New York, now at the Shelburne Museum of Vermont. No signature was found in this tavern, but the great number of shared designs warrants attributing the Farmersville Tavern to the same hand as the Shelburne Museum house.

One design shared by this building and the Stencil house, the "cabbage rose," was seen before, stenciled in vermilion on Vermont walls by Erastus Gates (I.31).

Over many years, the unadorned white sections of the tavern's ballroom walls proved irresistible to numerous visitors. Among much graffiti this nostalgic poem was found:

> When the years are fast elapsing
> And the shadows of old age fall
> Then I hope you will remember
> This was once a dancing hall.

Other buildings in western New York apparently were visited by this talented artist, since the Culper Tavern in Watkins Glen, plus two houses in Genesee County and one in Pittsford, all have enough matching designs to credit the same artist with their superb ornamentation.

(Top) Facsimile of one of three stencil schemes from ballroom of Farmersville Tavern. *From tracings by Annabelle Schwab, Elizabeth Nibbelink, and Norma Annabal.*

(Bottom) Facsimile of second stenciled panel from same ballroom. *From tracings by Annabelle Schwab, Elizabeth Nibbelink, and Norma Annabal.*

View of Davis house with inscription "The whole family and damn dog too," circa 1915. *Courtesy Ronald and Jane Towner.*

I.39. Davis House, 1811
Cohocton, New York
Artist: Unknown, 1815–1825

THE DAVIS HOUSE was built in 1811 by Daniel Davis, lumber tycoon, lawyer, and hostler, who at one time owned over three thousand acres that comprised much of the present-day Cohocton Village. His mother was a sister of Ethan Allen, leader of Vermont's Green Mountain Boys of Revolutionary War fame.

Not inhabited since about 1920, this interesting house almost succumbed to highway construction in the 1960s. Fortunately it is still standing, aloof and forlorn on a high bank overlooking the old Route 15.

Without central heating, electricity, or indoor plumbing (except for a hand pump in the kitchen sink), this house and its stenciled walls were in a sort of time warp dating to the end of the nineteenth century. Prior to that a few changes had been made to its original condition; the chimney and fireplaces on the right side of the structure were removed, probably when a kitchen wing was added to the left side, and of course wallpaper was added but only to some of the walls, leaving a great number never covered with paper or paint.

The Davis house contains a great volume of stenciled rooms, ten to twelve to be exact, among the best extant stenciling, in terms of quality and degree of preservation, known to the author.

Finding all original rooms of this house stencil-decorated was not the major discovery, since the author long ago sensed that early stencil artists were often commissioned to decorate every room in a house, not just a select few. The significant discovery was that they all survived into the twenty-first century—a most remarkable accomplishment, due partly to benign neglect!

After assuming ownership in 1990, new owners added a central heating system and electricity but no indoor plumbing. They also covered, for its protection, much of the stenciling with Sheetrock, but only after thoroughly recording it in photographs.

This stencil work is very impressive in its competent execution and great variety of designs utilized, with four different friezes and numerous secondary borders and fillers, executed on yellow ocher ground in four colors: red, green, blue, and black. Two layout styles, the paneled and the open, were used. This is the work of an experienced, talented craftsman with a vast portfolio of designs, many of which were also used in Connecticut.

Gina Martin, the aforementioned Connecticut stencil authority, recorded these designs in many areas of Connecticut, including Andover, East Haddam, Windham, and Glastonbury, attributing many to "Stimp." However,

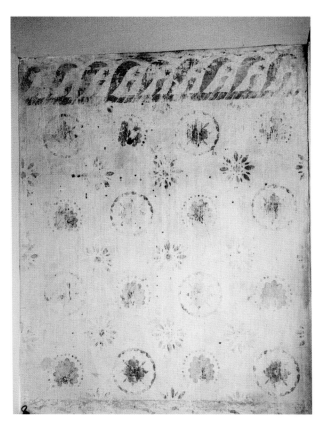

Extant stenciling in first-floor front stair hall. *Courtesy Ronald and Jane Towner.*

the work in the Davis house and other New York houses is more elaborate than that in Connecticut, an indication that it is either the work of a more mature "Stimp," at peak artistic capacity, or that of a very talented and experienced copyist. In either case this artist had been putting stencil brush to wall for a good many years.

It is hoped that when the necessary technical and financial resources are gathered, this fine example of New York stenciling, currently used as a gift shop, can be retrieved and conserved, allowing the Daniel Davis house of Cohoton, New York, to take its rightful place as one of America's most important stenciled houses.

Extant stenciling in a front parlor of Davis house. *Courtesy Ronald and Jane Towner.*

I.40. Ephraim Cleveland house, 1794

Naples, New York

Artist: Stephen Clark, 1828

THE STENCILED Ephraim Cleveland house is located just west of New York's Finger Lakes district, a short distance north of the previous example, the Davis house. All the designs found in two surviving stenciled rooms, a second-floor chamber and a first-floor parlor (now plastered over) were also used to decorate the Davis house, seemingly by the same anonymous artist from Connecticut. However, a name has come to light as the decorator of the Cleveland house.

Stephen Clark (1810–1900), a Naples native, noted in a youthful but very well-written diary that "I returned home [from the nearby Franklin Academy] and engaged in the business of decorating walls of rooms—a sort of frescoing using pasteboard patterns—I made this a profitable business for the summer of 1828—making from 2 to 5 dollars a day."[20] Clark family history has long credited Stephen with stenciling the Cleveland house, which was located very near the Clark farm. But it seems very precocious of an eighteen-year-old without benefit of tutelage by an experienced master craftsman to execute stenciling of such a high quality utilizing such a vast number of designs without some previous training. Perhaps he apprenticed with a Connecticut artist earlier (fourteen was considered an optimum age to commence an appren-

A beautifully preserved fireplace wall in bedchamber of Cleveland house. *Courtesy Ephraim Cleveland House, c. 1794.*

ticeship in those days), or perhaps he worked the summer of 1818 as an apprentice to an artist who had been working the area for some time. Either way it seems fairly certain that young Stephen had a hand in stenciling this house and probably other similar houses in the area.

After Franklin, Clark attended Amherst College in Massachusetts, after which he returned to western New York to teach at several area academies. His specialty was English grammar; in fact he wrote six widely utilized books on the subject. At the end of his long life he returned to farming, specializing in grape cultivation.

One can't help but wonder if the summer of 1828 was his only stenciling experience or if he continued to use his artistic skills first to finance his college education in Massachusetts and later to augment his teaching and farming income, both of which had off seasons. Perhaps walls decorated by S. Clark are still to be found in Massachusetts dating back to the 1830s, and in western New York well into the nineteenth century. If he was responsible for a significant body of work, it is a shame that such a literate person did not pause to scribe a signature or two for posterity!

I.41. Elijah Northup house,
first quarter nineteenth century
Stafford, New York
Artist: Unknown, 1825–30

ELIJAH NORTHUP, who was originally from western Massachusetts, where much stencil activity by artists such as Betts and Langdon and Stimp took place, came to western New York by way of Little Falls, New York, where he learned the textile business. About 1825 he opened his own textile mill in Stafford and shortly after added a store to sell his wares in his home. Stenciling was found in the store and an upstairs chamber of the house. Most of the designs used in this house were seen in the previous two houses with Clark connections, with the addition of a few new designs—an indication that this stenciling is by a different hand or, more likely, that the artist was constantly inventing new motifs or was constantly copying from fellow artists in order to offer the latest in wall decoration to his customers.

The stencil work in the store is now covered with paper, but the bedchamber retains a well-preserved example of extant western New York stenciling.

This house probably contains work by Stephen Clark, but there is always the possibility that another of the many artists attracted to this area of rapid growth and building activity visited the Northup house. Genesee County was a popular destination for itinerant artisans.

Extant stenciling in a second-floor bedchamber of Northup house.
Photo courtesy of Dan and Rose Barber, Stafford, New York.

THE VERY INTERESTING stenciling found in two first-floor rooms of the Deshon house is reminiscent of the Counterpane house in Vermont (I.32). The large repeat design, or diaper design, is very similar in style, proportion, and coloration to decoration found appliquéd on mid-eighteenth-century cotton quilts, often made by the lady of the house. We could subtitle this house the "Appliquéd Counterpane" house. The Vermont house, of course, suggests counterpanes decorated with stenciling; it could be the "Stenciled Counterpane" house.

The artist who stenciled the Deshon house utilized two motifs popular with all types of early artisans: the oak leaf, which was very popular with English wallpaper stampers, and the heart motif used throughout the ages.

Most likely this decoration was worked by Mrs. Joseph Deshon, whose husband built the family's center-chimney frame house in 1828 on one hundred acres of farmland purchased from the Holland Land Company.[21]

This free expression of creativity, most likely inspired by a favorite quilt, is another reminder of the great variety of artists and design sources used to create the vastly diverse body of work under the heading of early American wall stenciling.

(Below) Quilt appliquéd during first half of nineteenth century, probably in New England.

(Below right) Facsimile of unique stenciling found in two first-floor rooms of Deshon house. From tracings by N. Annabal.

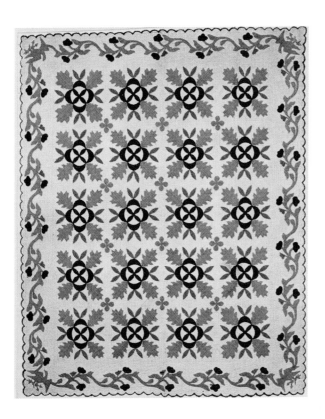

I.43. *Daniel Gould house, 1815 Walworth, western New York Artist: Leroy (signed), 1825*

Stenciled signature found in a bedchamber in Gould house. *Photo by William G. Frank. Courtesy Rochester Museum & Science Center, Rochester, New York.*

IT IS VERY SATISFYING to add a new name to the small list of stencil artists who left signatures on their work. An artist known simply as "Leroy" can be attributed with stenciling at least three structures in western New York thanks to research by Philip Parr, the aforementioned stencil researcher. Two of these examples are located in Wayne County, in the northwestern part of New York bordering on Lake Ontario.

The first structure is a large farmhouse built by Daniel Gould[22] between 1810 and 1815 with stone cut from a nearby quarry. It housed thirteen of his children and before the Civil War is said to have provided refuge for slaves escaping to Canada. Daniel and his wife Carintha came to Walworth from Canada in 1807.

Five rooms of stenciling survived to the 1970s. Probably many more of the original ten rooms were also stenciled in red, green, and black on gray walls by Leroy. His name was stenciled above a window in one of the two

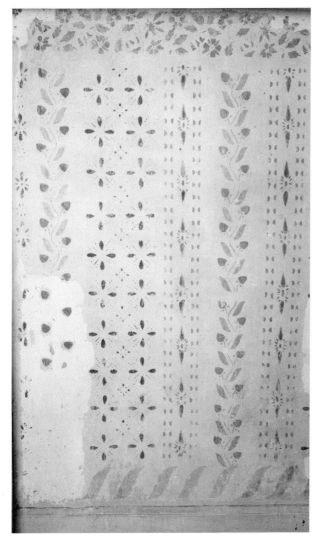

Original stenciling in first-floor alcove. *Photo by William G. Frank. Courtesy Rochester Museum & Science Center, Rochester, New York.*

stenciled bedchambers. Also, similar to an attic wall in the Sage house in Massachusetts (I.16), a sort of sample of Leroy designs was found on a second-floor stairway wall. Unfortunately most of this stenciling is no longer extant. All that remains is one panel of original work and tracings of five rooms in the collections of the Rochester Museum & Science Center (RMSC).

A second Wayne County sample of Leroy's stenciling was in the Cole house[23] in Wolcott, which was named for a Connecticut governor. Walls were reportedly covered with established Leroy designs plus neoclassical elements such as urns and fluted columns at the corners. Unfortunately all this work is now covered with paint or paper. Tracings of one room are in the RMSC collections.

Fortunately we have a name for this artist, but we do not know his origins. Since his work is definitely not under the influence of the New England folk-genre tradition, he could be a native talent. Or he could be from the mid-Atlantic area to the south. The initial settlers of this area were mainly from New England, but by 1780 conditions were favorable for the development of greater social and commercial communication with areas to the south. "Since the improving of a wagon road to the southward, it is found to be considerably easier to remove from Philadelphia, Lancaster, Trenton and Baltimore, than from New England."[24]

Considering that the Goulds were originally from Canada, a third possibility is that Leroy also came from Canada, most likely from the area conveniently joined to northwestern New York State by water and overland routes.

This part of Canada was adopted as home by many colonists, called Loyalists, who found themselves on the losing side of the Revolutionary War and were forced to give up all their holdings in America and move to a new country. These expatriates, including some of the earliest and most successful settlers in the colonies, had significant family, social, and decorative ties to America—cultural ties between Canada and America strong enough to last into the twenty-first century.

Southeastern Canada, in addition to sharing a border with America, has long shared strong cultural and social ties with its neighbor to the south. In the 1760s, when both were under England's rule, many colonists from heavily populated areas of New England immigrated to Nova Scotia simply to better themselves financially.[25] The region had recently been cleared of French Acadians, and King George was anxious to repeople the area before its rich farmland returned to a wilderness. His generous offer of large tracts of cleared land, lowered taxes, and religious freedom was too enticing for many New Englanders to refuse. However, many of these new Canadians remained loyal to the American patriots during their war with England and therefore were forced to remove from Nova Scotia back to their roots in New England at the end of hostilities.

A much larger influx from the new nation of America to Canada occurred after the Revolution as Loyalists, or Americans who had remained loyal to England, arrived. Many of them left by way of the port of New York City, which had been occupied by English troops and a Loyalist stronghold during much of the war. By June 1783 an estimated ten thousand Loyalists had accepted the English offer of free passage with the English fleet.[26] It is estimated that three out of four of these emigrants, many from Connecticut, New Jersey, and Pennsylvania, went to the Canadian Maritime Provinces.

Many other Loyalists, from inland areas of New York, New Jersey, and Pennsylvania, removed overland to Upper Canada by way of the Niagara Peninsula, an area settled almost entirely by retired Loyalist military personnel following duty in the American Revolution.

These transplanted American colonists left valuable real estate and possessions behind, but family and cultural ties remained strong. This sharing of aesthetics seems to be reflected in much of the painted decoration found on furnishings and interiors of early-nineteenth-century Ontario.

Jeanne Minhinnick, who conducted extensive research on the use of paint in nineteenth-century Upper Canada, had this to say: "In the decorated rooms that I have seen, only one did not include at least one or two motifs either reproducing or modifying those found in the United States. The Yankee Pedlar was a familiar traveler on the roads of Upper Canada and it may be that the itinerant wall decorator was another."[27] Her research also indicates that the stenciled wall was a rather common occurrence in Upper Canada between 1810 and 1840, particularly in towns bordering on Lake Ontario.

This area of obvious early housing starts and wealth attracted the interest of numerous itinerant artists early in the nineteenth century. Between 1800 and 1840, advertisements placed by artists in local newspapers included the following services: ornamental painting, fancy house painting, house painting, distemper coloring of walls, and painting in imitation of wood and marble. One ad in an 1810 paper was particularly curious. Its author offered to paint housing inside and out, and referred to something called "Patent Painting," a term now very obscure. It could refer to a set of designs registered with the authorities for a period of time or to a tool for applying decoration, perhaps a stamp or roller.

Most of the wall stenciling in Canada seems to be of the folk genre, with only two examples thus far falling under the classical heading (II.40). Examples of wall stenciling from other areas of eastern Canada, such as Lower Canada (Quebec) and the Maritime Provinces, have not come to the author's attention as yet.[28] However, numerous examples of floor stenciling, which was occasionally executed by wall stencil artists, have been found. A recent survey of interior decorative painting in Nova Scotia, conducted in the 1980s by the Art Gallery of Nova Scotia, noted a floor in a circa 1840 house in Smithville, Shelburne County, painted with geometric designs with the aid of a stencil. In New Brunswick, the Kings Landing Museum has re-created floor stenciling in at least two of its period houses. And finally, the Upper Canada Village, in Morrisburg, has several re-created stenciled floors.

Recently (February 2000) floor stenciling was discovered on the risers of the winding central staircase of a circa 1825 stone house located on the outskirts of Ottawa. The stenciling, found under several layers of paint, is described as brown swags and drapes on a dirty mustard-yellow background. This discovery is now part of a restoration "to as original a condition as possible" by the owners.

New examples of Canadian wall stenciling are being found under layers of paper and paint every day. Perhaps in the near future examples from the Maritime Provinces and stenciling in the French taste from Lower Canada will come to light, in addition to the numerous interesting and varied examples from Upper Canada.

John Brown house. *Courtesy Jon K. Jouppien, Heritage Resource Consultant.*

I.44. John Brown house, 1805
St. Catharines, Ontario, Canada
Artist: Unknown, 1820

Facsimile, utilizing much educated guesswork, of stenciling found between chair rail and baseboard in a front parlor of Brown house.

JOHN BROWN, a descendant of an early and prosperous agrarian family from the Schoharie area of eastern New York,[29] was among the close to 15 percent of New York residents who remained loyal to England during the American Revolution.[30] Finding himself on the losing side at the end of the war, he was forced to abandon his home, property, family, and friends in New York and start over across the border in the wilds of Upper Canada. Brown had served with Butler's Rangers,[31] and therefore he was granted compensation by the English government with a tract of land in St. Catharines on the Niagara Peninsula.

His new home was constructed in two stages, much as his ancestors had done nearly one hundred years earlier. First, John and his eldest sons built a small, rude, one-and-a-half-story structure, comprised of one large first-floor room and a sleeping loft above.

The second stage was the construction of an imposing "Loyalist Georgian"–style house, large enough to accommodate a family of twelve, which utilized the first section as the kitchen and its loft as a sleeping area for domestic help. John died in 1804, possibly before the completion of his mansion house, which, due to its position on the Pelham Road (heavily traveled by British soldiers during the War of 1812), was pressed into service as a public house.

When John's wife, Magdelena, died in 1818, she willed the property to her two youngest sons, who probably were responsible for structural modifications to the house made to accommodate a growing tavern business while protecting the privacy of a growing family. It is not clear if the stenciling found in a parlor to the left of the spacious front hall predates these alterations or not; therefore precise dating of the stenciling is difficult at this time.

The stenciling, which uses familiar designs in a very atypical way, is executed mostly in green with a few motifs in blue, on a yellow ocher background. It was revealed when many layers of wallpaper were removed by new owners around 1980. A precise re-creation was performed, leaving areas of wall where no stenciling was found disturbingly blank. Most of the designs re-created on the walls represent only the first half of a two-part stencil design. Several of the vertical oak-leaf borders are exact copies of those just seen in western New York, the difference being that they are missing the second part of the design. Details such as veining on the oak leaves, which was executed in black in New York, are mostly missing on these Canadian walls. This is a phenomenon that is often seen. For various and often inexplicable reasons, one paint pigment will be more transient than others used on the same wall and exposed to the same conditions. For example, when paper was removed in the Steere house (I.2), only the red units survived, with the green units almost completely invisible. Fortunately the designs by the same hand had been previously recorded in other houses.

The designs in the Brown house have been recorded on walls in Connecticut and New York. Even the frieze, which is completely missing except for a small section at the bottom of the design, seems to match in depth and composition the bottom of one previously recorded by tracing and photographing.

These similarities, however, do not imply that the Brown house stenciling is by the same artist (or artists) responsible for the work in Connecticut and New York. Since the designs in the Brown house are applied to the wall in a manner atypical of any seen before, they are probably the work of a copyist, who had access to them while en route to the Niagara Peninsula. The layout features the use of closely spaced vertical borders with no fillers in between. Also, several designs are cut in a new manner: the "undulating leaf" border design now has diminutive clusters of berries alternating with the leaves, and the "pollywog" border now has a serrated disk between each repeat. The artist traced the designs well but added his own touches during the cutting process, and used his own creativity in planning the room layout.

Original floor stenciling, perhaps the work of the same artist, has been re-created in the spacious front hall with a section of the original retained.

There is stenciling still to be retrieved from under wallpaper in the room to the right of the front door. In 1981 portions of a birdcage bar were found, an indication that this room had early on been converted to a taproom. This room, with its interesting bar and its enticing stenciling, is due to be restored by the owner, Jon Jouppien, a historic building restorationist, in the near future. Perhaps this stenciling will provide clues to when all the stenciling was executed, and will help to identify the missing stencil units in the opposite parlor.

A museum-quality restoration has been ongoing since the house was purchased by Jouppien in 1979. Appropriately, the Ontario Heritage Foundation plaqued the site in 1984 as being of great historic and architectural significance.

One cannot help but wonder if originally the front hall and perhaps the second-floor ballroom of the important "Loyalist" house were also ornamented by this mysterious early-nineteenth-century artisan who traveled the Niagara-to-Dundas stagecoach route with a satchelful of "Yankee" stencil designs.

I.45. Lewis Haynes house, 1829
Jordan, Niagara Peninsula
Artist: Unknown, circa 1830

THE HAYNES HOUSE, built around 1829 in the little town of Jordan, originally had extensive stenciling according to Jeanne Minhinnick.[32] Found under wallpaper in a hallway, it is described as dark crimson on a light crimson background with black walnut woodwork.[33] It is not clear if this woodwork was painted or a natural wood finish. This decorative work, which was possibly throughout the house, is now painted over, with but few design motifs recorded by Minhinnick. They include a cabbage-rose design similar to but not exactly like that used by Gates in Vermont (I.33) and also seen in western New York (I.36). Large and small flower-filled, very stylized baskets were alternated with the rose motif to form vertical borders on the walls of the stair hall.

Reportedly the Van Sicle house, also originally on the Niagara Peninsula, had several rooms of stenciling by a different hand than the previously mentioned Niagara

Three stencil designs reportedly found in Haynes house, which once stood on Niagara Peninsula. *Renderings by W. N. Minhinnick, circa 1970.*

I.46. *Duetta-Mouck house*

South Bay, Ontario

Artist: Unknown, circa 1830

---

examples. This house was carefully dismantled and moved in the 1980s; its present location and the condition of its stenciling are unknown.

It has not been established if the stenciling in the Haynes and Van Sicle houses was definitely of the folk genre. It could have been of the classical genre, since stenciling of that type has also been found in the peninsular area. It is clear that little of the once seemingly plentiful and varied wall stenciling in the Niagara area has survived into the twenty-first century. Hopefully as the historic, aesthetic, and ever increasing monetary value of early-nineteenth-century interior painted decoration becomes recognized and understood by preservationists and homeowners alike, more stenciled rooms will be preserved or at very least recorded.

✦

THE STENCILED Duetta-Mouck house is located on the northwestern shore of Lake Ontario across from the Niagara Peninsula. The house is situated in Prince Edward County, one of Ontario's earliest settlements.

This is the area Jeanne Minhinnick described as having large enough numbers of stenciled houses to make their existence quite common. She went on to say this about the location of the Duetta-Mouck house: "Other stenciled walls are known to have existed within a ten mile radius,"[34] an indication of a grouping of houses with stenciled walls perhaps by the same itinerant artist.

In the 1960s stenciling was found in a parlor under wallpaper but on top of a bright blue wash, a very common first treatment in Upper Canada.

The stencils correspond closely to those used in Columbus, New York (I.36), Farmersville, New York (I.38), and the Western Reserve area of Ohio (I.61) and were most likely executed by the same hand. The colors in all four buildings are similar to those used in New England, namely red and green stenciling on yellow ocher, with the happy addition of the brilliant Prussian blue for accent.

The current status of this house is unknown, but one wall of its fine stenciling, including baseboard, chair rail, and door, is reportedly safely stored in the collections of the National Museum of Canada.

Stenciling has been recorded in several other houses in

Facsimile of Duetta house stenciling. *From tracings by Gina Martin.*

this north shore area bordering on Lake Ontario. The MacLean house, built around 1830 in Brockville, reportedly had stenciling in a parlor and front stair hall. Many designs on these walls were identical to those seen in the Duetta house but executed in a different coloration. The same pigments—moss green, Venetian red, yellow ocher, and of course Prussian blue—were used, but this time the Venetian red was used to tint the background paint a soft pink with a deeper pink at the frieze area. The stenciling, executed in green, blue, and yellow, was very striking on pink walls. These two fine rooms of Canadian stenciling were plastered over long ago, with only a freehand facsimile of the parlor dating to 1958 remaining.

Stenciling was also found in the Player house, built in the 1820s in Lansdowne, Ontario, just west of Brockville. All that remains of this early work is a black-and-white facsimile that clearly shows a strong resemblance to a frieze seen in Farmersville, New York, joining this house to a group of houses probably decorated by the same artist who worked in New York, Canada, and Ohio sometime between 1820 and 1840. The origin of this artist, with a penchant for Prussian blue, is not known, but it appears that he started his career in eastern New York, or possibly New England, and worked his way west on early road systems and waterways that connected New York, Upper Canada, and the Western Reserve of Ohio, with a goodly supply of Prussian blue pigment in his poke—a welcome addition to the rather repetitious and limited color schemes of his early New England counterparts.

Chapter 6

The Middle States
of Pennsylvania
and Maryland

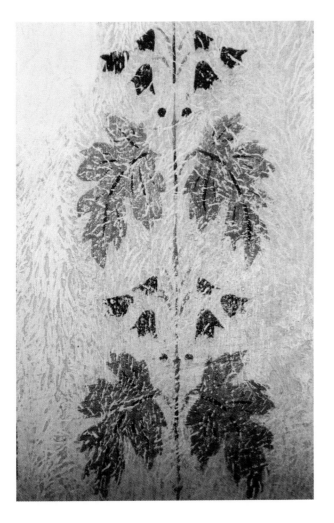

Leaf motif from a vertical border found in second-floor ballroom of
Martin Rohrer house, Hagerstown, Maryland.

The mid-Atlantic area of America has long been described as the quintessential American region. It is an area with a wide mixture of nationalities, a great variety of economic and social systems, and many religious sects, mostly descended from Protestants fleeing persecution in Europe.

During the founding of the nation, this area acted as a mediator between the New England colonies and the colonies to the south.

The mid-Atlantic state known as Pennsylvania was granted to William Penn, a Quaker, in 1681 by King Charles II in payment of a debt due to his father. Originally it included western New Jersey and all of the present state of Delaware, totaling about forty-five thousand square miles. Penn set up a liberal type of government that granted asylum to Quakers and all oppressed people of Europe. Large numbers of Scotch Presbyterians, many from Northern Ireland; French Protestants called Huguenots; Palatine Germans of the Reformed and Lutheran faiths; and numerous other nationalties and religions arrived in great numbers at the ports of Philadelphia and New Castle.

The Scots, in addition to being strong, dependable farm and iron-furnace workers, provided early artistic talent to the area. In a 1769 Philadelphia newspaper, Alexander Stewart advertised that he had studied at painting academies in Glasgow and Edinburgh and was desirous of painting "picture panels—at a very moderate rate." Twenty years later, in 1792, Anthony Stewart (perhaps related to Alexander) advertised in nearby Maryland to do "many things related to the decorations of elegant rooms."

French Huguenot emigrants included numerous craftsmen skilled in many disciplines, including a surprising number of silversmiths. They are also said to have been very well versed in the painting of faux bois and marbre as practiced on the Continent. These almost tromp l'oeil techniques were found in colonial homes along the entire eastern seaboard.

The German love of decorative painting can be seen in the homes and furnishings of the many early German rural communities radiating out from Philadelphia. They developed a mid-eighteenth-century type of wall decoration that could have been a precursor to the stenciled walls of a later period. Small one-color designs were applied uniformly on the entire wall surface. The tool is said to have been a stamp made by undercutting a design into a potato half; the resulting work was therefore called "potato stamp" decoration.

Decoration of this type was used on the bulbous stone kitchen walls of the Henry Antes house,[1] built 1736 in Upper Frederick Township, Pennsylvania. This important example of Germanic architecture, owned and restored by the Goschenhoppen Historians, was named a national historic landmark in 1992. The fragmentary decoration includes a stamped or stenciled four-petal daisy-like motif, executed in red on whitewashed walls. Throughout the house are remnants of at least two layers of painted baseboards, the earliest of which appears to be in red paint and the next in yellow ocher. This early paint is scheduled to be expertly conserved in the near future.

Another mid-eighteenth-century Germanic house, the Rex house in Schaefferstown, owned by Historic Schaefferstown, has an in situ panel in the kitchen with at least three different layers of colonial-period decoration, featuring white stamped, stenciled, and/or freehand motifs on a lively red ground. One of the motifs is very similar to the four-petal daisy found in the Antes house kitchen. All decoration appears to have been executed in water-based paint originally. This decoration was re-created on three walls by a previous owner. At one time the Rex house also had black dots on lively red in the stair hall and decorative painting in at least one parlor. Both early paint treatments are now painted over.

Pennsylvania's great port city, Philadelphia, in addition to being the "City of Brotherly Love," was also a very active center for the arts in colonial times. Alfred Coxe Prime noted in his *Arts and Crafts in Philadelphia, Maryland and South Carolina, 1721–1785* the great availability of paint materials, imported and domestic; design and instruction books both English and American; and of course artists eager for commissions in numerous artistic fields.

By 1790 Philadelphia was the largest commercial and artistic center in America and the second-largest English-speaking city in the world. The rapid building of handsome Federal-style homes created a great demand for craftsmen to build and ornament them in the popular clas-

sical style. This period also ushered in an ever increasing appreciation of and demand for painted ornamentation.

The new nation's first capital city, with its many home-grown artisans and recently arrived craftsmen trained on the Continent, was a fertile incubator for producing fine American Federal-period architecture, interior design, and room furnishings, much of which utilized the new passion for the painted surface—a passion that soon spread throughout the inland rural communities and on to the western frontier.

View of re-created "potato stamp" decoration found in kitchen of Rex House. *Courtesy Historic Schaeﬀerstown Inc.*

THE HANDSOME, three-story, double-width brick town house built in 1788 by Thomas Harper, a very affluent Philadelphia gentleman, is located in a section known as Society Hill. This neighborhood was not named for affluent English socialites but rather for a short-lived organization of craftsmen and artisans that was founded by William Penn around 1770. During the nineteenth century the area suffered a slow but steady decline, and almost total disaster during the early twentieth century.

After World War II there was a concentrated effort by national, state, and city agencies to save the great number of eighteenth- and nineteenth-century houses that had miraculously survived in the area. Restoration work, which began in 1951, was ongoing for at least thirty years.

Work on the Harper house began in the 1960s. During this process elaborate wall stenciling believed to date to the late eighteenth century was found under wallpaper in a large second-floor front room. Most likely a ballroom, it measured eighteen feet in depth and was thirty-eight feet long with a four-window frontage. It is quite remarkable that this eighteenth-century decorative painting survived in such an urban setting as the thriving port city of Philadelphia.

The stenciling, though lost during the rehabilitation of the building, was thoroughly recorded in photographs[2] and by tracings and paint analysis.[3]

The builder of this fine house died in 1790, only two years after its completion, leaving his wife, Mary, as head of household: four sons under sixteen, four daughters, and two slaves.[4]

It is quite possible that another Philadelphia resident by the name of Thomas Harper played a part in the interior decoration of this house. A Thomas Harper who had arrived from London in 1775 advertised in the *Pennsylvania Packet* that he was an "Upholsterer, appraiser and paper hanger" who had "served nobility in London." By 1784 he was advertising that, in addition to upholstery and paperhanging, he also "colors and ornaments rooms —and ceilings." It seems doubtful that Thomas was multi-talented enough to execute all these various artistic disciplines himself. It is more likely that he imported and sold fine fabrics, wallpaper, and other items to embellish the room interiors of Philadelphia society—being more of a merchant than an artisan, who employed upholsterers, paperhangers, and painters to serve his clientele.

Perhaps Thomas the upholsterer arrived in Philadelphia under the auspices of a rich relative. Perhaps the

View of Harper house, Philadelphia, showing right half of the double-width house where wall stenciling decorated second-floor ballroom.

wealthy uncle or cousin who shared a name with him called on his services to decorate the interior of his new town house. Having "served nobility in London," he certainly had proper credentials for such a lofty commission.

The Thomas Harper house now houses a fine restaurant, which utilizes the once stenciled second-floor ballroom as a dining room. Its very rare example of urban late-eighteenth-century stenciling is gone, but the exterior of this grand town house looks as handsome today as it did when new, over two hundred years ago.

Facsimile of ballroom stenciling.

Ironworker's House. *VanLeer-Potts House, 1780–1824. Wesley Sessa/Maureen Noonan.*

I.48. *Ironworker's house, 1828*
Pottstown, Pennsylvania
Artist: Unknown, 1830

FRAGMENTS OF WALL STENCILING, very unlike that seen before, were found under paint in the front room of an 1828 Pottstown farmhouse that once housed a worker or even manager of the Warwick Furnace, one of the numerous eighteenth-century iron-making facilities in Pennsylvania, particularly in this southeastern corner of the state.

This stenciling is very similar to, probably by the same hand as, that in the next two Pennsylvania examples, located a bit farther west in southern York County. Executed in shades of blue, green, yellow, and red on an undetermined ground color, it suggests—in its use of small, light flower sprays and motifs composed of diamonds—the circa 1800 wall stenciling on wood sheathing from Lower Dairy Farm, Little Horkesley, England.[5] The palette, however, is quite different, with the English version done entirely in dark gray on a white ground.

The stencil preservationist commissioned to reclaim this work should expect to find stenciling on the ceiling, which seems to be the format for this artist.

A recession in the iron industry occurred after the War of 1812. During this time the Warwick Furnace was purchased or inherited by Thomas Potts, grandson or great-grandson of John Potts, perhaps the most famous and affluent eighteenth-century ironmaster. Thomas upgraded his new holdings by building this stucco-on-stone farmhouse to replace the original two-over-two-room eighteenth-century log house. Perhaps he also commissioned the stencil artist.

Thomas's ancestor, the elder ironmaster, also enjoyed colorful decorative painting. His fine mid-eighteenth-century home, called Pottsgrove,[6] has been restored as a museum house by the Montgomery County Department of History and Cultural Arts. A second-floor chamber contains paneled doors and an overmantel covered with black on white veined faux marbre framed with lively red molding. The painted marble, which is said to represent that quarried in nearby King of Prussia, was re-created by York, Pennsylvania, artist Othmar Carli in 1988.

The Warwick Furnace was early and important. The first ironmaster, Robert Grace, was a close friend of Benjamin Franklin, whose famous stove design was first cast in 1742 at the Warwick facility. In 1757 the bell for Philadelphia's Congressional Hall, which warned of enemy troops during the Valley Forge encampment, was cast here. During the Revolution, cannons and ammunition were made here using, it is said, six thousand cords of

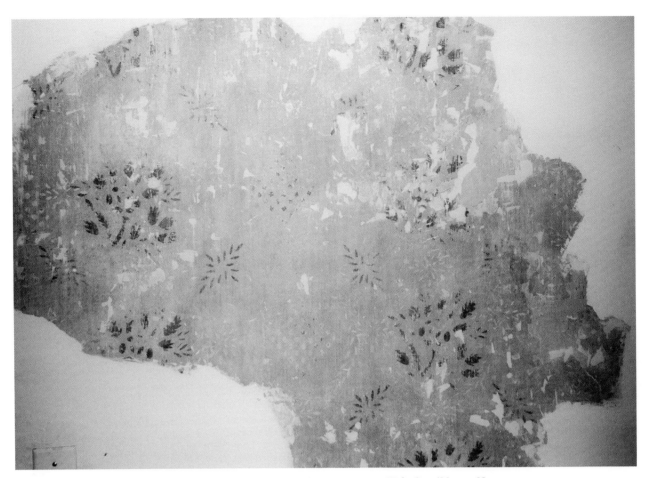

Fragment of stencil decoration found in a front parlor. *VanLeer-Potts House, 1780–1824. Wesley Sessa/Maureen Noonan.*

wood, or the product of two hundred and forty acres of woodlot.

Recently the current owner of the 1828 Pottstown house, Wesley Sessa of Eighteenth Century Restorations, moved a circa 1780 log half-house from York, Pennsylvania, to the site. It is positioned exactly where the original log structure stood, conveniently just to the left of its 1828 replacement. Now the eighteenth- and nineteenth-century ironworkers' dwellings stand side by side, depicting a charming vignette of Pennsylvania's early iron-manufacturing industry.

Robert Turner house.

I.49. Robert Turner house, late eighteenth century
Airville, Pennsylvania
Artist: Unknown, circa 1825

THE TOWN OF AIRVILLE is said to be one of the earliest communities in the township of Lower Chanceford, which was settled by Scottish immigrants as early as 1735. Its first industries were lumbering and shad fishing. Later, farming and iron production emerged as leading businesses. By 1820 large quantities of wooden chairs were manufactured in the area.

The stenciled Turner house, with its massive stone walls, is located just west of the Susquehanna River and north of the Mason-Dixon Line.[7] It was built by Pennsylvania legislator Robert Turner around 1780 on a once thriving corner where early railroad tracks bisected the early road and Muddy Creek. It was surrounded by clapboard mill buildings, a county store, an early post office, and a train station.[8] When visited by the author in the late 1990s, this stenciled house was run by Ray Hearne as a charming bed-and-breakfast located in a now sleepy corner of southern York County, its neighboring buildings long since abandoned. Well-preserved folk-type stenciling in red, green, and blue, much smaller and more delicate than that found in New England and New York, was retrieved from under wallpaper by Hearne in one bedchamber. The frieze interestingly included freehand-painted elements in addition to the stenciled ones. Of special interest is the rare ceiling stenciling, which ornaments that area with alternating closely spaced delicate green and blue motifs. This room with its unique panoramic stenciling provided a very pleasant overnight stay for the author and her husband.

The paint used to execute this stenciling seems to be of the distemper type. The pigments are unknown, but the author's visual impression is that the blue is not Prussian blue, since it shows no evidence of fading or graying. Perhaps the lake pigment, indigo, was used. The red, which is also very well preserved, is darker than straight red lead (minium), and is probably a mixture of red earth or ocher with a healthy dollop of lead for durability and brightening. The green is the least durable and in numerous areas has turned yellow, possibly an indication that it was made by mixing yellow ocher with a blue pigment of an unknown type. The background color for the main part of the wall is difficult to determine but is probably white or soft yellow. The four-and-a-half-inch frieze is a light shade or tint of the green used for the stenciling.

Hearne also discovered evidence of nineteenth-century stenciling, probably by the same hand, in other locations of the house. Also fragments of two layers of faux bois have been revealed on several paneled doors, with eighteenth-

View of extant stenciling found under wallpaper in a second-floor bedchamber.

century pecky bois found under nineteenth-century-style wood graining.

The delightful stencil work in the Turner house, which is now a private residence, is undoubtedly by the same talented artist who visited the Ironworker's house (I.48), which is located just a short distance northeast of this one.

❧❧❧

I.50. Stewart house, circa 1820
Airville, Pennsylvania
Artist: Unknown, circa 1830

THE STEWART HOUSE was built around 1820 on land granted to Patrick Stewart in 1808 by the Commonwealth of Pennsylvania.[9] It is not clear if it was built by Patrick himself or by one of his descendants. The Stewart family first arrived in the southern York County area several generations before, just after the mid–eighteenth century.

Without question this house was stenciled by the same artist as the previous two houses, with several motifs, including one found on the ceiling, exactly matching those in the Turner and Ironworker's houses. Fortunately this stenciling was recorded by Ray Hearne, the previous owner of the Robert Turner house, which is located just three miles away. Tracings were taken and sections of the stenciled walls were retained before the long-abandoned dwelling collapsed around 1980.

The nearby town of Stewartstown was named after Anthony Stewart, the son of the aforementioned Patrick Stewart. Anthony, who is said to have been a craftsman, probably a carpenter, removed to Mechanicsburg[10] in order to be part of its creative atmosphere. In 1832 the name of the town was changed from Mechanicsburg to Stewartstown in honor of its first postmaster—Anthony Stewart!

One cannot help but wonder if the two Stewarts who advertised their artistic talents in local newspapers, Alexander in Philadelphia in 1769 and Anthony in Baltimore in 1792 (see page 98), were somehow related to the Stewarts of Airville and Stewartstown. If so, was the later one responsible for the nineteenth-century stenciling in the Ironworker's, Turner, and Stewart houses? All three houses share stencil designs as well as Scottish heritage. Or was the earlier artist, Alexander, perhaps responsible for the eighteenth-century graining and marbling in Pottsgrove Manor and/or the Turner house?

It is interesting to note that the stencil work in these three Pennsylvania houses shares stylistic similarities with 1800 stenciling found in England at the Lower Dairy Farm, Little Horkesley, Essex.[11]

Fragments of plaster with stenciling removed from Stewart house before it collapsed around 1980. Top shows same frieze design as in Turner and Ironworker's houses. Bottom is same blue motif seen in both houses.

THE FACT THAT it was once a stillhouse is all that is known about a stenciled dwelling in Glenrock, southeastern Pennsylvania. Probably the distillation paraphernalia were housed on the first level, with the distiller's family residing on the second and third floors. Not much evidence of its original use remains, since the first floor was long ago converted into a typical residential living area.

The making of alcoholic beverages was an important and lucrative occupation during this period of universal family and social drinking. Distilled beverages were even supplied by farmers to their workers as part of their wages. Rum, wine, brandy, and whiskey were commonly sold at local country stores, with the customers bringing their own containers in order to avoid the extra charge for a bottle provided by the storekeeper.[12]

Unique stenciling originally decorated the wooden paneling in at least two second-floor rooms. A good-size section can still be seen in situ. It is in an excellent state of preservation due to the fact that it appears to have been covered with canvas or burlap while it was still in good

Stenciling on beaded pine sheathing still extant in a second-floor room of Stillhouse of Glenrock, Pennsylvania.

condition. The nails used to apply this protective covering can still be seen with bits of loosely woven cloth protruding from underneath.

A small fragment of the work once in a second room was found on the back of a panel of molded tongue-and-groove sheathing that was part of the original room divide. It was directly under a layer of blue wash, which was covered with a skim coat of plaster with at least two applications of wallpaper. This new design was a daisy motif in indigo blue, dissimilar to that in red on the in situ work. On the back of this same board is stenciling matching that still on the wall in the first room.

In some ways the Stillhouse stenciling is simplistic enough to suggest an in-house artist such as the German housefrau of the colonial period who applied potato decoration. On the other hand it is much later, definitely stenciled—not stamped—and utilizes at least five different stencil borders in a least three primary colors. Distemper paint pigmented with minium (red lead), indigo, and a green made by blending yellow ocher and indigo was used to decorate walls spread with a light blue wash.

The designs used are of curious origins and very ingenuous. Some, particularly the two daisy motifs, seem to be unfinished, as if only the first part of a two-overlay stencil motif. The distemper paint is applied with a very heavy hand and/or overloaded brush, producing much smudging, seeping under the edge of the stencil plate, and paint accidentally applied beyond the edge of the stencil plate, as if the brush was much too large for the job—obviously the work of a craftsman without benefit of academy or apprenticeship!

However, in spite of, or perhaps because of, its many technical failures, the stenciling in the Stillhouse by this anonymous nonacademic is very spontaneous, cheerful, and touching. For some inexplicable reason the creation of this "outsider" artist produces a goodly amount of visual pleasure and a smile!

I.52. Christian Oyer house, circa 1830
Saulsburg, Huntingdon County, Pennsylvania
Artist: Unknown, circa 1830

THE EXTREMELY REFINED Federal-style Oyer house, which is more related to those built by wealthy neighboring ironmasters than to those of other farmers in the area, is located in central Pennsylvania, not far from several early roads leading to the western frontier states such as Ohio, Kentucky, and Indiana.

Built in 1830 by Christian Oyer, a German farmer from eastern Pennsylvania, the house changed hands several times before 1880, when it was purchased by the Harmons, a farming family that retained ownership for a ninety-year period. During the Harmons' long occupation, practically no architectural modernization was made to the dwelling. No running water or plumbing of any kind, central heating, or kitchen or bath were introduced. Electricity consisted of a single lightbulb in the upstairs and downstairs hallways.

This extended period of benign neglect undoubtedly accounts for the great state of preservation of the structure and the superb original condition of a large amount of decorative painting found throughout the house. All

Christian Oyer house. *Courtesy Abe and Nancy Roan.*

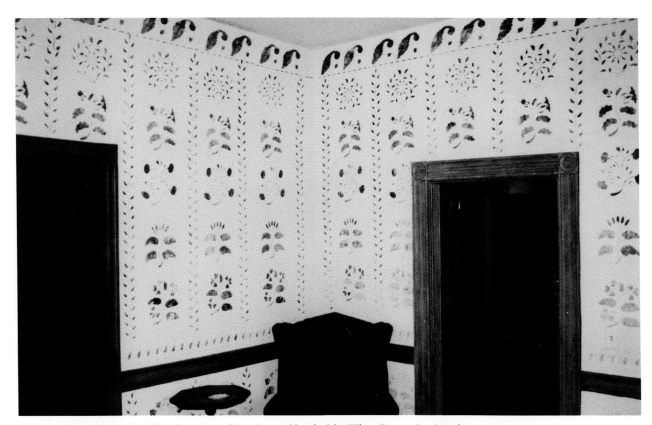

Conserved decoration in a back first-floor room of Oyer house. *Photo by John Wilson. Courtesy Jean Murphy.*

doors inside and out, the stairway from the first floor to the attic, baseboard molding, and chimney cupboards are either faux grained in figured maple, crotch mahogany, or bird's-eye maple, or marbleized in two types of faux stone. Only the woodwork in the kitchen and dining room was repainted in the late nineteenth century, in oak graining. All these techniques were practiced widely in German areas of eastern Pennsylvania, the original home of the Oyer family (of German ancestry). Of course the same techniques were also commonly practiced by New England itinerant artists. However, the matching exterior front and back doors, with contrasting light and dark faux bois decoration, are very Germanic in style.

A completely unexpected discovery was made by the new owner in the 1970s. Wall stenciling of the New England folk genre was discovered while stripping numerous layers of wallpaper from a back first-floor parlor. Executed in distemper paint in bright red and green on gray or blue paint,[13] it features motifs similar but not identical to those originating in New England and later used in Upstate New York. The panel layout and spacing of the elements above and below the chair rail also echoes work

seen in New York State, not far north of this central Pennsylvania location.

It is difficult to speculate on the travel route or origin of the artist or artists responsible for the vast amount of diverse painted decoration in the Oyer house. The stencil artist obviously must have traveled through the Northeast for his work to be so similar to that in New England and New York, but this type of faux work was commonly executed by artists up and down the eastern seaboard starting in the mid–eighteenth century. Therefore there is a definite possibility that the stenciling and faux graining were created by different artisans from different parts of the country.

Another puzzle on which to ruminate is that the stenciling was found only in one back parlor. Generally the commissioning of a traveling artist to custom decorate a new house was an event of great importance. Usually the best and most public rooms of the house were the first to receive this show of ostentation—especially if commissioned by a house builder such as Christian Oyer who was obviously striving to impress, and with such an affinity for highly ornamental painted decoration, as proven by

One of many fancifully grained or marbelized baseboards throughout Oyer house. *Photo by John Wilson. Courtesy Jean Murphy.*

the fact that he commissioned faux graining and marbling for every room of his house. The author senses that there was originally more stenciling in the Oyer house, but because it was executed in very unstable and vulnerable distemper, it was washed off many years ago, especially in the front hall and parlor, which tended to be tidied up more often than back rooms.

Several other houses in the area contain painted decoration from the same period as the Oyer house. The Curtin mansion, an elegant ironmaster's house in neighboring Centre County, had doors with wood graining, which unfortunately have been completely repainted. Also the Adam Fisher homestead, the next Pennsylvania example, has remarkable stenciling on the front stairway and baseboards in a front parlor.

Obviously a wide variety of decorative painters, possibly from the North, mid-Atlantic region, and Southeast, passed through this central Pennsylvania area on their way to seek their fortunes on the western frontier.

IN 1796, WHEN HE WAS just one year of age, Adam Fisher III removed from Lancaster, Pennsylvania, to the southwestern part of that state with his mother and father, John Adam Fisher, and his grandfather, Adam Fisher, Sr.

When the father, John Adam Fisher, died just ten years later, his land and part of the grandfather's property was put in trust for Adam III, the eldest son, and his siblings. It totaled some ninety-five acres.

Upon turning twenty-one in 1817, Adam III petitioned the orphans' court for this acreage and was awarded the land on the condition that he pay his siblings thirty-two dollars per acre for their shares, a substantial sum in those days.

The Fisher family raised rye to distill into whiskey, a popular cash crop for this area and time in history. Barrels to store and ship the whiskey were made on the premises. The rye whiskey was shipped all the way to Philadelphia instead of the much closer Pittsburgh, since the price paid in the capital city was eighty cents per barrel, twice as much as that in Pittsburgh. This trip east could also afford a visit with friends and relatives still

Stenciled front stairway risers and baseboards in Adam Fisher house. *Courtesy Karen Artuso.*

One of many faux bois doors in Fisher house. *Courtesy Karen Artuso.*

residing in Lancaster, which was on the route from United to the coast.

Obviously the family distilling business was very lucrative, since around 1837 Adam III was able to build a large, impressive, late-Federal-style red brick house that included many special features denoting a fine homestead rather than just a simple farmhouse. The walls (of brick made on the estate) were three bricks thick in exterior areas and two bricks thick for interior walls.

The Fishers also paid special attention to the woodwork, which was milled from the family's own woodlot. The moldings are carved, door and window frames have bull's-eye lintels, and there are carved panels on the wide door frames between rooms. Most of this handsome woodwork originally had expertly executed stenciling and graining.

The stenciling, with much freehand overpainting, does not exactly fit the profile of the rest of the stencil examples in this book, but because it is unique and, although not on the walls, is on vertical surfaces, it has been deemed appropriate for inclusion. It was found in at least two areas: the best parlor and the front stair hall.

In the best parlor it ornaments the baseboard with a fruit-and-vine motif, executed with yellow and black freehand work on yellow, red, and green stenciling on a light red ground. This work miraculously has never been overpainted and remains in a marvelous state of preservation.

Unfortunately, the stenciling in the front stair hall was covered with faux oak graining in the late nineteenth century, plus several coats of white oil-based paint later. This work has been partially recovered by the owners using a dry chipping method under direction of paint consultant Peter Dean of Lancaster. This dry method, as opposed to using a wet substance such as paint solvent or stripper, involves putting pressure on the top layer of paint by rubbing with a smooth rounded object such as a porcelain doorknob for large areas or a small spike from a deer antler to get into small areas and corners. Once paint is loosened, it is carefully scraped away. This technique works best if the top layers have begun to chip or craze due to some sort of paint incompatibility between earlier paint materials.

The decoration revealed by this tedious process is quite remarkable. Five different floral patterns were discovered in baseboard areas and on the stair risers, all executed in red, yellow, and green with yellow and green overstrokes. The background in most areas is gray, with one small area executed on a tan ground.

The second paint treatment used extensively throughout the Fisher house is faux bois graining of two types, tiger maple and a very red mahogany or rosewood. Much of this work was also overpainted with nineteenth-century oak graining and more contemporary white lead paint. Extant examples are still found in the formal parlor and the chamber above the kitchen. It is believed that most of the interior doors and all the five built-in cupboards had graining originally.

The styles of both stenciling and graining used to ornament the interior of this house would be equally suitable for the decoration of early-nineteenth-century Pennsylvania painted furniture. In addition, both types of decoration seem to be by the same hand, with the choice of pigments and medium seemingly the same for both techniques. Futhermore, the baseboard is an area traditionally decorated by a painter of wood, not an ornamenter of plaster walls. Thus the decorative work in the Fisher homestead seems to be that of a multitalented artisan trained in wooden furniture decoration who took to the road and plied his craft on the woodwork of fine new homesteads along his route to the frontier. His origins could very well have been in the Lancaster area, the hometown of the Fisher family as well as numerous painters skilled in the various diverse Germanic decorative arts.

Fancifully grained Eckschand (corner cupboard) as seen in Die Kich (the kitchen) exhibit at Goschenhoppen Folklife Museum, Green Lane, Pennsylvania. *Photo by author. Courtesy of the Goschenhoppen Historians, Inc.*

THE BORDER BETWEEN northern Maryland and southern Pennsylvania was long disputed by Lord Baltimore and the Penns. Many Palatine Germans who arrived in Philadelphia settled in the Maryland part of this area under the mistaken impression that they were still in Pennsylvania.

Such seems to have been the case with the original owners of the Germanic-style Solomon Arter log house in northern Maryland, which apparently was visited by the same nameless artist who ornamented the second-floor parlor of the Stillhouse (I.51) in southern York County, Pennsylvania. Although only fragments of the original stenciling remain in one second-floor back chamber of the Arter house, family history strongly suggests the presence of floor-to-ceiling stenciled borders capped by narrow frieze borders in all eight rooms. The exception was a small, second-floor utility area. There is also evidence of earlier painted decoration beneath the late-nineteenth-century graining currently covering most of the doors in the house.

Logs, an expedient and inexpensive building material, were used for home construction well into the nineteenth century. The first generation of settlers built small log cabins, which were enlarged or replaced by the second generation of log houses as soon as the families were financially able to do so. These later, permanent log houses had exteriors covered with weatherboards and interiors finished with lath and plaster when they were first built.

The decoration in this typical log house is quite naïve, possibly suggesting the efforts of the homeowner. However, it is much more sophisticated than its decorative-arts predecessor, potato-stamp decoration. Since the same designs have been found in two houses located fairly far apart, they are surely the work of an itinerant artist who seems to have specialized in ornamenting homes in German communities. The extent of his travels and the size of his body of work are unknown at present, but it is possible that more of this colorful, charmingly simple work will be found in the future.

Stenciled panel from a second-floor bedchamber of Solomon Arter house, showing designs very similar to those in Stillhouse (I.51), located just over the border in Pennsylvania.

Martin Rohrer house. *Courtesy Mr. and Mrs. Stuart B. Abraham.*

I.55. Martin Rohrer house, circa 1790
Hagerstown, Maryland
Artist: Unknown, circa 1800

MARTIN ROHRER BUILT this late-eighteenth-century six-bay brick house of English design and construction on one hundred acres of land that he had purchased in 1765. Possibly it was the second house Rohrer built, since there is a smaller and apparently earlier house of similar construction on the property. Since brick was an expensive building material in those days, Rohrer must have been a man of some means.

Also indicative of Rohrer's financial and social status is the house's second-floor ballroom, ornamented by the same artist who decorated the ballroom of the Thomas Harper house (I.47). Interestingly, the Rohrer ballroom runs from the front to the back of the house's middle, fronting on two center windows—a convenient layout for a tavern business. The center ballroom cleverly divides the second-floor bedchambers, ensuring privacy for the family, who would have used the left side of the building with its less formal entrance, kitchen access, and back stairway. The more formal entrance and front stair hall to the right would have served guests. Such a layout would provide privacy for an innkeeper's family as well as for guests.

The present owners, who named the house Antietam Hall after purchasing it in 1954, discovered the ballroom stenciling under a thin layer of plaster or many layers of whitewash, which in turn was hidden under a layer of green oil-based paint. (Most likely, a skim coat of plaster was applied to prepare the walls for the green paint.) While it is unclear what sort of paint the stencil artist used, the fact that the water-based plaster or whitewash neither smudged nor absorbed the stenciling indicates that the stenciling was done in oil-based paint, as was similar work in the Harpers' Society Hill town house.

Utilizing only two colors, red and black, this stenciling is simpler than that in the Harper house. The background above the dado was white paint, and below the dado it was yellow paint. Two of the designs are exact matches to those in Philadelphia. The layout of the decoration is somewhat atypical: although the upper part of the wall is filled with vertical borders spaced rather closely together, the wall area below the dado features borders running horizontally, or parallel to the baseboard and chair rail.

The discovery in this fine Hagerstown house of stenciling by the same artist who worked in Philadelphia strongly suggests that more stenciling of this type might be found in houses along the many early road systems that radiated out from Philadelphia, particularly the one leading southwest to Hagerstown.

Stenciling on walls and ceiling of a second-floor ballroom by same hand as stenciling in Harper house (I.47). *Courtesy Mr. and Mrs. Stuart B. Abraham.*

Postscript

The middle states may be the location of the earliest and most English-like wall stenciling in America. Stencil work seen on the walls of the Harper house (I.47), the first example in this chapter, and in the Rohrer House (I.55) of Hagerstown, Maryland, the last example, are both by the same stencil artist, probably fresh from stenciling walls in Great Britain. Both houses date to the late eighteenth century; both are large, expensive brick houses in the English Georgian style.

Since Philadelphia was the second-largest English-speaking city in the world by 1790, it follows that English decorative painters would flock to this thriving seaport city and to nearby Baltimore.

The following advertisement by William Priest, long accepted as the earliest ad for wall stenciling to appear in an American newspaper, appeared in 1795 in Baltimore.

PAINTING

In imitation of paper-hangings, by a mechanical process, which, from its facility, enables the operator to paint a room, stair-case, etc. upon lower terms than it is possible to hang it with paper of equal beauty. This method of painting (lately invented in Europe) being totally unknown in America, so of course are its many advantages; but as paper-hangings in a warm climate, are a receptacle for contagious infection, and a harbor for dust and vermin, it is to be presumed, this mode of painting will be found to answer all the purposes of papering without any of its inconveniences.

Early-nineteenth-century stenciled room in Alderman Fenwick's house in New Castle-upon-Tyne, England. *Courtesy Tyne and Wear Building Preservation Trust.*

It is most curious that this process was described as "lately invented in Europe," since art historians generally believe that the stencil technique (perhaps by a different name) had been utilized for hundreds of years to add color and pattern expediently to interiors, decorative accessories, and textiles.

Surely, when the craft guilds were formed in the twelfth century in England and Europe to ensure the highest quality of the various crafts and to guard their formulas and techniques, the use of the stencil was included in the many secret and "mysterious" techniques restricted to members only. The monopoly of the guilds became diminished over the centuries, and by the seventeenth century manuals containing the secrets of the various crafts began to appear. During this same century stenciled walls were seemingly out of favor in England, with the use of wallpaper becoming popular by the end of the century.

In 1712 England placed a tax on all printed paper products, including wallpaper, creating a demand for a substitute that was more affordable. Inevitably house decorators returned to painting patterns, perhaps the same ones stamped on wallpaper, directly on the wooden or plaster interior walls by means of a mechanical aid called a stencil. Stencil-decorated walls regained their popularity throughout the eighteenth century, with more and more books containing instruction available to novice and professional alike.

Perhaps William Priest, seeking an occupation to support himself after migrating to America, and aware of the numerous fine houses under construction in Philadelphia and Baltimore, decided that his new method (at least new to him) for decorating walls, namely stenciling, would score a success in America. Thus William Priest reinvented the ancient craft of wall stenciling!

Chapter 7

The Southern States of Virginia and South Carolina

Detail of extant stencil and freehand frieze from a front parlor of Clover Hill Tavern. *Courtesy Appomattox Court House National Historical Park.*

The colonial southern states of Virginia, North and South Carolina, and Georgia had very little in common historically, culturally, or artistically with their mid-Atlantic and New England counterparts, to which they were joined by the Constitutional Convention of 1787–88.

The earliest settlers of Virginia, in the 1607–24 period, were English gentry, sons of knights and barons, many graduates of Oxford University. Most of these original settlers either lost heart and fled back to England, died of fever, or were killed by Indians. The next generation, of the 1624–75 period, were people of middle-class origins who rose to wealth and power in the New World. The rigid hierarchy of seventeenth-century England made it all but impossible to climb out of the middle class if a man remained in Great Britain. The quickest road to nobility and wealth was by way of the southern American colonies. By 1672 Virginia's population had topped forty thousand, making that colony the first among all of England's continental colonies and second only to Barbados among all English colonies.[1]

Owing to the prevalence of the tobacco and cotton planters' culture, Virginia and the other southern colonies were settled in a dispersed, decentralized manner.[2] There was no need to build towns, since every large plantation was a self-sustaining unit, which raised its own food and had a full complement of mechanics and artisans to tend its needs. The majority of these workers were indentured servants, and a few were slaves. The taste of the plantation owners mirrored that of the English aristocrats in matters of architecture and interior design.

South Carolina's port city of Charles Town, as it was known before 1783, by the American Revolution had evolved into the fourth-largest city in Britain's North America and the preeminent southern seaport.[3]

According to early newspaper ads, many in Charles Town papers, artists arrived early and in sizable numbers to the South. In 1735 a Daniel Badger advertised that he was lately arrived from Boston and wished commissions in all sorts of house and ship painting. Richard Marten advertised, the next year, his willingness to execute sign and ship painting, and imitation marble and wood glazing. John Sisener, painter from London, offered house and ship painting and varnishing, including making wood into artificial stone in 1743. The majority of the early artists seem to have come from Great Britain (England and Scotland) or Ireland, but other countries were represented. In 1785 P. Tylsho from Amsterdam advertised as a coach and house painter, and glazier. France also contributed artistic expertise. In 1816 Francis LeCoq advertised in Georgia that he decorated apartments in the latest "Parisian Fashion."

This is just a small sampling of the numerous and diverse artists attracted to the southern states during the colonial and early Federal periods. The question is, Did any of them work in the American wall-stenciling tradition? Or did they work in a more formal continental style, being perhaps academically trained to paint freehand murals and overall pattern decoration, execute faux bois and marbre, or even highlight sophisticated carved woodwork with gilding?

Surviving examples of Federal-period stenciling in the South are extremely rare, perhaps due partly to the fact that a warm, moist climate is very detrimental to distemper, the paint of choice for most wall stencilers, and partly to the vigors of the Civil War on southern architecture. Or perhaps stenciled interiors were not as popular in the South, being somehow at odds with southern artistic sensibilities.

A canvass of the collections of the Museum of Early South Decorative Arts at Winston-Salem, North Carolina, and of numerous historic and preservation societies and departments in Virginia and the Carolinas, produced less than a dozen examples of Federal-period wall stenciling in the southern states. Many of these were found in Virginia's Shenandoah Valley along the Great Wagon Road, which ushered settlers to the southern frontier states. Stylistically they are equally divided between the Folk Group and the Classical Group, which will be examined in part II. None seem to be by documented New England artists.

An interesting artist by the name of S. G. West advertised in Richmond, Virginia, in 1813. Among numerous other techniques, he offered to decorate rooms in a "fanciful manner" and to imitate mahogany and marble. This is a very apt description of the first example of southern folk-genre wall stenciling. It was found in an early-nineteenth-century tavern that just happens to be located on an early stage road from Richmond to Lynchburg.

IN 1809 THE PATTESON BROTHERS, Alexander and Lilbourn, formed a partnership to develop a stage line between Richmond, Virginia's capital city, and the city of Lynchburg. In 1814 they purchased the Clover Hill farm acreage, with an existing small frame dwelling, located about halfway between the two cities—the perfect location for the headquarters of their successful stage business.

The brothers' enterprise benefited from a timely economic boom. At the end of the War of 1812, in January 1815, Americans responded with an explosive burst of optimism and expansionism. During those postwar years, the area known as Clover Hill developed into a thriving commercial village, with floods of people traveling through to the southwestern Virginia border and on into frontier states such as Kentucky, Tennessee, and Indiana.

In 1819 Alexander, whose brother Lilbourn had died in 1816, built a two-and-a-half-story, four-bay structure

Clover Hill Tavern, photograph circa 1900. *Courtesy Appomattox Court House National Historical Park.*

Re-created stenciling, faux graining, and marbling on fireplace wall of tavern parlor. *Courtesy Appomattox Court House National Historical Park.*

to serve as his large family's main residence and also as a tavern. At the same time, he built a three-story tavern guest house. Both buildings featured a high level of craftsmanship and fine detail.

About the same time that Alexander Patteson was building his house, an artist—perhaps from Richmond—was commissioned to ornament at least one of the parlors with stenciling, graining, and marbling. He covered the plaster walls with stenciled vertical borders, topped with a stunning frieze of flowers and seedpods embellished with numerous superbly painted brush strokes and tendrils. It is perhaps the most beautiful stenciled frieze this author has ever seen. The stenciled units were done in crimson, blue-green, white, and leaf green; their freehand accents were painted in a delicate reddish brown (probably alizarin crimson mellowed with burnt umber). The ground color for this frieze was medium-yellow ocher, and the background color for the main part of the wall appears to be medium blue.

The main section of the wall was covered with closely spaced vertical contiguous S-curve borders of alternating large and small proportions. The larger consisted of alternating green leaves and crimson trumpet flowers on a green vine. The smaller undulating vine was in burnt umber, with alternating small green leaves and bunches of berries.

The larger vertical border is not unlike those in northwestern Rhode Island (I.7 and I.8). This similarity is probably not attributable to the work of a single artist, however, but rather to the likelihood that two artists, many miles apart, were influenced by the same wallpaper motif popular at the time. A narrow border used around the Clover Hill house's architectural elements, however, is very similar to one used by New England stencil artists working in the classical genre (such as II.14). In addition, the general layout and proportion of this stenciling is very similar to work done in New England. Once again this is probably due to the fact that artists in both the North and the South were influenced by the same wallpaper designs. It may also be attributable to the mobility of early wall decorators, who seemed to travel freely between major East Coast seaport towns. Perhaps this artist visited Kennebunkport, Maine, or Boston, or Wickford, Rhode Island, before seeking employment in the southern states.

The baseboards and fire surround of the parlor at Clover Hill were covered with black-on-white feather graining with subtle red veining. The doors and wainscoting were grained in contrasting red mahogany and maple. The risers on the central staircases were marbleized, and there is evidence of similar grained wainscoting in the parlor to the right. Most of the doors on the second floor were also grain-painted in a mahogany finish.

When Alexander Patteson died in 1836, his estate inventory included eleven adult slaves, a library of books, numerous beds, stage property, plantation tools, and so forth, indicating that Clover Hill was a small working plantation as well as the capital of a small empire. The Patteson family owned land in many different areas of Virginia, but Alexander's wife and family moved to Patteson-owned land in Kentucky after the estate was settled.

In 1845 Appomattox County was formed, with Clover Hill as its seat of government. County meetings were held in Patteson's Tavern for a year, until the courthouse was constructed in 1846. Although the tavern remained one of the most important elements of the village, both the village and tavern declined through the years, mostly due to the development of canal and railroad travel. However, the events of April 9, 1865, assured Appomattox Court House and the Clover Hill Tavern a unique place in American history.

After General Ulysses S. Grant and Confederate General Robert E. Lee signed a formal surrender signifying the end of the Civil War at the McLean farmhouse a short distance from the tavern, the Union army set up printing presses in the tavern to print parole papers for the Confederate troops. Operations proceeded in the tavern throughout the night, and in the morning tens of thousands of Confederate soldiers received their paroles at the tavern. A few days later, the operation was moved to Lynchburg, where larger presses were available.

The village of Appomattox Court House, which had started to decline before the war, suffered a great setback in 1892, when the courthouse was destroyed by fire and the county seat subsequently moved two miles south, to Appomattox Depot. While this shift resulted in the general demise of Appomattox Court House, it also served to preserve, virtually intact, an early- to mid-nineteenth-century rural Virginia community.

When the National Park Service assumed responsibility for the village from the War Department in 1932, preservationists suggested the establishment of a permanent park and the restoration of the buildings around the courthouse square. In 1935 a congressional act established what is now known as the Appomattox Court House National Historical Park, honoring the agreement reached by Lee and Grant that ended four years of bloodshed. The courthouse was rebuilt, and the other seven buildings were restored to a style consistent with the Civil War era. At the time of restoration, the tavern was well past its peak and in a state of neglect and decline, its rare extant example of rural Virginia stenciling either very much darkened by smoke and grime or covered with wallpaper.

Around 1950, during restoration, the wall stenciling was found under more than two layers of paper. The restorers left exposed the work on one wall, which was constructed of pine sheathing to enclose the center stairway. This stenciling is still in remarkably fine condition. The other three stenciled plaster walls, and the grained and marbleized woodwork, were re-created in 1990 by restoration artist Linda Crozson and Philip Ward of Locustville, Virginia, with paint analysis performed by George T. Fore. The wooden elements of the room were done in oil-based paint, but it was difficult to determine the type of paint used for the plaster elements since oil-based glazes were thought to have been used to spruce up the decoration on both plaster and wood. However, the delicate and semitransparent quality of the freehand-painted elements definitely suggest the use of oil-based paint for the decorations on the plaster walls. In addition, the similarity of pigments used for the stenciling, graining, and marbling suggest that all three were executed by the same, most talented artist.

We are very fortunate today that this important early-nineteenth-century tavern, with its decorative painting, was saved due to the part it played in a landmark Civil War event. It is equally fortunate that the parlor was restored to its original appearance from the first quarter of the nineteenth century, a time when a great many travelers passed through Clover Hill on their way to settle the frontier. Thus, thanks to much good fortune, we have a rare insight into the antebellum lifestyle of rural Virginia, adding extra historical significance to a fine Civil War park.

IF THE PRECEDING EXAMPLE, the Clover Hill Tavern, represents the successful survival of early-nineteenth-century Virginia wall stenciling into the twenty-first century, the Anderson house represents its antithesis. Unfortunately, the failure of wall stenciling to survive represents the "rule" rather than the "exception" to the rule.

When the Andersons built their home in 1785, Brownsburg was well on its way to becoming a thriving settlement on the road between Lynchburg and Staunton, with taverns, stores, blacksmiths, and other shops, plus a mill to service the local farms.

Built in the early classical style, the Anderson house, offered access to its second floor, which was the public and formal level of the house, by way of a large pedimented front porch reached by twinned staircases on either side. At each house end were decoratively shaped exterior chimneys.

The interior featured a spacious center hall on the second level and carved classical-style woodwork, making this house a high-style one for its time and location.

Later in the nineteenth century it changed hands and was used by the Lucas family as a residence and store for many years.

During the twentieth century it fell on hard times and was all but terminal when purchased by its present owner. All interior architectural elements had been stripped, and a stairway chopped up for wood to heat the house; the front porch was missing, and debris littered the house interior and grounds. Fortunately many of the missing house parts were found among the debris, and others such as the front porch were reconstructed from extant pictures in local historical society collections.

Considering the sad state of the house interior, it is remarkable that one very small fragment of wall stenciling clung tenaciously to the center section of a wall in the earliest section of the house. Executed in deep red on white paint or plain plaster, it seemed to be the fragmented center of a round filler-type motif. This small record of the visit of a stencil artist to the Brownsburg house, unfortunately, has now completely disintegrated, with no images to aid its verification.

The New England–style stenciling applied to a back stairway during the restoration does not represent motifs found in the house. It is only a reminder that this section of the Shenandoah Valley was visited by an anonymous stencil artist, probably working in the folk genre of wall stenciling.

I.58. *Middlebrook Tavern, 1820*
Middlebrook, Virginia
Artist: Unknown, circa 1830

Facsimile of stenciling found around 1970 in first-floor tavern room of Middlebrook Tavern. *Courtesy Roberta Hamlin.*

MIDDLEBROOK TAVERN is located on an early road connecting Staunton to the north and Brownsburg to the south. The town of Middlebrook was formed in 1799 by the Scott family when they divided their land into twenty-six lots and sold them mostly to descendants of the area's earliest Scotch and German settlers.

The town grew rapidly until by 1836 there were 150 people living in thirty dwellings, plus numerous businesses and this tavern that had been built of brick in 1820. This tavern was enlarged around 1835 to accommodate the ever increasing flow of travelers along this busy road to the southern frontier.

Stenciling found in the Middlebrook Tavern could date to the original construction of 1820 but, more likely, dates to the addition of 1835. This stenciling, which is quite dissimilar to any seen thus far, is applied to the walls in a layout that could be described as spot stenciling, which is similar to but much simpler than diaper stenciling. The latter type involves an intricate interlocking pattern that must meet exactly to form an overall repeating wall decoration, whereas spot stenciling involves placing the same motif, in this case a roundel, evenly spaced on the wall in a diamond grid, then filling the void between with a smaller repeat design, either floral or geometric. Thus the whole wall panel is ornamented with only two motifs using a less than demanding placement. Horizontal borders can then be placed at the ceiling, baseboard, and/or chair rail.

This Shenandoah Valley work is similar to some discovered by Christine Borkan (appendix B) in Ohio's Western Reserve. She reported several stenciled walls signed around 1843 by a Henry Wells Sabin (1795–1871), who was born in Vermont and removed to Cleveland in 1820. Sabin did not seem to be a typical itinerant painter, since he had well-documented roots in the Ohio community. Borkan suggested that he might have been occasionally employed by a Cleveland decorating contractor. Perhaps we should take it one step further and suggest that Sabin used designs supplied by this same employer. Both the work of this anonymous Middlebrook artist and of Sabin in the Western Reserve lack the spontaneity and creativity of earlier work by artists who designed and cut their own stencils and applied them in a never ending variety of combinations to create one-of-a-kind walls with great diversity and individuality. The examples being studied, with their mechanical and repetitious quality, could suggest the availability of published designs late in the stencil period. The idea of published designs has often been suggested but never confirmed, just as numerous other questions about American wall stenciling have yet to be answered satisfactorily. The list of wall-stenciling enigmas is one of substantial length.

~⚬~

I.59. *Robert Tate house, 1803*
Greenville, Virginia
Artist: Unknown, circa 1825

Fragments of original stenciling found in front stair hall of Tate house. *Courtesy Virginia Department of Historic Resources.*

THE STENCILED TATE HOUSE of Greenville was built on a two-hundred-acre tract purchased by Robert Tate in 1759. Robert's father, John, probably of Scotch descent, came to Virginia from Ireland via Pennsylvania in 1745.

Robert built his house, which he called Clover Mount, in two stages, both completed before 1803, in the middle section of the Virginia Valley at the headwaters of the South River. Constructed of cut limestone, it is one of several early stone houses in the area that illustrate a rich local masonry tradition, which developed here late in the eighteenth century. The house still retains most of its original interior woodwork, with raised six-panel doors enclosed with molded ovolo architrave trim throughout. It is considered one of the earliest and best-preserved examples of a small group of vernacular stone houses built around the turn of the nineteenth century in southern Augusta County.[4]

During an 1970s restoration, early-nineteenth-century stenciled wall designs were discovered under numerous layers of wallpaper. Apparently wall stenciling was fairly common in the area, since the Virginia Historic Landmarks Commission stated in 1982 that "stenciling is known to have been popular in the area, but few examples survive," and went on to say that Clover Mount is the most extensive discovered in the central Shenandoah Valley to date.

The Clover Mount stenciling is said to be extensive, and very elaborate. Seven rooms of stencil work feature red, green, and blue vertical stenciled borders on a yellow ocher or buff ground. Design motifs feature closely spaced vertical borders of geometric and floral designs, with abstract horizontal borders at the ceiling, chair rail, and baseboards—a most unique and very extensive survival of stenciling along the Great Wagon Road.

The author's initial reaction to this work was that it had no connection to that in the Middlebrook Tavern (I.58), located in the northern part of Augusta County; however, on closer examination, several similarities came to the fore. First, the colorations are of a similar palette;

second, the proportions of the designs and their dense placement compare favorably; and third, one motif, a small spray of leaves, can be found incorporated into designs on the walls of both structures.

Perhaps those similarities indicate that the same artist who stenciled the Tate house stayed at and stenciled Middlebrook Tavern, located north of Clover Mount on the early road between Staunton and Brownsburg.

~∾~

I.60. Colonel John Hearst house, 1825
Bradley, South Carolina
Artist: Unknown, circa 1830

APTLY NAMED SYLVANIA, the charming house of Colonel John Hearst is one of the oldest antebellum homes still standing in the southeastern section of what was Abbeyville County, South Carolina. Fortunately, this eight-room, one-and-a-half-story white clapboard dwelling, which stands in a grove of ancient oak and poplar trees, has been preserved almost exactly as it was originally.

Built by descendants of Scotch immigrants from northern Ireland, who arrived in Charles Town, South Carolina, in 1766, it retains three rooms with surprisingly well-preserved examples of decorative painting dating to the building of the house. A bold grapevine motif, stenciled with freehand-painted details, is located on the plas-

Exterior view of John Hearst house. *Courtesy South Carolina Department of Archives and History.*

View of faux graining on plaster wall below chair rail and marbling on wooden baseboard in front stair hall. *Courtesy Lisa Wideman.*

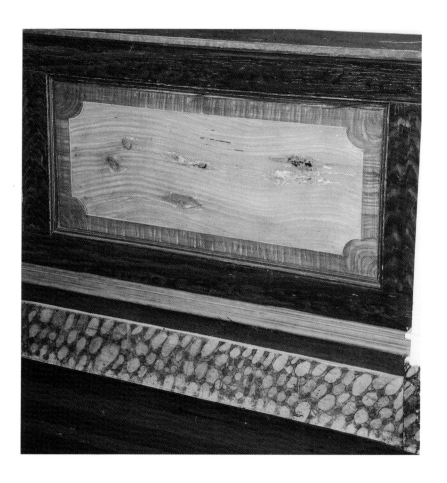

Detail of stenciled and freehand-painted border found above chair rail and at ceiling in two front rooms of Sylvania. *Courtesy Lisa Wideman.*

ter wall below the cornice board and just above the wainscoting in the central hall and up the staircase. Over eight inches deep, it is strikingly similar in composition, technique, and coloration to painted decoration found on country furniture of the same period, particularly that under the Germanic influence.

Also of interest is the craftsmanship manifested in the faux bois–decorated doors and wainscoting, as well as faux marbre baseboards, which ornament the front hall and both front parlors. Fanciful rather than realistic in feeling, this work suggests that seen in western Pennsylvania (examples I.52 and I.53).

Since the oil-based colors used to ornament both the plaster and the wooden elements have never been covered with paper or paint, the colorations remain almost as exuberant today as when applied some 175 years ago.

The Hearst house, in its bucolic setting, contains rare examples of extant Federal-period southern painted decoration, including a stenciled border in its stair hall that fits comfortably under the "Folk Group" umbrella.

Chapter 8

The Frontier States of Ohio, Kentucky, Tennessee, and Indiana

Fragment of a circa 1830 stenciled frieze featuring a 3-inch yellow and green bird being freed from its wallpaper covering. Picture taken in an abandoned Kentucky farmhouse in 1980 by John A. Diehl.

In 1787 General Rufus Putnam of Connecticut called a meeting of fellow Revolutionary War veterans at the Bunch of Grapes Tavern in Boston, Massachusetts.[1] The purpose was to propose a plan to purchase a large block of land in the Ohio Tract from the federal government, for resale to their military comrades. Their successful plan became the Ohio Company, which was composed of such Revolutionary War luminaries as Putnam, Generals Samuel Parsons and Benjamin Tupper of Connecticut, Commodore Abraham Whipple, and General James Varnum of Rhode Island, many of whom were among the first settlers of Ohio. In April 1788 the first detachment of forty-eight men, women, and children settled themselves in the southeastern corner of the tract near the confluence of the Muskingum and Ohio Rivers. This first settlement was named Marietta after the Queen of France, to honor that country for its assistance in winning America's war with England. Marietta at first was a stockade-like settlement with the threat of Indian raids ever present. In fact, in order to develop land on the outskirts of town, free land was offered to "warlike Christian Men"[2] willing to settle west of town. Not long after, close to the site of Ohio's first blockhouse or fort, the town of Cincinnati[3] developed, at the mouth of Kentucky's Licking River, where it meets the Ohio.

It's amazing to think that at the beginning of 1788 there was not a white American family legally settled within the bounds of the Ohio Tract, but by 1789 there were no fewer than twenty thousand settlers, mostly from Connecticut, Massachusetts, and Rhode Island, living on the banks of the Ohio River.[4]

In 1800 settlers began to migrate to a tract of land in northeastern Ohio that had been retained by Connecticut when it ceded the rest of its western holdings to the government. Appropriately called the Western Reserve, it attracted settlers mostly from Connecticut and Massachusetts. The area takes in that around Cleveland, named for General Moses Cleveland from Connecticut, who settled there with a number of his troops.

This new influx of settlers soon produced sufficient population for Ohio to gain statehood in 1803.

The large percentage of the Ohio population with origins in New England obviously contributed to the common occurrence of folk-style wall stenciling found in Ohio.

In 1990 Christine Edwards Borkan completed a study of wall stenciling in nine Ohio homes titled "Ohio Choices: Wall Stenciling in the Western Reserve before 1860" as her master's thesis while taking part in the University of Delaware's early American Culture Program.

Only five of her nine examples fit the time frame of this book. Of the five, three of the builders were from Massachusetts, and two had migrated from the state of Connecticut. Thus all were influenced by stenciling seen on New England walls, although the Ohio work was not necessarily executed by New England artists.

The popularity of wall stenciling in Ohio was quite widespread and seems to have peaked between 1835 and 1845, but it continued in use well into the 1850s, with designs becoming less like those in New England toward the end of that period. In southeastern New England, however, it peaked between 1820 and 1830 and by the 1840s was considered passé, with the earliest examples very dingy and old-fashioned, to be covered with a coat of paint or wallpaper in the newest Greek Revival style and coloration. Often one seldom seen room, such as a second-floor bedchamber, was retained as a reminder of an earlier time upon the request of an elderly family member.

In Ohio, as in the other areas studied, stenciling was the choice of middle- to upper-middle-class homeowners and many leaders of the community, on the basis of its artistic merit and not because of financial considerations.

As we will see in the following examples of Ohio stencil-decorated walls, the areas where this art form occurred are fairly well distributed throughout the early developed sections of the state, with examples in the earliest section around Marietta and Cincinnati to the south as well as the Western Reserve to the north. All known examples seem to be of the folk genre with definite similarities to that seen in New England. They all utilize designs that originated in eastern Massachusetts, moved westward with settlers and artists through western Massachusetts, New York State, and across the border into the Ohio Tract, bringing a bit of home to soften the vigors of frontier life.

Exterior view of Robinson house. *Courtesy Western Reserve Historical Society, Cleveland, Ohio.*

I.61. William Robinson house, 1830
Chagrin, Ohio (now Willoughby Township)
Artist: Unknown, circa 1840

THIS HANDSOME Greek Revival–style house was built around 1830 by wealthy mill owner William Robinson, who moved to the Western Reserve in 1827 from Lanesborough, Massachusetts, by way of New Haven, Connecticut, with his wife, a gentlewoman from Goshen, Connecticut.[5] Fortunately, by 1827 the trip from Connecticut to Ohio was greatly improved with the opening of the Erie Canal connecting the Hudson River of eastern New York State with Lake Erie, about 360 miles to the west. Some canal sections had been open as early as 1817, but the whole canal was not completed until 1825.

Robinson commissioned the preeminent Western Reserve architect-builder, Jonathan Goldsmith, to build his fine eleven-room house with four pilasters across the gabled facade and twinned one-story wings balanced on either side. The interior front stairway, with its fine carving and delicate spindles, is a good example of Goldsmith's fine detailing. Other examples of Ohio architecture by Goldsmith, who came to Ohio from New Haven in 1811 and died in Ohio thirty-seven years later, can be seen in Mentor, Cleveland, and Painesville. The Mathews house of Painesville, built in 1829, one year before the Robinson house, is a particularly fine example.[6]

The Robinson house was given to the Western Reserve Historical Society to become part of an authentic frontier village. Land for the village museum originally belonged to Jonathan Hale, a fifth-generation Connecticut farmer who headed west in 1818 and settled on five hundred acres, which he had exchanged for one hundred acres of depleted Connecticut farmland. This museum was appropriately called the Hale Farm and Village Museum.

During restoration of the Robinson house, stenciling was found in an upstairs chamber, which is probably just one of many rooms of stenciling original to this house. At that time, one wall of original stenciling was retained, and the other three walls were re-created over wallpaper. However, in 1999, the one remaining original wall was also re-created by Christine Borkan.

The stencil work in this house can, with a great degree of certainty, be attributed to the same anonymous artist who decorated the ballroom of the Farmersville Tavern (I.38) in western New York and the Stencil House (I.36) that originally stood in eastern New York. A very similar eagle, probably by the same artist, was discovered in a ballroom in Windsor County, Vermont, by Jessica Bond,[7] indicating the origins of this artist.

It is also of some importance to note similar work by different artists, including the "cabbage rose" filler and

"eagle with stars" used by Erastus Gates, President Coolidge's kin, in Vermont (I.33). Also the "peacock tail" motif was used as a filler and part of a vertical border, both in western New York (I.39) and in Ontario, Canada (I.44).

The talented artist responsible for at least three houses seen in this book seems to have worked in the later part of the stencil period, 1790–1840, adopting designs originated by earlier artists as his own. This homogenization of designs seems to be a common trend as stenciling moves westward, approaching the close of wall-stenciling popularity.

Facsimile of stenciling in a second-floor bedchamber of Robinson house. *From tracings by Philip Parr.*

I.62. *Warren Little house, 1830*
Aurora, Ohio
Artist: Unknown, 1835–40

THIS LARGE, TWO-STORY, center-chimney house with earlier ell to the rear was built around 1830 by Warren Little, who came to Ohio around 1812 with a group of settlers from Middlefield, Massachusetts. He was a dairy farmer and ordained Congregational minister.

It is interesting to note that Middlefield is located in western Massachusetts on the fringe of the Berkshire Mountains, just a few miles from two houses featured in this book with stenciling similar to that found in a hall of the Little house. The first, the Sage house of Sandisfield (I.16), has long been attributed to Stimp, but the second, the Gibbs house of Blandford (I.15), has the names S. E. Betts and L. W. Langdon, presumably the stencil artists, clearly stenciled over a chamber mantelpiece. The name Langdon has also been found stenciled on a wall in East Granby, Connecticut.

The unusual "pineapple vine" frieze in the Little house is similar to those seen in both Massachusetts houses with the addition of a "bell" motif seen before as part of the often-used "bell and swag" frieze shared by the Eatons, Gleason, Stimp, and the team of Betts and Langdon. The narrow acorn border is a favorite of Stimp used often by him in Connecticut and New York (I.35), but it is also

seen in work attributed to Stephen Clark in western New York (I.40).

This work in Ohio could very well be that of a documented New England artist, but probably not Stimp, since by 1840 he seems to have been beyond his prime and working primarily in Connecticut. However, Betts and Langdon, who seem to have worked later than Stimp, using many designs copied from earlier artists, are very strong candidates for the stencil work in the Little house.

It is very possible that this house originally contained more stenciled rooms. Perhaps studying more samples of this artist's work would provide a more definite attribution.

One panel of original work in the hallway has been preserved. The rest, after being carefully photographed and traced, was painted over and restenciled.

View of stenciling in a parlor of Little house. Original is to the right and re-created to the left. *Courtesy Warren Little House, circa 1825.*

I.63. Elixius Wooden house, 1832

Hudson, Ohio

Artist: Possibly Moses Eaton, Jr., 1835

IT IS QUITE POSSIBLE that the stenciling found in the unpretentious Wooden house on Hudson's Main Street was created by the country's foremost stencil artist, Moses Eaton, Jr. (see page 54). Discovered in the early 1970s under wallpaper in two areas, a parlor and stairhall (with only the designs from the parlor recorded in photos and tracings), all recorded designs from the Wooden house seem to match those in the aforementioned Eaton paint box in the collections of the Society for the Preservation of New England Antiquities. Plus most have already been seen in this book in two examples from Maine: the Thompson house of West Kennebunk (I.25) and the Perley house of Gray (I.24). The colorations used in this Hudson house, however, are the green/brown/orange on a white field as seen in the Thompson house, not the more common red and green on yellow ocher used in the Perley house.

This discovery of possible Eaton work in Ohio is not surprising considering his family's origins in eastern Massachusetts, which seems to be the birthplace for the folk genre of wall stenciling, and considering the fact that Moses, Sr., was a Revolutionary War veteran entitled to a land grant that was transferable to family members.

Four Eaton-type stencil motifs reportedly found in Elixus Wooden house. *Renderings of Eaton motifs by Polly Forcier.*

Moses Jr. probably had family and/or friends in Ohio. In addition it is said that after his father's death in 1833, Moses Jr. set out on an extensive trip to the western frontier. Perhaps Connecticut's Western Reserve was included in this itinerary as a good place to seek stencil commissions as well as visit with old acquaintances.

The house that Eaton seems to have visited was built as a residence and cobbler shop in 1832 on land originally owned by Owen Brown of Connecticut, father of abolitionist John Brown. It changed hands often over the next hundred years until in the 1970s it was severely renovated into a retail shop[8]—a renovation that included the removal of most fireplaces and walls on the first floor. Fortunately one parlor was spared, which is where the stenciling was discovered. This original work was carefully recorded, covered with plain paper, and scheduled to be re-created under the guidance of Cornelia Keegan, a Hudson resident and Historical Society of Early American Decoration charter member and master craftsman. She called this work "the only really old stenciled wall here in Hudson."[9] She went on to say that it was like figures 89 and 90 in the Janet Waring book, both of which Waring attributed to Eaton.

Unfortunately, this important in situ visual evidence of a documented New England stencil artist's visit to Hudson, Ohio, is now hidden under a coat of cream-colored paint!

I.64. Hiram Winchell Tavern, 1834
McConnelsville, Ohio
Artist: Unknown, 1835

A STATELY, FEDERAL-STYLE combination residence and tavern stands on the banks of the Muskingum River just a few miles from McConnelsville, in southeastern Ohio. It was built and named Unity Farm in 1834 by Hiram Winchell, who is said to have migrated to Ohio from Maine. The location he selected, on the main highway from Marietta to Zanesville, was quite propitious for a large, seven-bay public house.

However, the chief distinction of this fine structure is that at least ten rooms were originally stencil-decorated with variations of New England and New York designs and colorations.

Unfortunately, sometime before 1945, all but the walls of one room were covered over with white paint. Fortunately this paint was sheer enough to allow shadows of numerous motifs and layouts of rose or raspberry backgrounds to show through. This great number of seemingly well-designed cut and executed stencils suggests the work of an experienced artist with a portfolio of designs collected from many different sources.

One room still in original condition was pictured in a 1945 issue of *Antiques Magazine*.[10] It seemed in remarkably fine condition, containing many New England–inspired designs executed in red and green on a yellow ocher ground. Some elements resemble the work of Stimp, some that of Eaton, and others suggest those seen in western New York and the Niagara Peninsula. Most likely the Winchell house stenciling is not the work of a New England artist but rather that of a mature artist who originated in New York or Ohio.

The house changed hands in the 1960s and began a period of great neglect. By the early 1990s, when purchased by its present owners, all evidence of the original stencil work had disappeared along with many other architectural elements. In order to save the house, most of the original interior plaster with its stenciling was lost.

A variation of this Eaton design was used in a parlor of Winchell Tavern, according to a 1945 picture in *Antiques Magazine. Unity Farm was completely restored by Mr. and Mrs. James Eppley in 1992.*

I.65. *Eliphalet Ferris house, 1803–13*
Cincinnati, Ohio
Artist: Unknown, circa 1820

ELIPHALET FERRIS (1774–1859), son of a Revolutionary War veteran, at age twenty-five removed from Greenwich, Connecticut, to the Ohio Valley accompanied by his wife and two of his five brothers, Joseph and Andrew. They settled on 480 acres of land, which they purchased for about $1.68 per acre.

The Ferris brothers farmed their land and milled their own grain, and Joseph became one of the area's first distillers. Thus the Ferris settlement became known as "Whiskey Hollow." They transported the product on flatboats down the Little Miami River to the Ohio River and on by way of the Mississippi River to market in New Orleans.

Two Ferris brothers built homes. Joseph's, which was built between 1813 and 1830, is still standing in an area of Cincinnati now known as Fairfax.

Eliphalet first built a one-room structure in 1802 of handmade sun-dried brick, which he enlarged between 1803 and 1813 to the present three-story brick house with interior end chimney.[11]

This National Register house has an interesting history. It was used as a residence until 1923. A year later it

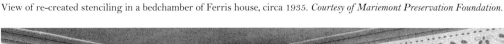

View of re-created stenciling in a bedchamber of Ferris house, circa 1935. *Courtesy of Mariemont Preservation Foundation.*

was purchased by philanthropist Mary Emery as head-quarters for her newly planned community of Mariemont.

During a 1930s restoration, wall stenciling was found under whitewash in the north or back left chamber. It was very indistinct but clear enough to be traced and re-created by Marion Bridgeman, who was paid $396.12 for her artistic services.[12] Some of the motifs such as the twinned vase over the mantel and the swag frieze were very fragmented and therefore difficult to interpret, which could partially account for their very atypical appearance. Most of the motifs are similar to those seen before in this publication, particularly those used by Stimp in Washington, Connecticut. The work below the chair rail was not re-created but was described as "Border of small leaves and dots" as seen in examples I.56 and I.59.

This stencil re-creation was part of a plan to turn the Ferris house into a municipal museum for the new town of Mariemont, a plan that sadly never came to fruition. Instead, for the next fifty years the house was used as office space for various organizations and businesses, including the Educational Services Institute. It was purchased in 1982 by Dr. Ann Grooms, who leased it to that organization, which now occupies the entire building.

After visiting her new acquisition, an appraiser advised Dr. Grooms to raze the Ferris house because "it was not worth saving,"[13] but instead she initiated an extensive renovation project, which included opening up all the fireplaces that had been plastered over and rebuilding an early lean-to on the north side of the house.

Unfortunately, by the 1980s the re-created wall stenciling was under several layers of paint and paper and therefore deemed impossible to retrieve.

This most interesting and important example of early-nineteenth-century Ohio architecture, said to be one of the earliest houses in the area, is now in fine condition, with the possibility that someday, utilizing the ever improving techniques for paint and paper removal, a facsimile of the stenciling commissioned by Eliphalet Ferris in the first quarter of the nineteenth century will once again ornament his bedchamber.

Kentucky and Tennessee

In 1790 Kentucky and Tennessee, which had been previously considered as the hinterlands of Virginia and North Carolina, respectively, were organized as the "Territory South of Ohio" by the federal government. This new territory was settled in a manner very similar to the Ohio Territory by military personnel, an arrangement desired by the government since it ensured protection from Indians, who were still a threat due to the continued agitation by the English well into the 1790s. Kentucky was settled largely by means of Virginian military land warrants, and Tennessee by veterans from North Carolina.

The procedure was haphazard at best. A veteran would obtain an authorization, proceed west, find an empty tract, survey, and record; if no contrary claim appeared in six months, the land was his. This method produced much litigation, which provided members of the western bar such as Andrew Jackson and Henry Clay much business.[14]

Despite the clumsy system, Kentucky gained enough population to become a state in 1792, and Tennessee gained statehood in 1796.

During the American Revolution, thousands of young citizens of France, many of them members of the French aristocracy, fought at the side of American soldiers, engaged in a common cause with the battle-weary Continentals and militiamen. Many of these French troops did chose not to go home, with post-Revolutionary America becoming a haven from revolutionary France.[15] It was natural that they would settle near their American counterparts. Many place names in Kentucky, such as Bourbon County and the early towns of Versailles, Paris, and Frenchburg, would make them feel right at home.

Other French immigrants arrived by way of New Orleans, which previous to 1803 had been in French territory. Many of these new arrivals seemed to be artistically inclined. Included were miniaturist Captain Favre, a defector from the French Army, who painted his self-portrait in 1820 in Frankfort, Kentucky, and Alfred Cohen, a native of southern France, who left numerous samples of his murals in Kentucky, including the walls of at least three fine Federal-style homes in Versailles.

In spite of this influx of French talent, several homes built by American military veterans in the "Territory South of Ohio" have walls decorated with artwork that seems to relate to that found on New England walls. The significance of this recurring phenomenon is unclear. It is most likely pure coincidence and nothing more.

IT WAS OBVIOUS from the onset that fathoming the stenciling found in Colonel James Coleman's impressive Georgian-Federal five-bay home with a facade of Flemish-bond brickwork would be a great challenge. In fact, when Nina Fletcher Little was sent pictures of the stenciling soon after it was discovered in 1987, she responded that she had never seen anything like it before—the author's exact feeling when viewing the same pictures some ten years later.

This National Register house was built by Colonel Coleman on a hundred-acre land grant for three years of service on the Continental line with the Virginia militia. It is located in northeastern Kentucky in the town of Cynthiana, where the Buffalo Trace meets the Licking River, about fifty miles downriver from Cincinnati, Ohio.

The stencil work was discovered in 1987 by the present owners in the back half of a ballroom that spans the entire left side of the second floor. It had been divided into two rooms, with the stenciling in the back section retained and that in the front whitewashed and papered over.

During the restoration process additional stenciling was discovered in the transverse hall (more than ten feet wide) on the second floor, and in the right front bed-

Re-created stenciling in the master bedchamber of Colonel James Coleman house. *Photo by M. S. Rezny Photography, Inc., Lexington, Kentucky.*

Stencil decoration in the second-floor ballroom. *Photo by M. S. Rezny Photography, Inc., Lexington, Kentucky.*

View of the stenciled second-floor stair hall. *Photo by M. S. Rezny Photography, Inc., Lexington, Kentucky.*

chamber. Traces of distemper paint, the same as that used for the upstairs stenciling, according to paint expert Mathew Mosca, were found in the left front parlor. This discovery of stencil paint in a first-floor room supports the theory that the first-floor stair hall as well as the right parlor were also stenciled originally, although all traces of paint seem to be missing.

The attic revealed additional information. Samples of all the colors used to stencil the walls were found, plus samples of designs not seen in surviving rooms can be seen—another indication of more rooms of stenciling originally. Inside an attic closet three initials were found playfully painted in mirror fashion—difficult to transcribe due more to the fact that the lower parts of some of the letters are illegible because of missing plaster. They seem to read BRP, but the middle initial could just as well be another B. However, they are painted freehand in large clumsy lettering, quite out of character for a stencil artisan who displayed great attention to detail when decorating at least four rooms of this house.

Restoration artist Chris Lemmon of Cincinnati, Ohio, meticulously restored the original work in the back half of the ballroom and re-created that in the front section, the second-floor hall, and the master bedchamber. Since

there was not enough evidence of the stencil designs in the parlor, a Rufus Porter–type panoramic mural using pigments found on the parlor wall was executed by Lemmon in that space.

Finally we turn our attention to who might have created this beautifully preserved stencil work. There were, by the late eighteenth century, two popular travel routes to gain access to northeastern Kentucky. From the southern states settlers followed the Shenandoah Valley Trail through Virginia, crossed through the Cumberland Gap, and proceeded up Daniel Boone's Wilderness Trail into Kentucky. Settlers from New England, New York, or Pennsylvania would procede inland through New York and Pennsylvania to Wheeling, West Virginia, which was just south of Pittsburgh. From this area they could travel to the frontier either by way of the Ohio River or overland by Zane's Trace, both of which came quite close to Cynthiana. The first route is the one probably taken by Colonel Coleman, but the second is most likely the one of choice for the stencil artist, who seems to have been influenced by New York–style stenciling. In fact, perhaps he stopped at a Cohocton, New York, tavern along the way, where he found stencil designs that appealed to his artistic taste.

I.67. General James McConnell house, 1820
Versailles, Kentucky
Artist: Alfred Cohen, circa 1830

A KENTUCKY MURAL exemplifies the use of the stencil by artists decorating walls with hand-painted murals depicting scenes of American rural life. It is located in the parlor of the James McConnell house, built in 1820 in Versailles, Kentucky, a settlement of many French immigrants on land that most likely had been a military grant.

The work is attributed to Alfred Cohen, a native of Bordeaux, France, who probably migrated to central Kentucky in the mid-1820s with his two brothers, John and Henry.[16] The parlor decoration includes murals in green, yellow, and blue, with touches of red above the dado, a stenciled red-fringed drapery swag at the cornice area, and a dado enriched with faux marbleized panels.

Two other examples of Cohen's work can be seen in houses located in Woodford County, both within a few miles of Versailles: Pleasant Lawn, built in 1829 by Daniel Williams, and Air Mount, built before 1813. The purely American primitive style of Cohen's work and his choice of motifs and pigment colors strongly resemble the work of the well-known muralist, educator, and scientist Rufus

View of mural and stenciled swag frieze in McConnell house parlor. *Photo by the late Clay Lancaster, special collections, University of Kentucky Libraries.*

Advertisement from 1822 Providence, Rhode Island, newspaper. *Courtesy The Rhode Island Historical Society.*

Landscape Scenery Painting.
RUFUS PORTER

IS desirous that every person in town should be informed, speedily as possible, that he has taken a residence for a *very* few days at Wesson's Coffee-House, and offers to paint walls of rooms, in elegant *full colors*, Landscape Scenery, at prices less than the ordinary expence of papering. Those gentlemen who are desirous of spending the gloomy winter months amidst pleasant groves and verdant fields, are respectfully invited to apply as above, where a specimen of the work may be seen, and where he will also paint "correct likenesses, in full colors, for two dollars." Nov. 20

Porter, who decorated walls in New England during the period from 1822 to 1845 (see page 55).

Porter painted panoramic backgrounds of rolling hills, lakes, islands, and trees freehand, but he carried with him a large collection of stock stencils of small houses, animals, boats, and people, to be placed on the prepainted background in mix-and-match fashion. He also sometimes used a stenciled border to ornament the ceiling or baseboard areas.

Since Porter was an educator and publisher as well as an artist, he published in 1823 a book, *Select Collection of Valuable and Curious Arts*, which included a section on "Landscape Painting on Walls of Homes." In the 1840s, when he was editor of *Scientific American*, he republished serially the original instruction for wall murals in an enlarged, more detailed form. This publication included the following advice: "The painting of houses, arbors, villages, etc., is greatly facilitated by means of stencils." He then went on to explain exactly how to cut the various stencil overlays to produce a house image.

Clay Lancaster, author of the 1991 *Antebellum Architecture of Kentucky*, in a 1948 magazine article describes the small elements in the McConnell mural as "cut-out silhouettes which would be changed from time to time."[17] This seems to be a precise description of the Porter method of applying stenciled units to a freehand-painted panorama.

Other similarities between the work of Cohen and Porter can be found in their choice of objects for the murals. For example, twin palm trees with evergreens in the distance appear in the overmantel decoration by Cohen in the parlor at Pleasant Lawn. This horticulturally improbable combination has been attributed to Cohen's nostalgia for the south of France. (Eaton also painted palm trees side by side with pine trees. His inspiration was said to be his fond memories of a sea voyage to Hawaii that he took as a young man.) Windmill-type structures can be seen in the work of both primitive artisans, as well as steamboats. Porter's was unnamed, but Cohen dubbed his the *Henry Clay*.

To fill the awkward diagonal wall space in a stairway, both men used a similar artistic device that involved painting an elongated, diagonal tree stretching from the first step almost to the landing. Lancaster noted this shared trick in the aforementioned magazine article.[18]

But, of course, the most obvious similarity is seen in the use of small houses and boats that are very much alike in style, execution, and coloration.

The final paragraph of Porter's directions for mural painting states: "We have seen an artist in this branch paint the entire walls of a parlor, with all the several distances, and a variety of fancy scenery, palaces, villages, mills, vessels, etc. and a beautiful set of shade trees on the foreground, and finish the same complete in less than five hours. And as we have before remarked, if there were a competent supply of artists who could accommodate the pubic with this kind of painting, it would nearly supersede the use of paper hangings."

It appears that just such a "competent artist," by the name of Alfred Cohen, left samples of his craft on the walls of at least three houses in Versailles, Kentucky.

❧

I.68. Deserted house, before 1840

Minerva, Kentucky

Artist: Unknown, before 1840

ANOTHER EXAMPLE OF New England's considerable influence on frontier stenciling can be seen in these remarkable pictures taken in the early 1990s of an anonymous house in eastern Kentucky. They depict two rooms of stencil work that displays motifs strikingly similar to Eaton-type work, but with equally striking atypical elements.

The first room, in traditional green, red, and yellow on a gray ground, uses four motifs; a diamond-and-petal vertical border, a pineapple, an asymmetrical willow tree, and a large carnation spray, all of which seem to be based on Eaton designs seen in numerous Maine homes (such as I.24 and I.25).

Panel of stenciling from a front parlor of an abandoned farmhouse that once stood in Minerva, Kentucky. *Photo by John A. Diehl.*

Stenciled panel from front hall of Minerva house. *Photo by John A. Diehl.*

All of these motifs show the work of a hand probably other than Moses Eaton, Jr., especially the pineapple, whose basic design is almost exactly like its inspiration as far as can be ascertained by eye but now is seen in more naturalistic yellow, with its green leaves reinvented and with green accents on its yellow triangular sections. The author would very much like to trace this pineapple for comparison with that in the Eaton paint box in the Society for the Preservation of New England Antiquities collection in Boston.

The second room—in green, yellow, and a now gray-blue that probably was a primary blue when newly painted—has mostly new designs, with the frieze of particular interest, being very atypical of stenciling seen in New England or New York. In green and yellow it features a small three-inch bird surrounded by tree foliage, framed and very much dwarfed by a six-and-a-half-inch diagonally positioned conch shell. Since conch shells are not often found naturally in the Kentucky frontier, this larger-than-life shell must be a nod to the coastal origins of the artist and/or the great majority of the area's earliest settlers. The vertical border of leaves and oval sunburst is a new design, as is the filler motif of four leaves with large blue circular center. The blue "snow flake" with its yellow center is the only familiar motif.

The location of Minerva[19] is probably significant, since it is just ten miles northwest of Maysville, Kentucky, which lies at the end of the famous Zane's Trace and is on the west bank of the Ohio River, the favored water route for those en route to new lives in the southern or northern frontier.

The exact location and present condition[20] of this structure and its intriguing stenciling is unknown but worrisome, since it was reportedly in extremely delicate condition and apparently abandoned in 1991.

More of this allusive artist's work will be seen as we proceed south into middle Tennessee.

I.69. General James Winchester house, 1795–1803

Gallatin, Tennessee

Artist: Unknown, circa 1830

THE ELEGANT, CUT STONE, Georgian-style house of General James Winchester, described as a Maryland manor house transplanted to the Tennessee frontier, was in sharp contrast to its neighboring log cabin–style dwellings. In 1800, when a stunned French naturalist named F. A. Michaux first spotted the general's house, he described it as "very elegant for the country!"[21]

James Winchester (1752–1826), its builder, was born in Carroll County, Maryland, where his father, William, had built the first and finest house in that area, which he described as his plantation house.[22] Like his son's house in Tennessee, it was considered very refined for the northern Maryland wilderness.

Brigadier General Winchester was a distinguished veteran of the Revolution who served continuously from his enlistment in 1776 to England's surrender at Yorktown in 1781. He moved to middle Tennessee in 1787 and settled on a large tract on the Cumberland River near Bledsoe Creek, where he became an Indian fighter, community leader, confidant and neighbor of Andrew Jackson, planter, and merchant. He started his fine house, which he called Cragfont due to its commanding position on a high rocky hill, in 1795 and imported artisans from Baltimore to complete its interior by 1803.

In 1802 the aforementioned Frenchman, Michaux, commented on the fine interior finishes of Cragfont, prob-

Exterior view of General Winchester house. *Courtesy Historic Cragfont, Inc.*

Restenciled panel from Cragfont's best parlor. *Courtesy Historic Cragfont, Inc.*

ably a reference to the very superior quality of the interior carpentry work by Frank Wetherred,[23] a carpenter known to have created much of Cragfont's woodwork. This reference to finishes could also pertain to the painted graining on the parlor fire surround, the front stairway, and on the paneled dados in numerous second-floor rooms. However, it seems more likely that the Michaux reference was to the woodwork and not the paint treatment, which most likely was applied at a slightly later time either by a Baltimore painter or by one of the many German and Scotch settlers who were swarming into Tennessee by 1800.

Also decorating the best parlor is, strangely, Eaton-like wall stenciling, quite unexpected and a bit startling in this fine Georgian frontier house! The author's initial viewing produced a flood of unanswerable questions. First and foremost was, Is this one of Junior's stops on his alleged trip west? and Did Moses Sr. know James Winchester from his Revolutionary War service? The second query seems doubtful, since Moses Eaton's service was entirely in the North while Winchester served in the mid-Atlantic and southern colonies.

The first query, however, cannot be dismissed that easily. Tracings made by the author in 1997 of three Winchester motifs—the "diamond and petal" vertical, the "sliced egg" border, and a "snowflake" filler—match Eaton designs perfectly. Also the layout and spacing are typical Eaton.

However, some of the motifs are completely new to the author, and others are slightly different from the Eaton version. Perhaps some of the differences occurred during the first re-creation of 1960. Often when original designs are very fragmented, unintentional misinterpretations occur. The best example of this variation is the "three carnation spray" filler, which now seems to have a fourth blossom growing out of what is traditionally the stem of the spray. This design was used by many New England artists including Eaton, sometimes without flowers, but when red carnations were applied only three were used.

The biggest difference, however, is the "shell and bird" frieze, which is new and somewhat out of character for Eaton. Moses Jr. was quite capable of using new designs, as witnessed in some of his attributed work in Maine (I.24). But this frieze is quite atypical of his previous work. Also this frieze has been found with the "sliced egg" border in other area houses as a borders-only layout without the Eaton-like vertical and fillers.

Most of the designs used are among the earliest used by Moses Sr. starting early in the nineteenth century, which continued to be used by Junior up to the 1840s.

Fancifully grained fireplace surround in same front parlor. *Courtesy Historic Cragfont, Inc.*

Thus they could have been traced from eastern New England walls any time during that forty-year period by any number of artists. The emphasis is on *traced*, since these designs are too similar to be memory copies of the originals. However, the author has a sense that this stenciling, which family history attributes to "an itinerant artist who spent some months at Cragfont and did stenciling as a gift,"[24] was executed around 1830–35, after the general's death in 1826. This mystery stenciling appears never to have been covered with paint or paper and was highly regarded by the Winchester family, who resided at Cragfont until after the Civil War.

During the Civil War, in August 1862, General John Hunt Morgan, renowned southern guerrilla leader, was entertained by the Winchester family in the stenciled parlor on the occasion of his chasing Yankee troops from the surrounding fields. Soon after, the Yankee chaplain and officers of Wolford's Regiment took complete and "entire possession" of the same parlor on an overnight visit, causing much "restrained indignation" to the general's young grandson George Washington Winchester.[25] The house and stenciling apparently survived the war unscathed, probably due to respect for the general and his family on the part of both sides of the Civil War.

The family reluctantly left for Memphis soon after the close of the war, leaving their beloved home, Cragfont, to change hands numerous times. A sales brochure of 1890 clearly shows the grained mantel flanked by stenciling still in fairly good condition.

Over the years, the grandeur of Cragfont continued in decline, until in 1956 the Sumner County Association for the Preservation of Tennessee Antiquities undertook to purchase and restore the Winchester homestead. Part of the restoration included the 1960s re-creation of the stenciling and graining on the parlor mantel and front stairway, leaving the graining on second-floor dadoes in original condition.

The house is now a beautifully restored museum house, furnished with an ever increasing number of original Winchester pieces, such as the Hepplewhite sideboard, which was purchased by the association at auction in New York City in October 2000.

Cragfont, with its mysterious bit of old New England, is now an important material-history museum demonstrating the development of the American frontier, an appropriate tribute to General Winchester, veteran of the Revolution and the War of 1812, frontiersman, and civic leader.

I.70. Hawthorne Hill, circa 1800
Castalian Springs, Tennessee
Artist: Unknown, circa 1830

KNOWN AS HAWTHORNE HILL, this house was probably built by North Carolina native John Bearden around the turn of the nineteenth century. He in turn sold this three-bay Flemish-bond brick house to Colonel Humphrey Bate in 1817. Bate, a carpenter, surveyor, and farmer, probably commissioned the stencil artist to ornament at least the best parlor of his home. The house remained in the Bate family until the 1930s.

The stenciled parlor at Hawthorne Hill was found under a layer of wallpaper in 1992 by new owners. The frieze design and narrow border are identical to that in Cragfont with the exception that the Hawthorne Hill version is in blue and green rather than yellow and green, making it identical in both design and coloration to the frieze in the Minerva, Kentucky, house; therefore all three can be safely attributed to the same hand.

In Hawthorne Hill the stenciling was executed on a background of blue sponge work that covers the entire wall surface, introducing us to another decorative treatment utilized by this artist. When paint restoration is ini-

Detail of "bird and shell" frieze in Hawthorne Hill front parlor, a frieze identical to that in Cragfont (I.69) and the deserted house (I.68).

Close-up of the "sliced egg" border also in Hawthorne Hill.

tiated on the interior of Hawthorne Hill, the discovery of more stenciling and graining on the wooden interior elements would not be surprising!

By combining the information from these three southern frontier homes, we are presented with a larger picture of the decoration skills of this artist (or perhaps this pair of artists), which include not only stenciling but many types of wood graining and sponging, all of which were well known to Moses Eaton and numerous other New England artists such as Rufus Porter, who hailed from the same New England area as Eaton and reportedly worked with Moses Jr. in the 1820s. The homes they decorated together had stenciling, murals, wood graining, and sponging.

Porter had many helpers and apprentices who are said to have been proficient in many decorative painting techniques. Jean Lipman, author of *Rufus Porter Rediscovered*, said, "in a large proportion of the frescoed houses in which Porter assistants or pupils worked, marbleized or grained woodwork and stenciled wall decorations are also found." Sponging used by the Porter School can be seen in figure 63 on page 116 of the Lipman book. It is in the Bidwell Tavern of Langdon, New Hampshire, and dates to 1824. It is also of note that most of the tree foliage in murals by Porter and his students is created by a deft use of sponge work.

It appears quite possible that the work in Minerva, Kentucky, and Gallatin, Tennessee, is by an artist from the New England area with access to Eaton stencil designs and a firsthand knowledge of Porter/Eaton-style faux finishes, possibly an apprentice and/or relative of Moses Eaton or his associate, Rufus Porter.

THE DOGTROT HOUSE is a superb example of the very democratic nature of American Federal-period wall stenciling, unrestricted by geographic location, ethnicity, or socioeconomic status.

Quite by chance, three rooms of decorative painting in good, original condition were found during the 1970s Historic American Buildings Survey of Tennessee in a simple log house in southern middle Tennessee, very close to the border with Alabama. Thought to be built around 1830 by a settler of Scottish origins from New Jersey, this stenciled house is a type of log house called a dogtrot, which originated during the colonial period along the Atlantic seaboard of the middle colonies,[26] mostly among German emigrants. It was later adopted by other settlers, including many Scots, as they moved to the frontier areas.

Dogtrot house. *Courtesy Library of Congress.*

View of hallway of "Dogtrot house" showing pine sheathing ornamented with stenciling on sponge work, like that in Hawthorne Hill. *Courtesy Tennessee Historical Commission.*

Stenciling on sponge work from the left parlor of Dogtrot house. *Courtesy Library of Congress.*

A dogtrot features two rooms of similar size, called pens, with an open passage between, which was commonly enclosed as a center hall. This Tennessee example is one and a half stories with chimneys at either end and an enclosed trot. The exterior is covered with later rough-sawn siding.

All three first-floor room interiors, completely fashioned of wood, are covered with painted decoration. Two have stenciling, sponging, and graining on walls, ceilings, doors, and stairway. The third is completely covered with sponging and graining. Reportedly one of the outbuildings, a smokehouse, said to date to the building of the main house, contains a sampler of the many designs used in the main house. Unfortunately no pictures of this work are available.

The stencil designs include those seen in the General Winchester house of Gallatin, which is often called the "finest house in Tennessee." These designs incorporate

the same idiosyncrasies seen in Cragfont. Also, the sponging and colorations seen in Hawthorne Hill, also of Gallatin, can be seen in the Dogtrot house, thus linking these three houses artistically.

Also seen are additional Eaton-type designs, some of which seemingly are traced from originals whereas others seem to be variations, such as the four-blossom "carnation spray" and a leaf frieze seen upside down. Some of the designs are in the Eaton paint box at the Society for the Preservation of New England Antiquities and others we have seen on Maine walls attributed to Eaton (I.24 and I.25).

The artisan responsible for this three-house grouping in Tennessee could have gathered these designs in a number of different ways: first, they could have been traced directly from Eaton work in New England or possibly Ohio; second, the artist could have apprenticed with Eaton during the tour he supposedly took of the frontier;

third, the tracings of the designs could have been mailed from New England to Tennessee, or the designs were somehow published and sold to aspiring stencil artists. Although the last suggestion is by far the least plausible, anything is possible.

It is interesting to note that a man by the name of Levi Eaton resided in Wayne County, close to the Dogtrot house.[27] Also, there are Eatons in neighboring Rardin County as well as in Sumner County, where Cragfont is located. The Eaton family was very early and large, with members spread throughout the country. Perhaps this Tennessee work is that of a distant relative of Moses Eaton who was carrying on the family's wall-stenciling tradition.

Unfortunately, the house containing this intriguing stenciling is abandoned and will soon be extinct. The one saving grace for the decorative painting is the fact that it is executed on wooden paneling, which is much easier to remove than work that has been done on plaster. Hopefully a preservation group will manage to remove these rooms, which are replete with decoration, before nature consumes a valuable example of southern Tennessee wall stenciling of a type more endemic to Maine than Tennessee!

Indiana

Indiana, the final state to be examined in this section, became a part of the United States with the signing of the 1783 treaty with France.

Not until the end of the War of 1812, however, did the territory west of the Appalachian Mountains, which includes Indiana, become safe enough to attract a steady flow of legal settlers. Indiana finally gained sufficient population for statehood in 1816.

Although one stenciled structure in Indiana is included in this study, the author has heard references to several others. This lone example is located in the southwestern corner of Indiana, not far from the Ohio River, which forms the state's southern boundary with Kentucky.

I.72. Jonathan Jaquess house, 1825
Poseyville, Indiana
Artist: Possibly Moses Eaton, Jr.,
before circa 1841

Portrait of Rebeckah Jaquess seated in the best parlor of her home in front of recently stenciled walls. *Courtesy Abby Aldrich Rockefeller Folk Art Museum, Williamsburg, Virginia.*

THREE REMARKABLE MEN, all born more than two hundred years ago, are responsible for the creation and survival of a unique example of late Federal-period frontier wall stenciling still extant in Indiana. Additional credit is due scores of dedicated late-twentieth-century material-history preservationists.

Of primary importance, of course, is the house's builder and the commissioner of its stenciling: Jonathan Jaquess (1753–1843), a man of the sea, Revolutionary soldier, and pioneer.[28] Born in Woodridge, New Jersey, before the Revolution, he was master of a sloop in the West India trade and a privateer. During the war he was a minuteman,[29] and he was with General Washington when Cornwallis surrendered in Yorktown, Virginia, in 1781. After the war he returned to New Jersey to farm and engage in coastal trading. In 1789, at the age of thirty, he abandoned the sea to migrate into Kentucky, settling in the Cynthiana area, where he spent about twenty-five prosperous years.

In 1811, at age sixty-one, Jaquess and his two brothers-in-law purchased two hundred acres of wilderness in the Indiana Territory, which had been carved out of the Old Northwest Territory in 1800. The move was inspired by a Pentecostal experience Jaquess and his large extended family had had several years earlier.[30] Their new utopia was located in what is now known as Posey County, and it was there that Jaquess and his family would spend the rest of their lives.

During the next four years, Jaquess and the other men in his party worked on their Indiana property: surveying, dividing, building cabins, planting orchards. Finally, in 1815, the tract was ready to receive forty-four settlers, all linked by kinship and marriage—the largest group to migrate to southwestern Indiana from Kentucky. Some men with the wagons and animals traveled by land, following the Red Banks Trail from near Cynthiana. The rest floated down the Ohio River on three flatboats loaded with belongings. From Henderson they followed an old buffalo trail to their new homes. The trip required more than three weeks.

Soon the original Jaquess cabin evolved into a larger, more proper house. Sometime before 1840, an itinerant wall stenciler—second of the three remarkable men—visited the home of Jonathan and Rebeckah. This artist applied familiar designs to at least the best parlor and stair hall, using layouts and colorations previously used in eastern New England by none other than Moses Eaton, Jr. (1796–1886), a sixth-generation American,

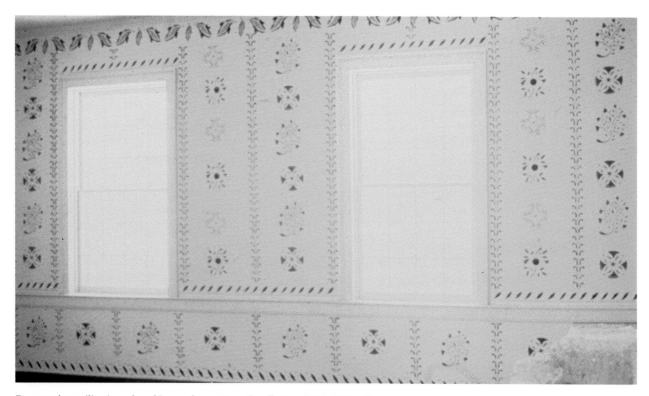

Re-created stenciling in parlor of Jaquess house. *From the collection of Historic New Harmony.*

New Hampshire farmer, and multitalented folk artist. Moses Jr. had learned his craft at an early age from his equally talented father, Moses Sr. (see page 54). Every stencil design in this parlor has proved to be a near match either to stencils in the famous Eaton paint box at the Society for the Preservation of New England Antiquities or to those used on other Eaton-attributed walls in New England. In addition, several have been noted in other frontier homes. The snowflake and small carnation without buds were used in the General Winchester house (I.69), and the leaf frieze appeared in an 1832 house (I.63) in Hudson, Ohio.[31]

It is impossible to make a definite attribution for these frontier stencil examples of what was probably Eaton work. Most, if not all of them, have been re-created or lost, with very few pictures of the originals still in existence, and no signatures have come to the fore. However, a large and persuasive body of evidence supports the Eaton family's contention that Moses Jr. toured the western frontier in his thirties. In addition, a Stephen Eaton, son-in-law of Rebeckah's sister, was listed among the forty-four Kentucky migrants with the Jaquess party. Either Moses Eaton, Jr., was responsible for the trail of

his designs along routes leading westward, or a very clever copyist was on the same trail.

The third member of this unique trio of renaissance men was a folk artist, Jacob Maentel (1778–?).[32] Born in Kassel, Germany, he served as secretary to General Napoleon for seven years and trained as a physician as well as an artist. Tired of the turmoil in Europe, Maentel fled to the New World, arriving at the port of Baltimore, Maryland, just in time to serve in the War of 1812. He lived and worked in Maryland and Pennsylvania until 1838, when, at age sixty, he followed the western migration to Texas. Due to an illness, however, Maentel and his family stopped in Posey County, Indiana, seeking assistance from an old friend from Pennsylvania, the Reverend Schnee. Maentel was destined to spend the rest of his life in Indiana.

Maentel painted portraits of his neighbors, Jonathan Jaquess and his wife, Rebeckah, in 1844. Jonathan was pictured in a nautical setting representing his early life and career. Rebeckah was painted seated proudly in her beautifully decorated best parlor, with a Bible prominently positioned on the chair arm. The stenciling in the background clearly showed Eaton-type motifs on a bright blue background. Since the stenciling was later covered with wallpaper for so long that it was eventually forgotten, this Maentel painting was the only obvious evidence of its existence to survive into the twentieth century.

The paintings and their creator caught the interest of folk-art historians such as Mary Black and Nina Fletcher Little in the 1960s, when they were sold by the Jaquess family to the Abbey Aldrich Rockefeller Folk Art Center in Williamsburg, Virginia. Since then, numerous portraits by Jacob Maentel have come to light in Maryland, Pennsylvania, Indiana, and Illinois. He is now considered one of America's foremost nineteenth-century folk painters.

In 1975, when the Jaquess farmhouse was in imminent danger of being demolished, a family descendant contacted Mary Lou Fleming, a local art historian. Fleming in turn alerted Ralph Schwarz, president of the Historic New Harmony Site, and Charles Hirsch, an Indiana artist and historian, who suggested that the stenciling depicted by Maentel might still be intact under the wallpaper. The owners agreed to give the old farmhouse to Historic New Harmony in exchange for moving the building. Soon the Jaquess homestead began is short journey to a field outside the town of New Harmony, where preservation architect Rose A. Broz began the tedious work of wallpaper removal. Under seventeen layers of paper, she discovered the stenciling still in relatively good condition. Further investigation revealed similar, but somehow different, work in the stair hall. After Broz traced, measured, and analyzed the painted decoration, preservationists chose the best-preserved panels, carefully cut them from the surrounding wall, and crated and safely stored them.

After the decision was made to save only the parlor, hall, and porch, they were dismantled and stored until they could be incorporated into New Harmony's decorative arts series[33] as the 1840s unit. Its installation into a connecting corridor between two in-place buildings was completed in 1980, at which time the Jaquess Parlor Museum opened to the public. Thus, a most important example of frontier American wall stenciling attributed to the country's preeminent stencil artist was preserved for the public's edification and delight.

PART II

The Classical Group of American Wall Stenciling

A second and equally important (though less well known and widespread) style of stenciling developed during the Federal period. It seems to be slightly earlier than the Folk Group, commencing perhaps as early as 1780.

The Classical Group seems to have originated in urban seaport cities both north and south in the latter part of the eighteenth century. Traveling from port to port and along navigable rivers, it seldom strayed farther west in New England than the Connecticut River Valley. Its practitioners then moved inland seeking commissions in the pockets of urban commerce and culture that sprang up sporadically along the early road systems.

The Classical Group is feminine and attenuated and more diminutive in proportion than the Folk Group. The Classical Revival, the rage of Europe since the mid–eighteenth century, influenced not only American stenciling but also its architecture, poetry, music, and dress.[1] The Age of Classicisms can be divided into three periods: The first, from 1750 to 1775, is identified with Georgian architecture and Chippendale furniture; the second, from 1765 to 1830, had the most influence on America's Federal period, producing Federal-style architecture, Hepplewhite and Sheraton furniture, and Adamesque painted decoration. The last period, from 1810 to 1850, produced America's Greek Revival architecture and Empire furniture.

Rooms decorated with solid-colored wallpapers, called "plain papers," and embellished only with borders, were very fashionable beginning around 1780.[2] These plain papers and borders were at first imported and later manufactured in the United States. Many were in the classical style, with the favorite "plain" colors being pink, Pompeiian red, soft yellow, and empire blue.[3] Patterns were often printed in water-based paint using stenciled and freehand painting first, and later wooden blocks.

Commonly, a combination of all three techniques was used.

Stencil artists borrowed directly from such wallpaper designs. More often than not, classical stencil decoration appears only on the border areas of the wall panels (thus this style is sometimes referred to as the "Border Group," but since this is also the name given to a type of freehand wall decoration, "Classical Group" is a less confusing title). Occasionally the best or most ostentatious rooms received decoration covering the entire wall space, executed in three or more colors. Overmantels were frequently adorned with classical flower-filled urns. Swags, festoons, urns, bellflowers, and quarter fans were favorite motifs of artists working in this style.

The practitioners of this style were generally anonymous; no signed walls have been discovered, or notations in family journals pertaining to the decoration of the family parlor. Only a few early newspaper ads give us clues as to the identity of some of these artisans. William Priest advertised in a Baltimore paper in 1795 that he did "painting in imitation of paperhangings by a mechanical process" and "laying plain grounds in distemper with plain or festoon borders"[4]—an apparent description of classical-style stenciling.

A thorough study of all the known classical stenciling suggests the existence of numerous and diverse stencil artists influenced by the classical craze. Among this great variety, two distinct bodies of work have emerged, each the work of a prolific, widely traveled, but stylistically identifiable artist or artists.

The first group of all decoration by the same hand has been dubbed "Classical I." Its identifying characteristics include straightforward, conservative, well-executed classical motifs, applied only to the border areas of the room. It has been found on walls of buildings along the New England coastline from Kennebunk, Maine, to Guilford,

(Facing page) General Schumacker's Daughter, painted circa 1812 by Jacob Maentel in York, Pennsylvania, or Baltimore, Maryland. The decoration on the wall behind is either classical-style wall stenciling or the wallpaper border that inspired that type of stenciled decoration. Notice the faux pecky bois painted decoration on the dado and the classical style of dress and hair. *Courtesy National Gallery, Washington, D.C. Gift of Edgar Williams and Bernice Chrysler Garbisch. Photograph © 2001 Board of Trustees, National Gallery of Art, Washington, D.C.*

Federal-style lowboy, circa 1810, with classical inlaid motifs, such as swags, fans, and bellflowers, motifs often utilized by stencil artists working in the classical genre.

Connecticut, on the eastern shore of Narragansett Bay in Rhode Island, and inland well east of the Connecticut River.

The second group is called, predictably, "Classical II." The work of this artist or pair of artists is much more freely and imaginatively executed, and often covers the entire wall surface with exuberant vertical borders. Examples of this body of work have been found in southeastern New Hampshire, eastern Massachusetts, the west side of Narragansett Bay, along the Connecticut River, and on the south fork of Long Island, New York.

The clients of these painters were mostly well-heeled, upwardly mobile middle-class merchants, craftsmen, and tavern owners in seaport cities. Although only 5 percent of the country's population in 1790 resided in these areas, they were of vital importance to the other 95 percent living in rural areas because their control of the maritime trades provided the means for disseminating the produce and wares of inland farmers and craftsmen to national and international markets.[5] The end of the Revolution saw a great depression in most of America's seaports, but by 1790 the maritime industry had recovered and was flourishing. This return to prosperity up and down the East Coast created a building boom, with many homes being built and decorated in the newest styles to arrive from England and the Continent, often copied directly from the numerous pattern books inspired by the Classical Revival.

Chapter 9

The Southern New England States of Rhode Island, Massachusetts, and Connecticut

The small state of Rhode Island has two major port cities, Providence and Newport, and numerous smaller seaport towns on the east and west sides of Narragansett Bay. Nineteen of Rhode Island's thirty-nine cities and towns are located on navigable water,[1] which makes it an appropriate starting place to illustrate a type of wall stenciling that seems to have proliferated by water travel.

As early as 1763, packet ships ran twice a week between Providence and Newport. Soon there were vessels connecting other Rhode Island seaports, which made regular runs to leading ports along the coast, including New York, Philadelphia, Baltimore, Savannah, and Charleston.[2] After the war, increased trade among coastal towns reflected the emergence of manufacturing. Sloops of seventy-five to one hundred tons burden, built for speed, were fitted to carry passengers as well as freight.

Smaller ports that prospered during the postwar boom included Warren and Bristol on the east side of Narragansett Bay and Pawtuxet, Apponaug, East Greenwich, and Wickford on the west side. The author has discovered classical wall stenciling in four of these: Apponaug, Wickford, Bristol, and Warren, as well as Federal-period floor stenciling in Pawtuxet, Providence, and Warren. Classical wall stenciling has yet to be found in either Providence or Newport. The lack of wall stenciling in the former may be due to the fact that many middle-class neighborhoods were torn down in the later eighteenth and early nineteenth centuries to make way for the robust growth of industry. (As Janet Waring wrote, "Urban development with its rapid growth does not preserve for us the handiwork of the past.")[3] Newport, on the other hand, suffered a long and difficult British occupation during the Revolution and a deep recession during the postwar period. George Channing wrote in his book, *Early Recollections of Newport, Rhode Island,* covering the years 1793–1811, "Carpenters there were but few of these. It was only at long intervals that new houses were built, and generally of very small dimension."[4]

Wallpaper was readily available in Rhode Island after the war. In 1784 the East Greenwich firm of Casey, Son and Greene was importing wallpaper borders from an

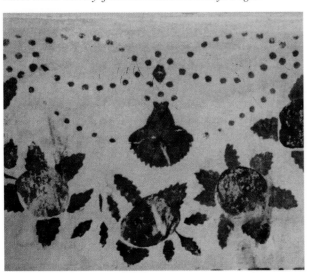

Detail of an 8-inch-deep frieze from Peck house (II.10) of Wickford, Rhode Island. *Courtesy of Martha Grossell and Marilyn Weigner.*

PAPER-HANGINGS.

THOMAS S. WEBB has for Sale, at his Paper-Hanging Manufactory, in Westminster-Street,

A VERY large Assortment of PAPER-HANGINGS, suitable for Parlours, Keeping Rooms, Entries, Halls, &c. with Festoon, Patch, Lace and Fruit Borders, of various Widths, at Wholesale or Retail.— Also, a large Assortment of COMPOSITION ORNAMENTS, for Chimney Pieces, Bed and Window Cornices, &c. &c.
Providence, August 4, 1804.   tbc.

Early wallpaper ad that appeared in a Providence, Rhode Island, newspaper on May 14, 1803, depicting a very classical swag-and-tassel border utilized by numerous stencil artists. *Courtesy The Rhode Island Historical Society.*

English supplier.[5] By 1799 wallpaper was being manufactured in Providence by Thomas S. Webb,[6] who had previously made paperhangings in Hartford and Albany. In 1799, Webb announced in the *Providence Gazette* that he had for sale "a large assortment of paper, suitable for parlours, chambers and halls, with festoons and other borders, from one to ten inches in breadth." In 1803, Webb's ad was illustrated with a design that resembled a stenciled frieze of the type that was popular with artists of the Classical Group, who were always looking to wallpaper manufacturers to find examples of the latest styles from Europe.

Exterior of John Martin house. *Courtesy Robert and Janice Fancher.*

II.1. John Martin house, 1707
(remodeled circa 1780 and 1800)
Barrington, Rhode Island
Artist: Classical I, early nineteenth century

JOHN MARTIN'S ANCESTORS arrived in America in 1635 and were among the first settlers of Rehoboth, Massachusetts. When he built the first part of his house in Barrington, the land it stood on was in Massachusetts. A long-standing border dispute between eastern Rhode Island and Massachusetts was finally settled in 1744, and four new towns on the east side of Narragansett Bay—Warren, Bristol, Tiverton, and Little Compton—were incorporated into Rhode Island, along with one (Cumberland) in the northeastern corner of the state.[7] Barrington had been independent until this border agreement, when it was consolidated with Warren. In 1770 it became a separate town again, the last to be incorporated in colonial Rhode Island.

The Martin house was expanded to almost twice its original size around 1750, and around the turn of the nineteenth century, it was remodeled in the new Federal style, probably by John's second son, Benjamin (1755–1836), who inherited the house. Part of this renovation was the creation of a wonderful dancing room in a second-floor front room. This has fine carved woodwork, a domed ceiling, and a resilient floor made of crossed pieces of flexible wood (similar to one in the Wayside Inn in Sudbury, Massachusetts).

Most important, it had classical-style stenciled walls, long since painted over but recorded in a black-and-white photograph from the early twentieth century. The colors will probably never be known, but the designs, including the narrow border and classical fans, are clearly the same ones used throughout New England. The frieze design was also recorded by Gina Martin in a house in Preston City, Connecticut.

Early photo of stenciled fireplace wall in second-floor dancing room. *Courtesy of Robert and Janice Fancher.*

II.2. Samuel Martin house, 1750
(remodeled 1797 and 1820)
Warren, Rhode Island
Artist: Classical I, circa 1800

WATER STREET IN WARREN, a prosperous post-Revolutionary maritime community, is the location of our second example of classical wall stenciling on the eastern side of Narragansett Bay. In 1790 the street was lined with shipbuilding establishments, sail makers, coopers, ironmongers, and blacksmith shops. In fact, the earliest part of the Martin house, the back ell dating to 1750, was a cooper's shop owned by the prosperous Maxwell family. Sea captain Samuel Martin (1750–1826), eldest son of John Martin (see previous entry), purchased the property in 1797 and altered the shop to accommodate the addition of his new Federal-style home fronting on Water Street.

Shipwrights were probably employed to construct the new Martin residence, since during the period 1790–1810 Warren was second only to Providence as a shipbuilding center, where skilled wood craftsmen were plentiful.

The stenciling, located in the front hallway and a front parlor, seems to be by the same hand as that in the elder Martin's house in Barrington and the Ballou house in Lincoln, even though the three houses feature different frieze motifs. The frieze design seen in the Warren house was also discovered by the author in a Pomfret, Connecticut, house in November 1997.

This may be the oldest classical stenciling in Rhode Island, since the owners, who are well versed in both history and restoration, believe the stencil work to be the first decoration on plaster in the house, dating to 1795.

Other decorative features include a front parlor ornamented with hand-painted, scenic wallpaper, which has been attributed to the French studios of either Zuber, Papillion, or Reveillon. This room also features beautifully carved woodwork throughout. A handsome portico was added to the front entrance during a later renovation,[8] perhaps by the Driscoll family, well-known Warren sea captains and whalers, who resided in this house from about 1820.

The Lynch family rescued this fine house from demolition in 1981, painstakingly restoring it to its former elegance, and now run it as a fine restaurant with lodging. It is called the Nathaniel Porter Inn after a Revolutionary War–era ancestor of the Lynch family.

Re-created stenciling in second-floor stair hall of Samuel Martin house.

Front door surround of the Wardwell house featuring such typical Federal-style elements as a triangular pediment, fluted columns, and a window over the door in the shape of a half-fan, which is known as a fanlight.

II.3. Samuel Wardwell house, 1808

Bristol, Rhode Island

Artist: Classical I, after 1808

Fragment of stenciled quarter fan found in 1970s under wallpaper in Samuel Wardwell house.

THE PORT OF BRISTOL was somewhat larger and more active than Warren, but because of their close proximity (Bristol is only four miles south of Warren), the two acted as partners rather than rivals. In fact, in 1801 the two seaports became an independent customs district, separate from Newport.[9]

Samuel Wardwell and Shearjachub Bourne, operating as the firm of Bourne and Wardwell,[10] manufactured rum and sent ships to the West Indies and Africa for merchandise and slaves. At one time the firm is said to have owned forty-two vessels. Wardwell built two nearly identical four-bay, center-chimney Federal houses on a Bristol street formerly known as Wardwell Place, as speculation houses to accommodate Bristol's population explosion during the first decade of the nineteenth century, when its census increased by more than half.

One of the Wardwell houses was carefully restored to its original appearance in 1970, aided by a Rhode Island Historical Preservation Commission grant. At that time, traces of classical stenciling original to the early plastered walls were found in a front parlor under multiple wallpaper layers, and the faint remnants were photographed by the owners. Though badly faded and with many elements missing, the stenciling was clearly by the same hand as that in the Ballou house in Lincoln (II.6), the two Martin houses in Barrington and Warren, and the William Taylor house (II.20), built in 1803 in Kennebunk, Maine. This discovery links the stencil artist or artists who traveled through Rhode Island early in the nineteenth century to work found throughout New England.

II.4. Lindsey house, 1803
Bristol, Rhode Island
Artist: Classical I, early nineteenth century

ONE OF ONLY a few double houses built in Bristol, Rhode Island, the Lindsay house was constructed in 1803 by Bristol housewright William Lindsey, probably for his two sons, John and Jonathon.

Stencil fragments were found under wallpaper during a recent restoration by Bristol restoration architect Lombard Pozzi, thus far only in the front stairway and a small second-floor chamber. However, there very likely was more stenciling in this house and in its twin next-door.

The stencil work is by the same hand as that seen in the Wardwell House (II.3), also in Bristol, located just a short way east of this one. This exact frieze was used in the dancing room of the Martin house in Barrington, Rhode Island, and more important, it was used to decorate the present kitchen area of the Governor Benjamin Pierce homestead of Hillsborough, New Hampshire (II.25), thus joining this group of Rhode Island houses with a group of stenciled houses considered the finest examples of this artist's work. It is not clear, however, which group of stenciled houses represents the earlier work of this artist.

Detail of original stenciled frieze found under wallpaper in late 1990s on second floor of Lindsey house.

Once again, serendipity, defined by the *Random House Dictionary* as "an aptitude for making desirable discoveries by accident," has played a role in saving an early-nineteenth-century stenciled structure from oblivion. The fine old Angell Tavern with its long-forgotten stenciled ballroom was scheduled to be razed before the beginning of the new millennium. Fortunately it was purchased in mid-December 1999, on the condition that it be dismantled and moved to a new location.

While surveying his new purchase, the owner, much to his delight, discovered stencil decoration under wallpaper in the second-floor, twin-fireplace ballroom. Fortunately, he was knowledgeable enough to sense the importance of his discovery and quickly called the author. Several serendipitous factors contributed to preserving this stenciling: first and foremost, it was purchased by an individual aware of the artistic and monetary value of early American decorative wall painting; second, a knowledgeable stencil preservationist was readily available to advise on procedures for recording and preserving as much of the original work as possible.

Another very "desirable accident" was caused by a serious leak in the roof over the southeastern corner of the ballroom ceiling. The water damage had caused the many layers of ceiling paint to flake, quite unexpectedly revealing stencil-like markings on the ceiling, including the familiar quarter fan. This water damage also caused a large chunk of ceiling plaster to loosen and fall. Miraculously it survived the fall in one piece, its landing softened by a fluffy pile of pink insulation that had been piled in that corner waiting to be installed by the previous owner. This cushioning saved the plaster from smashing into tiny unrecognizable pieces. In addition, had the insulation and its Sheetrock covering been completely installed, the stenciling certainly would not have been discovered until well into the dismantling process, which unknowingly would have destroyed much of the original stencil work.

Amazingly, when this ceiling plaster was turned over, it revealed a beautiful oval fan motif in black on a yellow ground, seen before in the John Martin house in Barrington (II.1). Vigorous ceiling scraping revealed a border around the entire ceiling periphery, which matched that in the Samuel Martin house of Warren (II.21). Further scraping in the center of the room unearthed a large, impressive, thirty-inch fan with alternating red and black rays on a yellow ground. This is the first recorded example of ceiling decoration by the Classical I stencil artist.

Wall stenciling recovered from under wallpaper in Angell Tavern. *Courtesy Daniel and Kirsten Romani.*

Perhaps he decorated numerous ceilings that are still totally buried under layers of water- and oil-based paint, without the benefit of a leaky roof to expose their existence.

This stenciling, by the same artist as that seen elsewhere in the East Bay area of Rhode Island, was undoubtedly commissioned by Daniel Angell (1777–1869), a fifth-generation descendant from Thomas Angell, who settled in Providence in 1636 with Roger Williams. He built this two-and-a-half-story tavern and farmhouse shortly after 1800 on the Douglas Pike, one of a series of early-nineteenth-century toll roads radiating out from Providence to towns and villages in Massachusetts and Connecticut.

The Douglas Pike ran from Providence to central Massachusetts, where it connected with roads leading north into New Hampshire and west into New York State. (The aforementioned ancestor of the author's husband traveled this road on a sultry August day in 1816,[11] "stopping at Angell's for breakfast and a cool drink" on his trip by horseback from Providence to the Adirondack area of New York state.)

Reportedly this artist also decorated a tavern on the Putnam Pike, which ran west from Providence to Putnam, Connecticut. Viola Lynch, owner of the Samuel Martin house in Warren, recalls seeing designs similar to those in her house many years ago in another Mowry Tavern across the pike from the Paine-Mowry Tavern (I.4). Unfortunately no image or tracings of this work survive.

Previous to dismantling, panels of original stenciling in the Angell Tavern ballroom were carefully removed and stored. Designs, placement, and colorations were precisely recorded in preparation for re-creating this room of perfect symmetry, fine proportion, and subtle balance of color and placement. Hopefully, the Daniel Angell Tavern and its fine classically stenciled ballroom will rise again in time to celebrate the beginning of its third century!

II.6. Nathan Ballou house, date unknown
Lincoln (Smithfield), Rhode Island
Artist: Classical I, circa 1800

Facsimile of upper wall stenciling once in Ballou house. *From notes and pictures by Margaret Fletcher.*

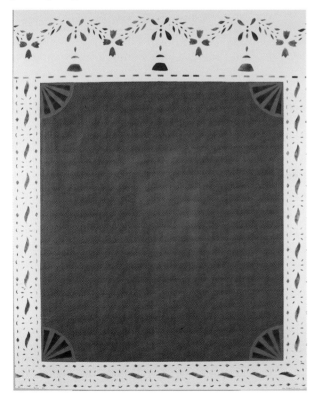

AN EXAMPLE OF the Classical Group is (or was) located in an area once known as the North Woods of Providence. It was part of Providence until 1730, when the colonial legislature divided the northern section of the colony into the towns of Scituate, Glocester, and Smithfield. The town of Lincoln, with the Blackstone River as its eastern border, was part of Smithfield until 1871, well after the period covered in this book. Lincoln is situated in the lower Blackstone Valley, named for William Blackstone, who established himself in this wilderness by 1635, preceding Roger Williams by over a year.[12] The Arnold family, however, are regarded as the real founders of the area. Their patriarch, Eleazer, is said to have been the son of Thomas and the nephew of William Arnold, one of Roger Williams's original party, but the Arnold genealogy, written in 1935, disputes this.[13] Perhaps the Smithfield Arnolds were related to the Apponaug Arnolds mentioned in example II.7.

The Nathan Ballou house,[14] which reportedly contains classical stenciling in a second-floor room, has been a long-standing mystery for the author, who has tried unsuccessfully for twenty years to locate the house. The first reference to its stenciling was in a report on Rhode Island wall stenciling written in 1973 by Margaret Fletcher, a member of the Providence Preservation Society's Consultant Bureau. Referring to a style of stenciling mentioned in Nina Fletcher Little's 1952 book on wall painting, which says that examples of this type are "located in each of five New England states, Rhode Island excepted,"[15] Mrs. Fletcher (no relation) writes, "I have found the same stenciled wall in Lincoln." (When Mrs. Little's book was expanded and updated in 1972, it included a reference to the Ballou house in the chapter "More Examples of Varied Kinds," noting that its stenciling closely resembles that in the ballroom of the Governor Pierce house in Hillsborough, New Hampshire.)[16]

Margaret Fletcher describes the colorations of the Rhode Island wall thus: "The walls at the top are rose, and bottom below the chair rail gray-blue. The borders are a white or light gray band, and the stenciling is done in blue." She goes on to say that there were "witty fans in the corners." She also photographed the stenciling; the author has a photocopy of the picture dating from 1980, clearly marked "Nathan Ballou house, Lincoln, Rhode Island," but has never been able to find either the original photograph or the house itself (which may have since been demolished.) Thus, the location and condition of this classical stenciling remain a mystery.

Exterior of Thomas Arnold house.

II.7. Thomas Arnold house, circa 1800
Apponaug (Warwick), Rhode Island
Artist: Classical II, early nineteenth century

DESCRIBED AS "undoubtedly the grandest Federal-era residence in Apponaug,"[17] this two-story gable-roofed dwelling was built in the early nineteenth century, probably by Thomas Arnold, great-great-grandson of William Arnold, one of the original thirteen proprietors of Providence and Pawtuxet and said to be the area's largest landowner.[18] Its location, Apponaug (from the Narragansett Indian word for oyster), was an early and very active seaport and shipbuilding center.

After falling into extreme disrepair, this fine house was moved in 1985 by Steve Tyson, local housewright and restorer, to the Buttonwoods section of Warwick. Prior to dismantling the house, Tyson noted stenciling in two rooms. The front right parlor, the "best" parlor, featured classical stenciling in the entire wall surface above the dado molding. The plaster wall below the dado was grained to resemble red cedar, a treatment also used on the wooden fire surround, which featured a folk-genre painting of a large rabbit, two large trees, and ten small trees[19]—thought by some to symbolize the fertility of the couple who originally occupied the house.

The second stenciled room, located directly behind the first, had stencil designs only in the border areas, above and below the dado molding. A delicate six-inch blue swag in the compose technique decorated the ceiling area. (We have seen such blue swags in colonial decor and Folk Group stenciling, but this classical version is much smaller in proportion.) The remaining architectural elements of the room were set off with a dainty two-inch border design. The quarter fans in the corners of the upper wall panels were larger than the ones used on the lower panels, a treatment often seen in the Classical Group.

The only original decoration that could be saved was a fragment of the blue swag from the back room and the rabbit overmantel, which was reinstalled in its original position. Designs in this Warwick house have been recorded in other homes in the New England area, including the Salmon Wood house in Hancock, New Hampshire, and the Manse in Peterborough, New Hampshire.

Facsimile of wall stenciling in a back parlor of Arnold house.

THE ROBERT POTTER HOUSE stands on the main thoroughfare of an early seaport town that was once, after Newport, the largest port in Rhode Island. The colonial and Federal homes and shops of merchants and mechanics engaged in maritime endeavors lined this bustling street, which connected with Ten Rod Road, joining the farmers and craftsmen of inland rural Rhode Island and Connecticut to the port of Wickford. Merchants, mariners, and even farmers invested in the many ships built in the area, and much trading of ownership occurred in the shops and taverns along Main Street.

The Potter house, built in 1770 and typical of the five-bay, center-hallway dwellings built in Wickford in profusion after 1776, was visited by a stencil artisan working in the classical genre early in the nineteenth century. Classical-style stenciled festoons of roses and tassels[20] in shades of red and bluish green alternate with plain wall sections in pale yellow ocher. No stenciling was found under the wallpaper on the first floor, perhaps because the first level was commercial in use, with the family living quarters on the second floor, a common practice in this type of neighborhood.

This anonymous artist was well traveled, since the designs in the Potter house are similar to work in the Salmon Wood house in Hancock, New Hampshire,[21] and the Temperance Tavern in Gilmanton Four Corners, New Hampshire.[22] The secondary border was found in Connecticut by Gina Martin,[23] who did extensive research on local stenciling while living in Connecticut.

A tavern located next to this house, called the Narragansett House, built in 1773 on land purchased from Robert Potter, reportedly had stenciling in its front hall, which is now painted over. Benjamin Franklin supposedly stopped there not long after it opened.[24]

Facsimile of stenciled frieze in second-floor bedchamber of Potter house.

II.9. Samuel Carr House, 1797
Wickford (North Kingstown), Rhode Island
Artist: Classical II, circa 1800

AT ONE TIME the Samuel Carr house served as a tavern, one of many on Main Street in Wickford that accommodated the many seamen, businessmen, and dignitaries who visited this leading port, which served as North Kingstown's political and economic center. For many years the tavern was owned by the James E. Reynolds family.

Upon removal of wallpaper in an upstairs room, stenciling was revealed. Although re-created by the owner, with no photographs available of the original, it is clearly recognizable as the work of an artist working in the classical manner, with narrow borders at the ceiling and around architectural features of the room. Similar motifs have been found in the King Hooper (II.11) house, built long before the Revolution in Marblehead, Massachusetts.[25] The blue-green colorations used in that fine Marblehead house match others in Wickford, and the narrow border around the architectural elements is very similar to that in the Arnold house in Apponaug (II.7), suggesting a connection among the three and the possibility that all three were executed by the same hand.

A second stencil artist apparently traveled through Wickford during the mid–nineteenth century and left a sample of his work in the front stair hall of the Carr house. In his portfolio were designs utilized by earlier folk-genre stencil artists, plus ones new to this study, which were possibly derived from the free-form, foliate vine borders found in Pompeiian decorations used so profusely by Scottish architect Robert Adams a century earlier, and illustrated in early design books such as that by Guillaume Zahn, published in Berlin in 1828.[26]

Given this house's proximity to the shore (as the easternmost house on Main Street), it is likely to have sustained water damage during the hurricane known as the Great Gale of 1815, which caused extensive flooding in the upper Bay. Flooding was disastrous for stenciling executed in distemper on whitewashed walls, not to mention for the plaster itself. The stencil artist who created the unorthodox stairway design, quite unlike those found upstairs, may have been hired to redecorate walls whose original stenciling was destroyed in the hurricane.

Facsmile of later stenciling found in the front stair hall of the Carr house.

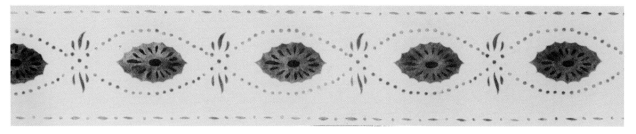

Facsimile of guilloche-type frieze found in a second-floor bedchamber of Carr house. *Courtesy Mr. and Mrs. Thomas E. Steere.*

Early-nineteenth-century wallpaper border, showing renaissance of guilloche motif in interior decoration during the Federal period. *Courtesy Old Sturbridge Village.*

II.10. Aaron Peck house, 1785
Wickford (North Kingstown), Rhode Island
Artist: Classical II, circa, 1800

Facsimile of stenciling in second-floor chamber of Peck house. *Martha Grossel and Marilyn Weigner.*

STENCILING WAS FOUND in a second-floor room of the four-bay, gambrel-roofed Aaron Peck cottage, located a short distance down Main Street from the previous example. The first floor is thought to have been used as a business of some sort. A stenciled festoon of roses and leaves in colors very similar to the Potter house, dark blue-green and red, with yellow ocher used for the plain wall areas, was found under wallpaper.

This interesting design, very typical of the Classical Group, with its delicate secondary border and quarter fans in the wall corner, was found in the Oliver Warner house in East Haddam, Connecticut,[27] on the eastern bank of the lower Connecticut River, as well as in an early house in Walpole, New Hampshire,[28] on the eastern bank of the upper Connecticut River, and in Hinesburg, a town in northwestern Vermont.[29]

Perhaps the Wickford stenciler sailed from Rhode Island to East Haddam, continued up the river by raft to Walpole, stopping along the way to decorate dwellings in prosperous towns en route, and crossed into Vermont over an early bridge (built by Colonel Enoch Hale in 1784) that connected Walpole and Vermont.[30] A similar route may have been used by the numerous other artists who have left examples of their painting, stenciling, graining, marbling, and so forth in the Connecticut River Valley, an area rich in early American decorative arts.

Massachusetts

Boston, the premier seaport in Massachusetts, soon became the taste- and style-setting center of New England. A newspaper, the *Boston News Letter*, was established in the city by 1704,[31] an indication of early culture and commerce. Newspapers provided invaluable information about craftsmen working in the area, as well as a possible design resource. Embellishments called "printer's flowers," which were cast or engraved mostly in England, were used by the early printers to decorate their pages. Many were similar to, though much smaller than, designs used to ornament walls at a later time.

According to an ad in the aforementioned newspaper, Boston received the first calico printer in America.[32] George Leason (an early spelling for Gleason) arrived from England in 1712 and set up shop on Cambridge Street. Many early newspaper publishers also stamped textiles, as is noted in a 1713 ad placed by James Franklin, Benjamin's brother and founder of another early Boston paper, the *New England Courant*.[33] The ad announced that Franklin printed linens, calicos, and silks in addition to his paper.

Wallpaper was imported into Boston early in the eighteenth century and made locally from about the middle of that century. It was practically a first cousin to early calico, with the same people in England, France, and America designing motifs for both. Thus the designs were practically interchangeable.[34] Many early print works produced both patterned textiles and wallpaper. The stencil technique was well known to cloth as well as paper printers, since it was used to ornament some of the earliest of both. Esther Brazer had this to say about wallpaper manufacture: "The earliest process of manufacture in America was that accomplished by stencils, a reversion to the crude method used in the very infancy of wallpaper in France two centuries earlier."[35] Later, when block printing was adopted, the stencil was still utilized to apply additional colors to block-printed designs.

These "stamping" crafts (newspaper printing, textile stamping, and wallpaper staining) all utilized techniques closely related to stenciling. It is therefore not surprising that patterned textiles and wallpaper from the Boston area shared many design elements with the earliest wall stenciling. It would have been a natural progression for the work of a wall stencil artist to evolve from one of these late-eighteenth-century disciplines.

Another major design source for classical-style stencil artists was the numerous neoclassical design books, which arrived in Boston during the second half of the eighteenth century from England and the Continent. These books, and the fine Federal-style room accessories and interiors produced by Boston and Salem cabinetmakers and architects under their influence, contained designs that found their way into the portfolios of most Classical Group wall stencilers. Quarter fans, round fans, and oval fans, often seen inlaid on Federal furniture, were used so often by the Classical I artist that they are considered his signature designs. Swags, festoons, bellflower chains, urns, fluting, and reeding, as seen on fine inlaid and carved furniture and woodwork, were all used by stencil artists to complement homes built in the Federal style. Often, if a room was not fortunate enough to have fine carved woodwork, the stenciling was used to suggest high-style carving, a sort of faux Samuel McIntire treatment!

This vast confluence of a great variety of fine craftsmen in early Boston, many working in the new classical Federal style, which so perfectly mirrored the social and political atmosphere of the new nation, without doubt created optimum conditions for spawning a classical-genre wall stenciler.

King Hooper mansion. *Courtesy Marblehead Arts Association.*

II.11. *King Hooper mansion, 1728*
Marblehead, Massachusetts
Artist: Unknown, circa 1800

MARBLEHEAD, AN EARLY seaport town just sixteen miles northeast of Boston, was settled nine years after Plymouth, in 1629, by fishermen from Cornwall and the Channel Islands, who emigrated not in search of religious freedom but to establish a fishing colony in the New World. A very independent lot, they obeyed or ignored the laws of the colonial government as they pleased, but since the main export of the region was fish, their independent ways were tolerated. It is said that Puritan Massachusetts derived its ideals from the Bible but its wealth and power from the cod.[36]

Marblehead in 1744 had ninety vessels, two hundred acres covered with drying fish, and an annual catch worth thirty-four thousand pounds sterling. In 1765 it was the sixth-largest town in the thirteen colonies, behind Newport but ahead of Salem, Baltimore, and Albany.[37] The provincial merchants of the area had great influence on society and politics; they owned not only merchant ships but also fishing craft, whalers, and coasters, and sent their vessels to all coastal ports and all great ports of Europe and the West Indies. In addition they sold merchandise from their own shops and engaged in land speculation, banking, and insurance underwriting.[38]

One such entrepreneurial merchant family, the Hoopers, commissioned a stencil artist to ornament their stylish homes in the center of Marblehead. The first family house was known as the King Hooper mansion; its original five-story section had been built by Greenfield Hooper, a well-heeled candle maker, in about 1728. His son Robert became one of the wealthiest traders in New England. With a fleet of merchant ships, he engaged not only in the colonial trade but in trade with Europe and Asia as well. In 1747 Robert, known as King for his integrity and fair dealings with the local fishermen, created the King Hooper mansion by adding a shallow Georgian-style three-story house onto the front of his father's spacious colonial home, which became the leg of a T-shaped structure. The Georgian addition featured a facade constructed of wide grooved clapboards made to resemble stone blocks, finished with coined corners, an impressive entrance hall stairway featuring carved balusters with three different twists per stair, superb paneling, and double dentil molding in a drawing room, plus a ballroom that occupied the entire third floor.

During the Revolution, King Hooper, who was greatly liked and respected, made no secret of the fact that he was a Loyalist. In 1774, as many of his neighbors were becoming more and more disturbed by England's oppressive

Re-created stenciling in front stair hall of Hooper mansion. *Courtesy Marblehead Arts Association.*

tactics, Hooper entertained the newly appointed English governor of Massachusetts, Major General Thomas Gage,[39] just one year before Gage's troops marched on Lexington and Concord. When the war began, Hooper removed from Marblehead to his country estate in Danvers, Massachusetts,[40] which was also used by Major General Gage as his summer headquarters.

After the war Hooper, though financially diminished, was able to return to Marblehead, where he lived quietly until his death in 1790. His descendants resided in the mansion until about 1819. The stenciling most likely was commissioned by one of King's descendants who inherited the house in 1790, perhaps his eldest son, Thomas.

Another Hooper family house, the Nathaniel Hooper house, located diagonally opposite this building, contains remnants of stenciling similar to that in the King mansion. It was built in the mid-1700s, purchased and handsomely enlarged by Nathaniel Hooper in 1801, a probable date for the stenciling in both houses. There is also a possibility that the stenciling dates to the mid-1700s, when the Georgian front was added to the King mansion and the Nathaniel house was built, making this stenciling the oldest known example of its genre.

In the century after it passed out of the family, the King Hooper mansion was used for everything from a rooming house to a YMCA (which turned the ballroom into a bowling alley). Amazingly, little permanent damage was sustained to this lovely mansion.

It was purchased and restored in the 1920s by the antique dealer Israel Sack, as an ideal "showroom" for displaying his fine collections of early American furniture. In 1938, when a prospective buyer proposed stripping many of its decorative elements, a group of local artists purchased the mansion, restored it, and made it their headquarters.

In 1991 English artist Leonard Stubbs was commissioned by the Marblehead Arts Association to re-create much of the early stenciling. Mr. Stubbs, originally from Cheshire, learned his craft through the still functioning apprentice system in England. Stenciling, which had been found earlier under many layers of wallpaper, was carefully re-created in the center halls and stairways from the front entrance to the third floor. The first- and second-floor halls and stairway are in deep red ocher with black stenciling. The less important stairway to the third floor is in yellow ocher with the same dark stenciling. Sections of original work have been retained in all areas. Two areas not re-created also have samples of early stenciling, one in the first-floor "borning room" and the other in a small back room[41] on the fifth level of the original colonial structure. The ballroom most likely also had stenciling.

This early border stenciling, devoid of the typical swag and quarter-fan motifs, is a most interesting example of the abundant decorative interior painting found in the North Shore area of Massachusetts.

Early photograph of stenciling in second-floor ballroom of Fuller's Tavern.

II.12. Fuller's Tavern, 1807
South Walpole, Massachusetts
Artist: Unknown, early nineteenth century

IN ALL PROBABILITY the same anonymous artist who stenciled the Hooper mansion early in the nineteenth century traveled by coach to Fuller's Tavern over the newly opened Norfolk and Bristol Turnpike (now Route 1). A picture in a 1928 publication[42] showing the tavern's second-floor ballroom after a 1926 restoration clearly depicts stenciling identical to that seen in the front hall of the King Hooper Marblehead mansion. The accompanying article states that "many-colored stenciling was found throughout the building."

Built in South Walpole, situated exactly halfway between Boston and Providence, the tavern occupied a very financially rewarding location, since the trip was of a day's duration—which placed hungry travelers at Fuller's just in time for a hearty meal. Food at this establishment was as famous as the tavern itself, an added incentive for this artist to seek the plum commission of decorating the walls of this handsome new Georgian/Colonial-style public house. Itinerant artists usually boarded free at taverns while decorating was in progress and also might be invited to stay while completing other commissions in the area, using the work in the tavern as a sample for interested clients.

Built by John Needham in 1806, soon after the Norfolk and Bristol opened to travel, this tavern was purchased soon after by Stephen Fuller, Jr., a distinguished innkeeper from Boston and Dedham, son-in-law of the turnpike's chief promoter.

Two innkeepers were savvy enough to locate in this halfway position. The Folly Tavern stood until the 1960s directly opposite Fuller's. Friendly competition developed, with all coaches stopping at the tavern to the right, thus ensuring equal business for both. One would catch them coming and the other going.

Both of these taverns were famous enough to be mentioned in several early twentieth-century books on nineteenth-century road systems such as Alice Morse Earle's book, first printed in 1900, followed by Frederick Wood's book in 1919.

Fuller's was converted to an apartment building in the 1960s. It is still there, its beauty much diminished, on a now quiet corner of South Walpole, removed from the busy route by the building of a new section of Route 1, which in an earlier time would have been a disaster for the tavern but now is its saving grace.

Exterior of Rider Tavern. *Courtesy Charlton Historical Society.*

II.13. The Rider Tavern, 1797–99
Charlton, Massachusetts
Artist: Unknown, 1810

THE RIDER TAVERN, a truly outstanding extant example of an unaltered Federal-period turnpike inn, was built in the Georgian style between 1797 and 1799 by local distiller Eli Wheelock and his partner Leonard Morey. After Wheelock fell to his death from the roof during construction in 1797, Morey continued building and charged the expenses to the Wheelock estate, giving historians a rare opportunity to identify the source and costs of every element in the building. The architect of this tavern, which boasted the only roof garden in New England outside of Boston, was John A. Haven, a local housewright.

By 1806 the Rider family had purchased the entire estate, and it was during their ownership (1801–24) that the tavern became an important center of community activity and a major stop on the Stafford and Worcester Turnpike. In the 1820s the tavern hosted a visit from the Marquis de Lafayette, with a full military muster followed by a sumptuous meal.[43]

The classical stenciling found in two Federalized rooms on the left side of the building, and in the second-floor ballroom, was probably executed during this period. Two of these rooms, one on the first floor and the other directly above, contain the only Federal-style woodwork in the tavern, indicating that they were stenciled to complement the newest in classical-style trim.

There is scroll-type freehand decoration in a small room directly west of the first-floor stenciled room. This room retains the earlier, simpler woodwork, perhaps an indication that the painted decoration was of an earlier period.

By the 1840s, the railroads' competition for stagecoach traffic and the transfer of the mail route to the Central Turnpike caused the roadside tavern business to dwindle and the Rider Tavern to be used almost exclusively as a dwelling. The ballroom continued to be used for dances and social gatherings, but the rest of the building was made into three apartments.

The Charlton Historical Society acquired the tavern in 1975 and launched a much-needed restoration. The stenciling in the ballroom was re-created in late 1980 by Nancy Garcia, a local artist, who also recorded and re-created other early stenciling in the Charlton area. Faded fragments of the original stenciling can still be seen in the two rooms on the most easterly side of the building. The original, executed in distemper, was re-created in acrylic.

Pictures shared with the author by Ms. Garcia show area walls that resemble the work of Stimp, Gleason, and

Re-created stenciling in second-floor ballroom. *Courtesy Charlton Historical Society.*

Eaton, plus decorated walls in the Nathan McIntyre house in South Charlton, which has both scroll painting and border stenciling very similar to that in the Rider Tavern. This south-central area of Massachusetts, close to the Rhode Island and Connecticut borders, was obviously a popular stop for numerous decorative painters in the early nineteenth century.

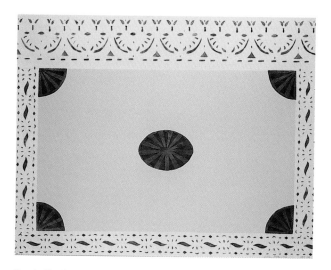

Facsimile of stenciling found in front parlor of Job Winslow house.

II.14. Job Winslow house, 1770

Dighton, Massachusetts

Artist: Classical I, early nineteenth century

STENCIL WORK FOUND in three rooms of the modest pre-Revolutionary Winslow house/tavern is clearly by the same hand as the previous examples found in Rhode Island on the east shore of Narragansett Bay. This area of Massachusetts is just east of the Rhode Island border; in fact, prior to 1744, the present-day Rhode Island towns of Barrington, Warren, and Bristol were all part of Bristol County, Massachusetts.

This two-story, three-quarter house was built in 1770 by Job Winslow, who served his town in many elected positions as well as being a colonel in the Bristol County militia. He sold the house in 1793 to Simeon Williams, who took advantage of its location on an early road from Boston, midway between Taunton, Massachusetts, and Bristol, Rhode Island,[44] and enlarged his residence to include a tavern and country store. The stencil decoration was probably commissioned to ornament the new stagecoach stop.

The author's re-creation of this stenciling clearly illustrates the stylistic influence of the inlay designs used profusely on fine Federal-period furniture. Designs such as the quarter fan, used as an accent in the spandrel areas of each wall panel; the oval fan, used as an accent in the center of overmantel plaster panels; and the bellflower motif, used as an element in the frieze and secondary borders in the second-floor chamber, were all found in early cabinetmaker pattern books,[45] which arrived on American shores in great numbers starting in the mid-1700s.

One room of stenciling was re-created by members of the Dighton Historical Society after they purchased the neglected house in the 1960s. Panels of original work were retained in all three rooms, and the rest of the stenciling was painted over with latex paint at that time. A visit by the author in 1999 found only fragments of original stenciling faintly visible.

II.15. Oliver Robbins House (Westbrook), 1800
Pittsfield, Massachusetts
Artist: Unknown, circa 1810

Original stenciling in front second-floor bedchamber of Robbins house. *Courtesy of Westbrook Farm, Pittsfield, Mass. 01201.*

THE STENCILING ornamenting the walls of the Berkshire-area Oliver Robbins house is an unparalleled example of the influence wallpaper exerted on wall stencil artists. This decoration features exact replicas of the two wallpaper borders, not just adaptations of a few motifs, as seen on the walls of the Goodale farm in the eastern part of the state.

The house was constructed by Oliver Robbins in 1800 on land purchased by his father in 1792. Town records show the sale to Joshua Robbins in 1792 of one hundred acres of the original settlement lot in the northwestern corner of Pittsfield, close to the Shaker settlement at Hancock. Oliver lived in the house until 1820, at which time his daughter Elizabeth French took up residence.

Three stenciled walls were found in 1930 by Miss Gertrude Watson, a wealthy society woman and music patron from Buffalo, New York, who purchased the estate in the late nineteenth century as a summer home, which she called Westbrook. She lavishly entertained artists and intellectuals at both Westbrook and her Italian-style villa across the street, where she resided during the winter because it had a modern heating system.

Stenciling under many thicknesses of wallpaper was found in two rooms on the second floor and one on the first. The stenciling on the first floor was also covered with a coat of blue kalsomine and could not be restored because it came off with the kalsomine, a water-soluble paint. This is a strong indication that the stencil field was executed in distemper. This room was repapered at that time, its design to be retrieved by the next stencil enthusiast to visit the home.

However, in the two upstairs rooms, well-preserved stenciling was successfully restored. One room also featured the familiar marbleized floor. It is in these two rooms that exact replicas of wallpaper borders made in Boston between 1790 and 1810 were found. One of these borders, the "feather and ribbon," was used in the Stephen Robbins house in East Lexington, Massachusetts, a possible family connection. The execution of this stenciling could only have been achieved by copying directly from the paper, either on the wall or from a segment cut from the paper roll and added to the artist's portfolio to be used for a special commission. (Wallpaper borders were printed much as they are today, lengthwise on a single-width roll of paper, to be cut by the paperhanger as needed.)[46] Perhaps this copying was the work of a family member who brought samples of favorite wallpaper from

Original stenciling in first- and second-floor back rooms of Robbins house featuring exact copies of early-nineteenth-century wallpaper. *Courtesy of Westbrook Farm, Pittsfield, Mass. 01201.*

a family home in eastern Massachusetts to a new home in the Berkshire Mountains.

When Miss Watson passed away in 1938 at age eighty, she willed the house and 328-acre property to two of her employees, who within five years sold it to a lumber company, which promptly logged much of Miss Watson's treasured stand of original trees. For many years the barns were rented for horse stables, and the house stood empty. When the author visited in 1990, she found the ell and stables occupied, with the house vacant and in extreme disrepair. A subsequent visit in 1998 found conditions unchanged, but this time it was possible to gain entrance to the house thorough a hole in the front door.

Surprisingly, the stenciling on the second floor, which was pictured in the Waring book, is still there and in fairly good condition.[47] The back room, with its full design on cheery red, is exactly as depicted. The big surprise was in the front room: the frieze described but not pictured in Waring, which proved to be an extraordinary example of the stenciled swag with beautifully hand-painted embellishments in a style that has been dubbed "compose," which made the stenciled version of the "cone and leaf" wallpaper border seem small and insignificant.

Examination of the first floor provided additional unexpected pleasures. Stripping back Miss Watson's 1930 wallpaper revealed stenciling in both the front and back parlors, with the latter identical to that in the room above. The front parlor, although its decoration is barely discernible, clearly had been a finely ornamented room, as befits the "best" room in a house. The frieze, not clear enough to trace, was obviously quite sophisticated. The main wall decoration, on light yellow ocher, was ornamented with alternating vertical borders placed about eight inches apart. One was a reeded column in soft gray entwined diagonally with a vermilion ribbon and a gray vine. The second vertical was a simple grape-and-vine motif in dark green. A Greek-key border was placed above the dado. The extensive decoration below the dado could not be deciphered.

This front room and the other three must have been very beautiful and definitely unique, but the fate of this singular house and its decoration is uncertain, for unless care is forthcoming in the near future the house and its important early American stenciling could be lost forever.

Connecticut's seaport town of New Haven was settled in 1683 by colonists of the English merchant class and became an early center for cultural, artistic, and intellectual pursuits with the founding of Yale University in 1708. During the early Federal period an active artist community developed in the city, including one well-known engraver and mapmaker, Amos Doolittle, whose painting rooms were situated near the university on College Street.

According to Janet Waring, classical-genre wall stenciling also came early to the New Haven area. A footnote in her 1937 book states that a house in Guilford, just east of New Haven, had stenciling similar to that in the Governor Pierce house in New Hampshire, probably dating to 1790.[48] This type of stenciling was found throughout New England.

Since southern Connecticut was easily accessible by packet ship or stagecoach from the mid-Atlantic and southern colonies, this southern New England area could have attracted stencil artists from the south as well as from New England.

Numerous artists, many trained abroad, advertised between 1786 and 1800 their willingness to accept many types of painting commissions, including "house painting," according to newspaper advertisements in Philadelphia, Maryland, and South Carolina collected and published by Alfred Coxe Prime in 1969. Perhaps some traveled north seeking commissions to ornament the fine Federal homes springing up along the banks of the Connecticut River.

~❧~

II.16. Isaiah and Ruth Tuttle house, 1803 Torrington, Litchfield County, Connecticut Artist: Unknown, early nineteenth century

THIS LARGE, TWO-STORY, transitional late Georgian/early Adam–style house was built in 1803 by Isaiah Tuttle, the fifth generation of his clan to reside in the New Haven section of Connecticut. He moved to Torrington in 1772, married in 1774, and erected his first house in the area soon after. He built his second house, the one pictured here, across the street from the first in 1803 and resided there until his death in 1831. He kept a tavern in the old and new house for many years. According to family history, the foundation stones were cut in New Haven and dragged to Torrington by ox team. Perhaps other New Haven resources and draftsmen were utilized as well in the construction and decoration of this house.

The interior features a second-floor ballroom, six beautifully carved Federal-style mantels, plus wonderfully exuberant wall stenciling in shades of scarlet, pink, black, and white on a yellow ocher ground. The stenciling was found by the present owners in the 1990s in four different areas: a left front parlor, front hallway, second-floor ballroom on the right side of the house, and a small back chamber to the left of the stairway, under as much as eight layers of wallpaper. The stenciling in the first-floor parlor unfortunately has been painted over, presenting a very difficult restoration problem. Three different horizontal frieze designs were used, two of which are similar

Tuttle House. *Courtesy Robert J. and Stacey duBell Mileti.*

Detail of "rose festoon" frieze in second-floor stair hall. *Courtesy Robert J. and Stacey duBell Mileti.*

Panel of original stencil work from second-floor ballroom with faux reeded columns and guilloche-like vertical borders. *Courtesy Robert J. and Stacey duBell Mileti.*

but not identical to ones seen in Wickford, Rhode Island (II.8), and another will be seen in the next example, also in Litchfield County. Several vertical borders are also similar to but not exactly like those in Rhode Island homes. Familiar motifs are combined with new ones to create a unique visual treat, especially for wall-stenciling enthusiasts. This seems to be the work of someone with more than a casual knowledge of classical stenciling in Massachusetts, Rhode Island, and areas of Connecticut but who is using these designs in a different, perhaps considered by some "superior," manner. However, there is something to be said for the refined, symmetrical work seen in previous examples.

The decoration in this house definitely falls into the classical genre with its repeated use of faux carved reeding, not seen before on a stenciled wall. First, it is used as a reeded column wrapped with a diagonal leaf, a treatment used on carved furniture and interior woodwork, and often depicted on wallpaper. Second, stop reeding is used to create a frieze, which features reeding stopped in such a way as to create and frame an oval space in the center to spotlight a design feature. The definition of "reeded," according to the glossary of terms in the *Book of Decorative Furniture* by Edwin Foley written in 1911 is, "Decoration by means of parallel lines of raised wood, usually placed in rows upon FRIEZES, legs and other plain

spaces or ENCIRCLING COLUMNS." This style of carved decoration is associated with the Georgian period in England and the American Hepplewhite/Sheraton or Federal period.

Definitely classical (but not the type that just decorates the periphery of the walls), vertical borders covering the entire wall panel are spaced close together in an alternating repeat with still visible lines scribed[49] into the plaster to ensure that they are plumb. Most rooms feature two or three alternating borders, with the ballroom having a grand total of four different designs in the overmantel area. The Tuttle house is a very elaborate example of the classical genre of wall stenciling.

There are also remnants of decorative work of some kind on the front hall stairway, suggesting a runner of woven carpet in colorations similar to those seen in the Rhodes house of Pawtuxet, Rhode Island.

Design elements seen in this house have traveled up the Connecticut River into New Hampshire and on into northwestern Vermont. For example, a large floral spray used in the overmantel area in the Tuttle house was also found in the Peter Farnum house of Francestown, New Hampshire, one of the many fine Federal-style homes decorated in the early nineteenth century in Hillsborough County, New Hampshire.

<hr>

II.17. Colonel Ithiel Hickox house, circa 1790

Washington, Litchfield County, Connecticut

Artist: Unknown,

early nineteenth century

<hr>

BUILT IN 1797, the Colonel Ithiel Hickox house was lived in by four generations in direct descent, some of the men of rank in the colonial army and in the judicial life of Litchfield County. The builder's great-grandson found hidden and long-forgotten stenciling when enlarging the opening between two rooms around 1930. The best parlor had been covered with stylish French wallpaper that had been on the walls for at least a century, helping to date the stenciling to the early nineteenth century.

Esther Brazer visited this house shortly after this discovery to record and photograph the stenciling, which she described as one of "singular beauty and taste." She so admired this room, often described as the most beautiful room in America, that she chose to re-create it in the dining room of her Flushing, Long Island, home called Innerwick.[50]

The author was very honored to be able to work from tracings of these stencils cut by Mrs. Brazer in re-creating this house for her own collection of sample boards. The

Facsimile of extant stenciling retained in first-floor parlor of Hickox house in Washington, Connecticut. *From tracings by Esther Stevens Brazer. Courtesy Mr. and Mrs. Adam Williams.*

Brazer stencils are part of the Historical Society of Early American Decoration collection housed at the American Folk Art Museum in New York City. A 1997 visit to the house by the author found the stenciled room still in fairly good condition.

This house shares much with the previous Litchfield County house, the Tuttle house of Torrington. The design, coloration, and masterful execution are undoubtedly by the same artisan without peer.

This very elaborate version of classical stenciling will travel up the Connecticut River into Vermont.

*II.18. Caleb Grosvenor house, 1750
Pomfret Center, Windham County, Connecticut
Artist: Classical I, early nineteenth century*

THE AUTHOR'S INITIAL VISIT to the Grosvenor house on old Post Road in Pomfret was a memorable one. In three obscured areas on the second floor, well hidden behind earlier renovations, remnants of familiar classical stenciling were waiting to be discovered. The frieze design from the Samuel Martin house in Warren, Rhode Island (II.2), was barely visible on plaster that originally was part of the front hallway, now well hidden behind a new doorway leading to the third level. Also, on the original back walls of two chambers on either side of this front hall, now hidden by closets enclosing the entire back end of each room, designs from houses in Bristol (II.3) and Lincoln (II.6), Rhode Island, can be seen. Tracings from the Grosvenor house are an exact fit for those from Rhode Island, linking this house with the artist who traveled from Dighton, Massachusetts, through Rhode Island and on into Windham County, Connecticut. It is highly possible that stenciling once decorated the first-floor rooms as well as the second.

This house was built by descendants of one of Windham County's most important and wealthy original twelve proprietors, Caleb Grosvenor. Located on the old Post Road, it served as a mail delivery post before the first local post office was established between Boston and New York. About 1765 it was improved as a well-known Revolutionary-period public house.[51]

Grosvenor's estate was insolvent at the time of his death in 1788 and was sold at auction in 1790 to Thomas Lee, Esquire, of Cambridge, Massachusetts. Lee probably was responsible for commissioning the stencil artist who decorated his newly acquired house/tavern.

The stenciling in this house, with its simple classical border designs, so familiar and predictable, is definitely by a different hand than the previous two exuberant examples of classical-genre stenciling.

Included in the Martin Collection at the American Folk Art Museum are samples of walls stenciled by the same hand as the Grosvenor house but located in other sections of Connecticut such as South Windsor, Salem, Hampton and as far south as Preston City. The latter features a frieze that is an exact match for those found in Barrington, Rhode Island (II.1), and just east of the Rhode Island border in Dighton, Massachusetts (II.14). The discovery of this three-state grouping of work by this early-nineteenth-century stencil artist, which is among the earliest in the classical genre, joins this area artistically to the Governor Pierce house of Hillsborough, New Hampshire, the Joslin Tavern of West Townsend, Massachusetts, and the Barry house of Kennebunk, Maine (all featured in the Waring book). Possibly a through study of the architectural history of the structures involved will shed light as to the chronology of this artist's travel and work itinerary.

⤳❦⤲

THE WORK OF YET another stencil artist to visit Connecticut can be found in the Pomeroy Tavern, an early stagecoach stop overlooking the old Boston Turnpike[52] (Route 44) located just sixteen miles east of Hartford. Built by Eleazer Pomeroy early in the nineteenth century, it remained a public house until the late nineteenth century, when it became the home of a local physician.

Stenciling was found under wallpaper in the second-floor hall by the present owners in the early 1990s. There is also evidence of similar but more elaborate work in the second-floor ballroom, which runs the length of the building front. The presence of stenciling on the first-floor rooms would not at all surprise the author.

Stenciling by this hand was fairly prevalent in the northern part of Connecticut, with sightings reported in the Windsor County towns of Salem, Hampton, and South Windsor.

The aforementioned ancestor of the author's husband, John Brown Francis, visited this tavern in 1817 when traveling by stage from the Adirondack area of New York back to his home in Rhode Island. The following notation appears in his diary dated July 23: "Leave Hartford at six, breakfast at Pomeroy's in Coventry 16 miles; Porter's in Hartford pretty good house, arrive in Providence before sun set."[53]

Stenciling similar to that in the Pomeroy Tavern, and probably by the same hand, was discovered under wallpaper by Sandra Tarbox[54] in the 1980s in a 1780 saltbox known as the Dr. Wheeler House of South Britain, Connecticut. It was located in at least two areas, a front parlor and the front hallway leading to the second level. In the parlor the coloration is the same as in the Pomeroy, black designs on a pink/red background. The ground in the hallway, however, is white, probably the bare plaster, with the usual black used for the stenciled decoration.

Work by this same artist was also found up the Connecticut River in the Thomas Everson House of Norwich, Vermont, according to Polly Forcier, a Vermont resident. Two border designs from the Pomeroy, plus a very unusual overmantel border of alternating tall and short trees, are stenciled in black on gray parlor walls.

II.19. Pomeroy Tavern
Coventry, Tolland County, Connecticut
Artist: Unknown, 1815

View of extant stenciling found on second level of front stair hall of Pomeroy Tavern.

Chapter 10

The Northern New England States of Maine, New Hampshire, and Vermont

Detail of 7-inch stenciled urn used above baseboard in several northern New England areas, including front stair hall of Temperance Tavern (II.16), Gilmanton, New Hampshire.

A good place to start our study of classical stenciling in the northern New England states of Maine, New Hampshire, and Vermont is on the eastern shoreline of the area. Seaport towns from Portsmouth, New Hampshire, to Portland, Maine, were thriving communities during the post-Revolutionary period with affluent merchants, shipbuilders, and sea captains building impressive homes influenced by the Salem, Massachusetts, architect and furniture maker Samuel McIntire. Classical stenciling drew heavily on the same design sources that influenced Federal-period architects and cabinetmakers, with the two art forms perfectly complementing each other.

Numerous artists were attracted by the great cultural and financial vitality of this coastal area. Sometimes new arrivals migrated to work in the new style. Often, however, two or three generations of the same family remained nearby, ornamenting the furnishings and interiors of homes in the coastal New England area.

Several examples of these artistic dynasties come to mind. The Gray family is said to have been decorative painters in the Salem area as early as 1770, offering a full range of utilitarian and decorative painting services. William Gray (1750–1819) and his father before him were said to be painters in the area.[1] John Gray, Jr., who probably apprenticed with his uncle William in Salem, moved to Portsmouth in 1800, working there for a number of years. Another possible family member, Breverter Gray, who was born in Hillsborough, New Hampshire, in 1785, worked in his hometown during the 1805–8 period, according to his account book and recipe book, which sold at the Little Collection auction in 1995.[2] Both John Gray, Jr., and Breverter Gray were well positioned to be part of the classical stencil tradition in this coastal area.

The Hamblens were another family to pass decorative painting techniques from generation to generation. Three generations starting about 1780 were "House, Sign and Fancy Painters" in Portland, Maine.[3] George was the first generation; his son Almery, the second; and Almery's four sons, Joseph, Nathaniel, Eli, and Sturtevant, were third-generation artists. Portrait painter William Prior married Almery's daughter, Rosamond, in 1828. Prior, like most portrait painters of the time, was not above accepting utilitarian commissions such as wall stenciling to supplement his portraiture income.

Unfortunately, there is no conclusive evidence connecting any of these surnames with the artists responsible for the classical stenciling in this three-state area of northern New England.

II.20. Taylor-Barry house, 1803
Kennebunk, Maine
Artist: Classical I, 1803

(Below right) Early photo of Taylor-Barry house. *Courtesy The Brick Store Museum, Kennebunk, Maine.*

View of first-floor stair hall showing stenciling and complementary classical carved woodwork. *Courtesy The Brick Store Museum, Kennebunk, Maine.*

KENNEBUNK LANDING, the shipbuilding area of the town, was the site of over twenty large shipyards that built sailing vessels from 1766 until 1879. Many of the fine homes that line the streets of Kennebunk were built by the shipbuilders, shipowners, and merchants whose businesses were sited at Kennebunk Landing.

The Taylor-Barry house was built for William Taylor in 1803 by housewright Thomas Eaton (no relation to Moses) from Salem, Massachusetts. It is a foursquare, five-bayed Federal structure with a hipped roof and woodwork carved in the style of Robert Adam, which is believed by some to be by Samuel McIntire (1757–1811.)

Classical stenciling, as befits a house with Adamesque-style woodwork, was discovered under wallpaper in 1940. Five generations of the Barry family, which acquired the house in 1818, had lived there unaware of the stenciling, which helps to date the work to the early years of the house, probably soon after its completion in 1803. The last Barry to live in the house was Edith Cleaves Barry, founder of the Brick Store Museum, who bequeathed it to the museum.

We have seen these designs before in Rhode Island, Massachusetts, and Connecticut. Indeed the designs seen here have become the "signature" designs of this artist, usually seen in the front halls of his commissions in the same color scheme as here, namely black and red stenciling on white bands, with Pompeiian red wall centers. Probably more rooms were stencil-decorated originally, since a second simple border design has been found in a second-floor dressing room.

Exterior view of the Foxcroft house.

II.21. Reverend Samuel Foxcroft house, 1765
New Gloucester, Maine
Artist: Unknown, late eighteenth century

THE STUNNING WALL DECORATION adorning the front stair hall of the Reverend Foxcroft house was not applied with the aid of a stencil. It was painstakingly painted freehand using various-size natural bristle brushes, called quills. The design similarity between this freehand work and stenciled wall decorations in central New Hampshire has long intrigued the author. It is an excellent illustration of the influence that late-eighteenth-century freehand work had on later wall stencil artisans. The translation of a decorative scheme from the labor-intensive freehand technique to one executed more quickly by stencil seems to have been a fairly common way for stencil artists to augment their design portfolios—or for freehand artists to make their work more efficient.

This Georgian-style house was built in 1765 by a descendant of English aristocrats to mimic the stylish homes of the Boston area. It became the home of New Gloucester's first minister, Harvard graduate Samuel Foxcroft. The house's fine painted decoration was first discovered under wallpaper before 1921 by the Chandler family, who were its owners then.

Since the 1920s ushered in a period of great interest in colonial and Federal-period American painted surface decoration on furniture, room accessories, and interiors, the discovery of the Foxcroft house decorations must have caused a stir in preservation circles. One wonders if the early researchers, such as Edward B. Allen (*Early American Wall Paintings*, 1926) and Janet Waring (*Early American Stencils on Walls and Furniture*, 1937), paid study visits to the Foxcroft house.

We know that the house was visited by Esther Stevens Brazer (*Early American Decoration*, 1940), a native of nearby Portland. In the 1790s, Brazer's ancestors founded the japanned-tinware industry in Stevens Plains, not far from New Gloucester and Portland. While researching her ancestors' tinware business, she discovered an ancestor named Phillip Rose (1771–1800), known to be a nephew of Paul Revere and thought to have been involved with tinware decoration in Cambridge, Massachusetts. Brazer learned that Rose was in Stevens Plain in 1796 when he painted two illuminated Stevens family records. From this evidence and more Brazer concluded that Rose almost certainly was the artist responsible for the Foxcroft wall painting.

It would, of course, be extremely satisfying to attribute this superb decoration to Phillip Rose, with his ties to a leading researcher and practitioner of early American decoration (Brazer) and to a Revolutionary War hero

View of freehand decoration in front stair hall of Foxcroft house.

(Revere). He was an artist, and he had been in the right place. Unfortunately, he may not have been there at the right time.

If Rose painted the Foxcroft walls in 1796, at age twenty-five, it would mean that the Reverend's fine home —completed in 1765—had remained unadorned for some thirty years. This seems unlikely, considering that the Foxcroft house was built to imitate the ostentation of fine Boston dwellings and that its builders probably employed Boston craftsmen. Indeed, it would seem probable that Reverend Foxcroft, who had family and social ties to Boston, would have chosen an artist practicing in one of the seaport towns, such as Boston, Salem, Portsmouth, or Portland, to decorate his home well *before* 1796. On the other hand, perhaps the impending blockade of the Boston coast by the English fleet interfered with the completion of the Foxcroft house's decorations.[4]

Whether they were done by Phillip Rose or not, the Foxcroft house's painted decorations are superb. The work in the front stair hall on the first and second levels

Panel of original painted decoration in a second-floor chamber.

is composed of large, vertical grapevines with stems and leaves in black, laid on a white ground, with touches of iron red on the terminating sprays. Each grape and the backs of some of the leaves are mottled in greenish blue. The frieze is a swag of numerous tiny brush strokes, almost featherlike, in black on white—very effective on a soft yellow ocher ground.

The decoration in the right front parlor, very different in coloration and style from the hall, seems to have been done by a different hand. It features marbleized columns emphasizing the architectural elements and swags and tassels at the ceiling in blue on white, on a dark green ground. This decoration was painted over in the 1990s after being photographed by the Greater Portland Landmarks Commission.

There are several existing samples of early work in a closet between the front parlor and the room behind it, which was constructed after the decoration had been applied. One section seems to have been done by the same hand, indicating the original existence of decoration in the right back room. The other decoration might have been added later to cover up the bare plaster of the renovation.

In the 1990s a small section of painted decoration in a second-floor bedchamber was exposed, revealing a field of diagonally spaced three-flowered sprays, perhaps on a blue ground. This diagonal-grid layout apparently was used for centuries in Europe and England, and it is seen often on New England walls decorated by many different artisans. The frieze in the chamber obviously was done by the same artist who did the work in the stair hall.

A small attic room in the house contains new designs connected by style and coloration to the work in the hall. These feature a solid swag at the ceiling, instead of the multitudinous-brush-stroke version seen on the walls in the first and second floors. This was expeditious for attic decoration!

Judging by the amount of decoration still preserved in this house, we may safely assume that every room was originally decorated. These choice examples of eighteenth-century freehand-painted wall decoration are echoed by some of the earliest wall stenciling in America, thus contributing early freehand motifs to the many design influences on American Federal-period stencil artists.

II.22. Stephen Robinson house, 1803
South Paris, Maine
Artist: Unknown, possibly three

FARMER STEPHEN ROBINSON purchased land in the southeastern section of Maine in 1787. He lived in a simple starter house while clearing land for the planting of potatoes, from which he planned to distill whiskey. This obviously was a lucrative business, since Mr. Robinson was soon prosperous enough to commence building a very fine house with an impressive late-Georgian-style front entrance. He completed the mansion, the finest in the area, in 1803.

Placed on the National Registry in 1990, the Robinson house contains samples of wall decorations by as many as three different artists, one of whom may have been a family member. The decoration in the left front parlor and the right front chamber contains designs that are related to work already seen in Rhode Island and Connecticut of the Classical II type. Similar designs will be seen as our survey moves westward through the northern New England states.

The right front parlor contains freehand decoration featuring a three-flower spray in a diamond grid, seemingly inspired by that in the Foxcroft house in New

Detail of original "rose festoon" frieze retained in a front parlor of Robinson house.

View of original stenciled and freehand panel in a second-floor chamber.

Gloucester but incorporating a border that seems to be a stenciled version of the freehand one in the Foxcroft house. There is nothing to indicate that this work is by the same hand as that in the other two stenciled rooms of the Robinson house.

The stair hall (first and second floors) is decorated with stenciling of a completely unfamiliar type. While very handsome and well executed, it is completely unrelated to the other two types of decoration.

Family history relates that "a decorator came in from Portland when the house was first built." That artist was probably responsible for either the rooms with the stenciled "three-rose festoon" or the freehand work in the right front parlor, or both. Another family anecdote relates that "the narrow stenciled border on the plaster walls of the front hall was by your great-grandfather, Albert Quincy—who married Adeline Robinson in 1831 at the old Homestead." Since the motifs in the front hall on the first and second floors seem to be by the same

hand, the hall might have been restenciled in the 1830s, some thirty years after its original decoration was applied.

No doubt the walls were shabby by then, since they had been painted with distemper paint, which was vulnerable in busy areas such as a stairway—especially one used by a family of thirteen! (The Robinsons had ten daughters and one son.) In 1801 a French artist by the imposing name of Antoine-Alexis Cadet-de-Vaux wrote about the disadvantages of distemper paint: "It comes off by the slightest friction, so that when it is used for staircases one is obliged to be upon one's guard against suffering clothes to come into contact with it."[5]

After thirty years of use, the front stair hall of the Robinson house may have been in dire need of refurbishing. How convenient it would have been, to have a new son-in-law who was talented with a stencil brush! Perhaps the name of Albert Quincy should be added to the small list of American Federal-period wall-stenciling artists.

Musterfield farm.

II.23. *Musterfield farm, 1798*
Parsonsfield, Maine
Artist: Unknown, 1800

BUILT ON A HIGH HILL in the late 1790s, reportedly by a Thatcher Bernham on land owned by his father, Noah, this farm was named Musterfield because it was a favorite place for the local militia to meet and drill. When members of the Greater Portland Landmarks Commission visited Musterfield farm in 1986, they found an early Federal post-and-beam structure that was remarkable for what had *not* been done to it. No electricity or plumbing had been installed. The fine Federal-style woodwork had but a few thin coats of paint, not the usual thick layer of multiple coats completely obliterating the details of the carving. Best of all, under the wallpaper the visitors found well-preserved stenciling, untouched by paint or particleboard. The house was a fortuitous example of benign neglect.

Numerous areas of Classical II stenciling in this interesting house suggest that all of its rooms—with the possible exception of the kitchen—originally were stencil-decorated. The artist was probably the same anonymous man who decorated the Robinson house (II.22) and the McDonald house (II.24) in Limerick, a few miles east of Parsonsfield.

Detail of flower vase and frieze in first-floor back room.

Original stenciling still decorating walls of a first-floor parlor and second-floor chamber, directly above.

The house's present owners have preserved the origi- nal stenciling in the front left parlor and the chamber directly above it, which have identical coloration and designs, including the "three-rose festoon" frieze. The only difference in the two rooms' decoration is that in the parlor it stops at a chair rail, while in the chamber it con- tinues down to the baseboard, where it meets an urn-and- shield vertical motif (II.45).

The third area to retain its original decoration is a first-floor left back room. Its feathery stenciled swag at the ceiling area is very similar to a freehand one seen in the Foxcroft house (II.21). The room's wall centers are covered with a red and black symmetrical floral arrange- ment, repeated in a square grid.

Many of the designs in the Musterfield house can be seen in other homes stretching westward through New Hampshire to Walpole, on the eastern bank of the Con- necticut River. They may have been done by the same artisan or by a copyist. It is also possible that the motifs traveled in the opposite direction. Perhaps the artist came up the Connecticut River from points south, copying ear- lier work along the way and incorporating the new de- signs as he stenciled his way to the East Coast.

JOHN MCDONALD, successful merchant, member of the Maine Senate, and a general in the state militia, bought the land where his fine mansion now sits in 1805.

This impressive three-story mansion, replete with ten fireplaces and an arched third-floor ballroom, is interesting because it has not just one layer of early-nineteenth-century painted decoration but two. The first, by a stencil artist working in the classical genre, was probably executed soon after the completion of the house around 1810; it can be seen peeking through the second decoration by a muralist known as Paine,[6] a student of Rufus Porter. The second application includes murals in the front hallway and a second-floor chamber, plus rather weak stenciling in another second-floor chamber.

The earlier work can be seen through the later in the stenciled chamber and the murals in several areas. The design is the "three-rose garland" seen in Rhode Island and Litchfield County, Connecticut, executed in black and red stenciling on pink or red background. In addition, evidence of a second color scheme—namely dark green stenciling on yellow ocher—was found under wallpaper in a small closet area.

Second layer of stenciling in a bedchamber of McDonald house with first frieze (rose festoon) showing through.

Fragment of original reeded border found over the mantel in a back second-floor chamber.

Of great interest are the stenciled fragments recently found under paper in a back chamber, which, in addition to the same rose frieze, contain a very unique overmantel border featuring faux stop reeding—not unlike that in Connecticut, but exactly like that yet to be seen by the reader in a beautifully stenciled room in Loudon, New Hampshire (II.27).

Some say that the Paine murals have only light retouching, but Jean Lipman[7] reports that they were entirely repainted before 1950.

THE HANDSOME, historically important Benjamin Pierce house is undoubtedly the best stenciled museum house in New England, with numerous rooms of re-created early-nineteenth-century classical stenciling. Built by Benjamin Pierce, governor of New Hampshire in 1827–28 and father of Franklin Pierce, the fourteenth president of the United States, it is now owned by the State of New Hampshire and administered by the New Hampshire Department of Parks and Recreation and the Hillsborough Historical Society.

Benjamin is said to have been one of the many Massachusetts farmers who literally dropped their plows in the field when hearing the news of the battle of Lexington in 1775 and marched off to join General Washington's army, which was gathering outside Boston.

After the war he moved his family from Massachusetts to a small farm in the pine-covered hills of Hillsborough County, New Hampshire. Six weeks after Franklin, their fourth son was born, the Pierce family moved into a massive, wood-frame house that had long been under construction.

One original panel of stenciling is retained in the best parlor of Governor Pierce mansion. The other three walls are covered with 1830s French scenic wallpaper, which can be seen reflected in mirror. *Courtesy The Franklin Pierce Homsestead.*

Re-created Classical I–type stenciling in second-floor stair hall. *Courtesy The Franklin Pierce Homsestead.*

Benjamin had obtained a tavern license and built this house to accommodate tavern guests as well as his large family. Perhaps an early visitor to the tavern, which operated only about six years, was an itinerant stencil artist who offered to stencil the walls in exchange for room and board—said to be a common occurrence in those days.

The installation of fine French scenic wallpaper in the best parlor around 1824 suggests a date for a general refurbishing of the house corresponding to Pierce's ascension into political life. A second stencil artist might have been retained at this time to redo rooms previously stenciled or to stencil those not yet adorned. Perhaps this explains the author's sense that the Pierce house contains two distinct styles of stenciling not seen in the same house before. The work under paper in the parlor, of the rose-festoon type, is representative of the earlier hand. Rooms decorated in a similar manner seem to be the best parlor, the second parlor, the side entrance hall, the front entrance hall (first and second floors), the downstairs bedchamber and dressing room, and the upstairs boys' chamber with attached dressing room. Rooms containing the distinctive quarter fan—signature of a second stencil artist—are the ballroom, kitchen, and dressing room of the girls' chamber. The chamber itself seems to be stenciled slightly later by a different hand and sensibility.

Three other fine houses built and probably stenciled before 1810 can be found in Hillsborough County: the Bleak house, built in 1797 in Peterborough; the Salmon Wood house, 1801, also in Peterborough; and the Peter Farnum house, 1790, in Francestown. All contain elaborate stenciling of a type consistent with and probably by the same hand as the rose-festoon frieze under paper in the parlor of the Pierce mansion.

In addition, the stenciling in the Elizabeth Pierce McNeil house (Franklin's sister), built in 1811 next to her father's house, has decoration consistent with the quarter-fan style, perhaps decorated around 1820 by the second artist to visit her father's mansion.

Temperance Tavern. *Courtesy Jacob M. Atwood.*

II.26. *Temperance Tavern, 1793*
Gilmanton, New Hampshire
Artists: Unknown, first 1790s
and second circa 1820

THIS MOST INTERESTING EXAMPLE, the Temperance Tavern has numerous rooms of original stenciling. It has been found in about eight of the fourteen rooms, some with two layers of early classical stenciling probably executed by different hands some twenty years apart. The first stencil treatment probably dates to the 1790s, commissioned either by Joseph Young, who built the tavern in 1793 on the Provincial Road connecting Dover, New Hampshire, to Canada, or by "innkeeper" Samuel French, who purchased it for nine hundred dollars in 1799. The second stencil treatment probably dates to the ballroom addition about 1815, a time of peak highway travel, necessitating enlargement of this popular stagecoach stop.

Stenciling was discovered by new owners in the 1940s when they stripped wallpaper to discover wide stenciled borders in shades of pink, rose, and black. Rose festoons were found at the ceiling, and beautifully rendered urns connected with ropes of bellflowers at the baseboards. A further surprise was in store when they attempted to wash the solid-colored wall centers. Earlier decoration was found under the paint on the whole wall area. The solid-colored pink paint was obviously distemper; therefore it was easily dissolved by water. Some of the first decoration was in the same red/pink/black color scheme, but other rooms were done in a second color scheme,

Original stenciling found in a bedchamber, possibly the second layer of early-nineteenth-century stencil work. *Courtesy Jacob M. Atwood.*

Original stencil work in a second-floor room used as a Masonic meeting room. Two layers of stenciling are clearly visible. *Courtesy Jacob M. Atwood.*

namely dark blue/green on a yellow ocher ground, a combination we have seen before. It is interesting to note that the "three-rose festoon" seems to be shared by the first and second artist, with but one variation. It seems as if the second artist used the favorite frieze of the earlier one to redecorate many of the rooms. The only areas without two layers of stencil designs are the front hall and the ballroom, and perhaps the left front chamber. The remaining walls still retain a unique mingling of two different layers of stenciling, a sort of stenciled double image, providing a rare visual experience and a challenge to wall-stenciling connoisseurs.

This tavern had a great variety of uses over the years, including tavern, county court with private chamber for the judge, local post office, Masonic meeting place, and boardinghouse for a local boys' school. More recently: a bookstore, headquarters for a local weaving association,

private residence, and since the 1960s, a fine bed-and-breakfast located at Gilmanton Four Corners, a charming early-eighteenth-century village in New Hampshire's lakes region.

Folk-type stenciling was also in the Gilmanton area according to Margaret Fabian,[8] who found Eaton-type stenciling in a nearby house and on a fireboard that once decorated a fireplace in the Temperance Tavern. One wonders if this later folk-genre stenciler stayed at the tavern while working in the area and, if so, did he find this high-style stenciling to his liking?

This tavern shares design elements and perhaps artists with several other nearby buildings: the John McDonald house of Limerick, Maine (II.24), which is also on the road from Dover to Canada, and three houses in Loudon, New Hampshire.

THE TOWN OF LOUDON, formed in 1773 when set off from Canterbury, was founded by Scotch and English emigrants and named for one of its grantors, John Campbell, fourth earl of Loudon. It contains a most interesting group of stenciled houses by the same hand linked by artistic similarities to previous examples in Gilmanton, New Hampshire, and Limerick, Maine.

Loudon's first town meeting was held in 1773 in the first part of Captain Abraham Batchelder's home. The Batchelders were leading and influential citizens of Loudon for many years.

The front section of this house, a fine Georgian/colonial-style addition, was built around 1790 and stenciled soon after by a traveling artist who had an affinity for birds.

Red and black stenciling on a once bright blue ground, long under wallpaper in the right front parlor, was recently retrieved by the present owners. It features many new designs in addition to the diamond layout seen in the Temperance Tavern and an overmantel with faux reeding just like that seen in the home of John McDonald

Original stenciling in front parlor of Batchelder house.

Original stenciled compass or roundel stenciled in center of ceiling in same room.

Detail of bird motif found on wall panel between two front windows.

in Limerick, Maine. These three areas are linked to an anonymous artist dubbed "Bird Man" since all three examples of his work in Loudon include a beautifully stenciled bird of unknown species[9] on a between-windows panel at the front of the house.

There is also a very interesting and nicely executed stenciled compass on the ceiling of this extraordinary room, and quite possibly the house originally contained other rooms of early-nineteenth- or late-eighteenth-century-stenciling.

After leaving the Batchelder family ownership in the twentieth century, this house became the country retreat for industrialist Elwyn Lovejoy for many years. Painstakingly restored and renovated by the present owners, it is now expertly run as the Lovejoy Farm Bed and Breakfast.

JONATHAN CLOUGH, SR., who built the initial part of his house about 1771, came from Salisbury, Massachusetts, with his five children and located on a wilderness tract of land in Loudon now known as Clough's Hill. A blacksmith by trade, he was a man of large business and community capacity, serving as town clerk for seventeen years and selectman for four years.

His son, Jonathan, Jr., probably built the large two-story addition to the front, which according to D. Hamilton Hurd's history of Merrimack County was the thing to do between 1790 and 1800.[10] He states, "When settling in town the old proprietors built very large, two-storied houses, and in most instances, upon the top of some eminence or high hill."

Junior was probably also responsible for commissioning an artist to embellish his new home with wonderfully spirited stenciling, which still remains in very good condition in the front hall and in one bedchamber.

Beautifully preserved original stenciling in front second-floor bedchamber.

Extant stencil work found in front stair hall.

The hall, with red and black decoration on yellow or pink backgrounds, is very colorful and visually stimulating. However, the best decoration is to be seen in the front left chamber, a room never fitted with a modern heating system and seldom exposed to sunlight, since it had been until recently shaded by a two-hundred-year-old maple tree. Its current owner treats this room with great care and reverence. He allows visitations only by special overnight guests or suitably reverent wall stencil researchers.

This room is a pristine example of the art of wall stenciling at its finest. And of course there is a panel between the front windows featuring a fanciful bird perched on a stylized flower-filled vase!

The artist apparently also decorated room accessories to match his walls. In the Bertram and Nina Little Collection there was a large (forty by fifty-nine inch) fireboard[11] with three of the same birds and bordered at the top with the same rose-festoon frieze in shades of black and gray with touches of vermilion on natural wood. Visitations to homes decorated by this artist now include measuring the fireplace openings to locate the one originally adorned by this board.

Hopefully the name of this ingenious artist will be discovered someday, but for now he is with great admiration called the "Birdman of Loudon."

Medium-size dome-top box, approximately 10 × 11 × 24 inches, with black and red stenciling on a medium green ground. The red was barely discernible to the naked eye but obvious under black light. Decoration on front is the same stencil design used as a frieze in Temperance Tavern (II.26), and the stylized flower-filled 6½-inch urn on box ends is the same as that stenciled between front windows of a chamber in the Gove house (II.29). *From author's collection.*

Detail of bird panel found between two front windows of front second-floor bedchamber.

II.29. Jonathan Gove house, circa 1800
Loudon, New Hampshire
Artist: "Birdman," circa 1800

THE JONATHAN GOVE HOUSE is the third house with similar stenciling found in the Loudon area by the author. Its builder is unclear, but the surname of Gove and the idea that he came from Gilmanton has long been associated with the history of the property. This is substantiated by the fact that a Jonathan Gove paid $2.69 in highway taxes to Loudon in 1801.[12]

Until 1979 this house contained at least one room, a second-floor chamber, of Birdman-type stenciling, described by the Wiggins brothers as "the best stenciled room they had ever seen." Considering their experience and background, this is high praise indeed.

The expected signature "bird panel" was between two front windows, and a dial-type roundel was stenciled on the ceiling. Both were larger and more elaborate than those seen it the Batchelder and Clough houses. It is interesting to note that the practice of ornamenting ceilings with horological motifs might be of seventeenth-century English invention. John White included the following heading in his 1651 how-to book: "A pretty way to make a sundial on the ceiling of a room, whereby you may know the time of day as you lie in bed."[13] It is hard to imagine how this could be functional, and probably the decorative aspects of this practice continued in favor long after its practical purpose had been forgotten.

This interesting example of the Birdman's stenciling fortunately was recorded by Margaret Fabian as part of her survey before being covered with paint in the early 1980s.

This house most likely had additional stenciled rooms, which were lost so long ago that they are totally forgotten. The best parlor, however, was papered with French wallpaper of the 1820s style. Perhaps more stenciling will be found under that paper someday.

Bird panel that once graced the panel between two front windows of a bedchamber in Gove house. From Fabian Collection. *Courtesy New Hampshire Historical Society.*

SAMUEL KELLY, the first settler of New Hampton, traveled to his new home by oxen-drawn sled in midwinter 1775. Kelly and his family reportedly spent their first night camped on a large boulder on top of Pinnacle Hill,[14] the site of their future home.

His initial, small functional dwelling grew in time into a spacious home with interesting wall decoration. Three rooms of decoration, which probably adorned most rooms at one time, can still be seen. One room, a second-floor chamber, remains in mostly original condition with only light inpainting; a second chamber and the second-floor hallway have been artfully re-created by David Wiggins.

The original work is most interesting because it combines freehand painting and stenciling. The coloration and freehand diamond layout strongly suggest the decoration in the parlor of the Batchelder house (II.27), which has an identical flower spray stenciled in the center of each diamond. The frieze in this room, executed either freehand or with a clumsy stencil technique, is yet another version of the three-rose festoon copied from wallpaper by other stencil artists. Painted freehand at the

Beautifully preserved stenciled and freehand decoration retained in second-floor chamber of Kelly house.

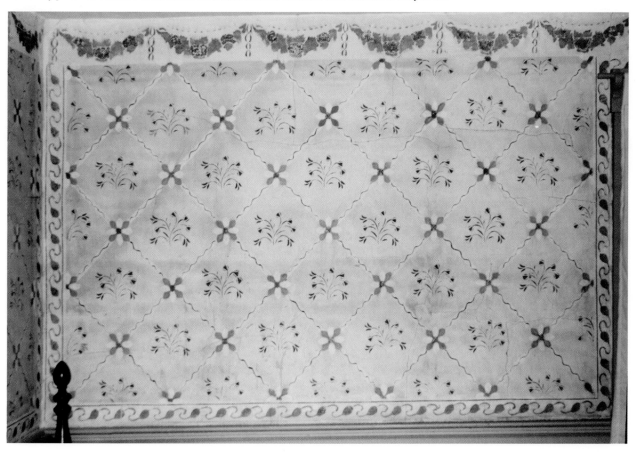

Freehand-painted bird panel between front windows of Kelly bedchamber.

baseboard is an undulating vine, which could have been the inspiration for a stenciled border seen in several sizes in the Clough House (II.28) in Loudon. Another similarity is a four-petaled blossom in the center of each diamond, which is either a badly stenciled or freehand version of one seen in the baseboard motif in the Clough and the Batchelder houses, as well as in the hall of this house. And, of course, there is a bird accenting the panel between the two front windows, but it is painted freehand, not stenciled!

The second chamber, with only periphery borders, is stenciled mostly with painted accents. The frieze is unfamiliar to the author, but the small periphery border was found in the MacDonald house in Limerick, Maine (II.24).

The hallway contains stencil borders and colorations seen before in the Loudon group of houses.

The first explanation for this mingling of techniques and designs is that it is the work of two different hands such as master and apprentice. The second, just as likely explanation is that this house shows two techniques by the same artist, perhaps in the early stage of his career when he is experimenting with the stencil as a more expedient yet very creative tool for a budding wall ornamenter.

This intriguing blend of freehand and stenciled decoration, which could be some of the earliest work of the Birdman, beautifully illustrates how stencil designs and the artists using them evolved during the late eighteenth century.

II.31. Colonel Caleb Bellows house, 1790
Walpole, New Hampshire
Artist: Unknown, circa 1800

A STATELY, FEDERAL-STYLE house was built for Colonel Caleb Bellows by his father, Benjamin Bellows, Jr., on the occasion of his marriage in 1791. Caleb's grandfather, Benjamin Bellows, Sr., had moved in 1752 from Lunenburg, Massachusetts, and presided from a one-hundred-foot-long palisade fort over the settlement of Walpole,[15] a community composed largely of his relatives. This unusual town, located on the eastern bank of the Connecticut River, soon evolved from a fortified family seat to a bustling center of hospitality and a supply base for settlers making their way into Vermont. This great traffic flow brought early social, economic, and intellectual development to the Walpole area.

In 1793 *The Farmers' Weekly Museum*, an early country newspaper, began publication in Walpole. It soon enjoyed unprecedented popularity as a weekly literary periodical, with subscribers in New York City, Philadelphia, Charleston, South Carolina, and all cities between. This paper might have made Walpole most attractive to artists in the middle and southern states.

The stenciling in the Bellows house is both early and high-style, as befits an area of early development. Whether the artist approached from the south or the east is unclear, since similar work has been found in Connecticut to the south as well as eastern New Hampshire.

There is evidence of stenciling in only two areas of this house, which no doubt once had stencil decoration throughout. The front hall stencil decoration was re-created in 1984 by Walpole artist Dutchie Perron. The only other remnant of stenciling is a fragment of plaster from a third-floor room showing black and gray atypical stenciling on a pink ground, which seems to be executed in distemper paint.

Re-created stenciling in front stair hall of Bellows house.

Original sign for late-eighteenth-century Watkins Tavern.

II.32. Alexander Watkins Tavern, 1790

Walpole, New Hampshire

Artist: Unknown, circa 1800

CURRENTLY SERVING AS the clubhouse of the Hopper Golf Club, the handsome Watkins Tavern was built by Alexander Watkins around 1790. A popular publican, he lived there until his death in 1824.

Many taverns flourished in Walpole, but this one seemed to be the choice of many Sunday churchgoers as a place to warm themselves inside and out during the noon break between long services at the unheated meeting-house.

Frizzell's history of Walpole relates this interesting insight into early churchgoing.[16] "Parson Fessenden sometimes preached a cold sermon, and on those occasions he drifted with his parishioners to Uncle Alex's, as he [Alexander Watkins] was called, and quaffed a generous quantity of flip with them."

Stenciling, which shares artistic similarities with that in the Caleb Bellows house, was found in at least four rooms of this ancient tavern and may still be under wallpaper in other areas. Fragments of original, classical stenciling have been preserved in one second-floor bedchamber; in another chamber, re-created stenciling by artist Ruth Wolfe can be seen. An interesting but unrelated roundel design was found in the center of one chamber wall. This was probably added at a later time by Erastus Gates, who stenciled numerous houses in the Plymouth, Vermont, area in the folk style.

Re-created stenciled frieze in bedchamber.

Re-created triple urn border used at baseboard in same bedchamber.

Carlisle house. *Courtesy Jeanne and Peter Jeffries.*

II.33. John Carlisle house, circa 1785

Walpole, New Hampshire

Artist: Classical II, circa 1800

THE MASSIVE, neoclassical-style Carlisle house seems to have evolved in various stages between 1760 and 1790. The first section, present in 1760,[17] was probably a simple "starter house," with the front section added in two parts sometime later. This was a fairly common practice in late-eighteenth-century New Hampshire. "It was very popular to build a large house and, if the expense was too heavy, a two-story half house was built first and the other half added whenever able."[18] The exact builders of the three eighteenth- or early-nineteenth-century sections are unclear, with at least five candidates suggested in the Frizzell *History of Walpole.*

John Carlisle, a well-heeled shoemaker, either purchased the property around 1790, at which time it was thought to be in its present form, or was responsible for adding the right front section to his very fashionable home. Either way Carlisle probably was responsible for commissioning a stencil artist of the classical genre, but not the same artist who stenciled the previous two Walpole examples.

Fragments of stenciling recently were found under wallpaper in three areas. This stenciling is related stylistically to that found in Hillsborough County, New Hampshire, and the West Narragansett Bay area of Rhode Island.

A stenciled faux swag frieze found in a bedchamber is very similar to that in Apponaug, Rhode Island (II.7), and in Hillsborough County, New Hampshire,[19] the coloration being the only difference. The rose-and-tassel festoon frieze found in a second bedchamber has more in common with the work in Hillsborough, New Hampshire, and Rhode Island than it does with a version of the same design in the Loudon, New Hampshire, area, indicating that the Walpole work is not by the "Birdman" but simply another example of the free exchange of designs between stencil artisans.

Fragments of a stylized flower-filled vase found on these walls are identical to a vase decoration used profusely in another Hillsborough County house, the Peter Farnum house,[20] which also has definite style ties to the West Bay area of Rhode Island. A faint, small swag frieze in a back first-floor room is also found in the Hillsborough area.

Dutchie Perron, the aforementioned Walpole stencil artist, has recorded other houses in the area with stenciling by this artist, including one with the five-rose-festoon frieze seen before in the Pierce house (II.25) and the Peck house in Rhode Island (II.10). One of these Walpole-area

Three borders from Carlisle house. *Top:* Frieze found in a bed-chamber. *Middle:* Border used as a vertical in same chamber, but seen as a frieze in a back chamber of Dering house (II.37), Long Island, New York. *Bottom:* Fragments of frieze from second chamber, which seems to be identical to that in a parlor in Arnold house (II.7). *Courtesy Jeanne and Peter Jeffries.*

houses, the Lewis-Hopper house, unfortunately burned to the ground in the early 1990s.

It would seem that this prolific, well-traveled artist working in the classical genre of wall stenciling had a lengthy and no doubt financially rewarding stay in Walpole, a town as architecturally beautiful and culturally alive today as it was two hundred years ago.

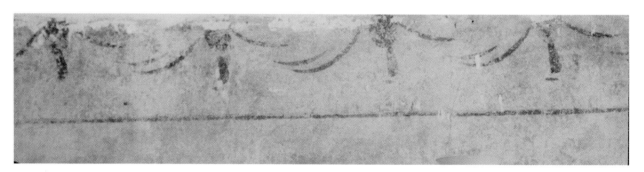

Grimes house.

II.34. *John Grimes house, 1801*
Keene, New Hampshire
Artist: Jothan Stearns, 1816–17

ACCORDING TO Marjorie Smith's 1971 book, *Historic Homes of Cheshire County*,[21] this southwesternmost part of New Hampshire was visited by numerous stencil artists. Built in 1801 in Keene, the John Grimes house is significant because it introduces both a type of work never seen before and, possibly, two new stencil artists.

John Grimes, of Scottish descent, came to Keene from Pelham, Massachusetts. He and his family lived in a log cabin while he built his Cape-style house.

The left front parlor is a room of exceptional beauty. Its decoration features a rare example of stenciling combined with freehand work by an artist of great talent. The walls are covered with a warm beige aqueous paint and decorated in red, green, and black with semitransparent white accents, all in distemper; the result is a very attractive color scheme. The stenciled frieze, a double swag in deep green and red with a diamond in the center of each, is beautifully accented with elongated white teardrop strokes. An airy stenciled black border, vaguely resembling one of the Classical II group, frames all of the architectural elements. The main part of the wall is divided into large, elongated diamonds by lines of delicate black brush strokes similar to those in the Foxcroft house (II.21). Centered in each is a very delicate, elongated freehand three-bud floral spray in green and red with filmy white accents. The overall effect is one of skilled and subtle workmanship.

Tradition holds that the Grimes house artist was twenty-one-year-old Jothan Stearns (1791–1832), son of Jonathan Stearns of Hopkinton, Massachusetts, who reportedly learned his craft while apprenticed to his uncle, Jedutham Bullin of Keene. While painting the Grimes house parlor in 1816 and 1817, Jothan fell in love with the Grimes's daughter, Mary. They married in 1817, lived in Keene for a while, and then returned to Hopkinton. After Jothan died in 1832, Mary returned to Keene, and her descendants lived in the Grimes house well into the twentieth century.

This family tradition provides us with two new names of possible wall decorators who worked in the Massachusetts and New Hampshire area, using the stencil technique or painting freehand, or both, between approximately 1800 and 1840. Jothan Stearns and Jedutham Bullin are welcome additions to a rather short list of artisans.

Extant stenciled and freehand decoration in front parlor of Grimes house.

While Vermont was the last of the New England states to be developed, it caught up quickly. After 1760, a new spirit of settlement traveled into the upper Connecticut River Valley, Vermont, and northern New Hampshire. Between 1760 and 1776, Vermont's population swelled from 120 white families to about 20,000 white settlers.[22] This growth, and the accompanying building boom that continued well into the first part of the nineteenth century, attracted a number of itinerant wall painters.

Over a lifetime of seeking out and recording examples of American wall stenciling, Jessica Hill Bond—a resident of Dorset, Vermont—discovered numerous stenciled walls in her home state. Beginning with the fall 1997 issue, her findings were published serially in the *Decorator*, the biannual publication of the Historical Society of Early American Decoration, of which Bond is a charter member and master craftsman.

Bond recorded diverse examples of wall stenciling in the classical as well as the folk style from all over Vermont, and by many different artists. Examples of the Folk Group include more work by Erastus Gates (I.33), work by several artists heretofore unknown by the author, and walls most likely stenciled by Moses Eaton, Jr., himself.

The most important Eaton example is one found by Bond in Hartland Four Corners, Vermont, that shows faint traces of classical stenciling peeking out from under an Eaton-attributed frieze. The classical work probably dated to the early part of the nineteenth century and thus was on the wall a good twenty years before Eaton visited the area to add his stenciling. This example provides impressive visual proof that the Classical Group of stenciling preceded the Folk Group by several decades in some cases.

Bond also recorded numerous diverse examples of the earlier classical type of stenciling by as many as four different artists. The only obvious missing examples are those of the Classical I artist or group.

Our first example of classical stenciling in Vermont is fortuitously located in one of the state's best museums. It could be among the earliest stenciling in the state.

II.35. Salmon Dutton house, 1782

Cavendish, Vermont

Artist: Unknown, circa 1800

BUILT IN THE center of the town of Cavendish by Salmon Dutton, who came to Vermont in 1781 from Ashby, Massachusetts, early in the twentieth century, the Dutton house fell on difficult times and was abandoned for some fifty years. In 1950 it was given to the Shelburne Museum by the Vermont Historical Society and moved to the museum site a year later.

Fortunately, the stenciling found in at least four rooms of the house was of the earlier borders-only type. Thus samples could be more readily removed before the dismantling process to serve as examples of the original during the re-creation of the stenciling at a later time. The stenciling was re-created by the late Duncan Munro soon after the house was reassembled at the museum.

This house is a two-and-a-half-story Georgian saltbox-style home, with low ceilings and small- to medium-size rooms with no chair rail molding. Thus the "border only" style was adequate to decorate this simple late-eighteenth-century house. However, as houses got bigger and more elaborate, with higher ceilings and more spacious plaster areas to ornament, artists working in the classical style felt the need to fill the larger wall centers as well as the peripheral areas with decoration. Thus vertical borders to be used on the wall centers were incorporated into their design portfolios.

The four stenciled rooms of the Dutton house were decorated with red and black borders on white or salmon-colored grounds, with plain yellow ocher wall centers throughout. The designs were of a small to medium proportion, many of which were seen before in New England plus many of new composition. Many of these motifs, including the urn baseboard, have been found in several other Vermont structures, including one in Chester.[23]

These designs have also been found in Massachusetts from Assonet[24] in the southeastern part of the state to North Orange,[25] located on a much-traveled route between Boston and Brattleboro, Vermont, which is close to Chester and Cavendish, in the southeastern part of the state. This could suggest that the stencil artist approached either up the Connecticut River or from eastern Massachusetts.

Having a house with four rooms of well-restored designs by the same early artist is an extremely valuable tool for assigning stencil work to a particular, though unknown, artist or pair of artists. The Dutton house, with at least four different stenciled friezes, baseboards, and vertical borders, is a virtual sampler of this artist's work.

It is interesting that one of the motifs from this sampler was used in the Grimes house of Keene, New Hampshire (II.34), which is mostly freehand decoration with a few stenciled accents including a narrow border used in the Dutton house parlor. Since the Grimes house work is attributed to Jothan Stearns and/or his uncle and teacher Jedutham Bullin, there is a very slim possibility that the Dutton house was stenciled by one of them. Of the two, the older Bullin from Keene is the best bet.

Renderings of stenciled friezes from Dutton house. *Top to bottom:* 5⅝-inch-high, three-rose festoon found in dining room/parlor, executed in black, red, and white on white band; 5⅛-inch border used in west bedchamber, stenciled in black, red, and white on a salmon serrated band; 5⅜-inch border in parlor, stenciled in black on a salmon pink band; 4½-inch border in bedchamber, stenciled in black and red on a white band. All wall centers are yellow ocher.

Secondary borders used in Dutton house. *Top to bottom:* 3⅛-inch-high border used above baseboard in west bedchamber, black and red on salmon; 2⅜-inch border used above chair rail in parlor, black on white band; 1½-inch border used vertically in parlor, black on white band; 2½-inch border used vertically in dining parlor, black on white; 1¾-inch border used as a vertical in west bedchamber, black on white band; 1⅜-inch border used in west bedchamber, black on salmon.

Seven-inch-high urn and bellflower swag border used above baseboard in dining parlor and east bedchamber, stenciled in black, red, and white on yellow ocher wall coloration.

II.36. Vermont Stenciled Houses

Unusual frieze from the Rich Hollow Tavern, North Montpelier. *Photo by Polly Forcier.*

Second frieze from Rich Hollow Tavern. *Photo by Polly Forcier.*

Border from Wright Farm, Chester. *Photo by Polly Forcier.*

VERMONT HAS A surprisingly large number of classical-genre stenciled walls, mostly located in early villages along or near the banks of the Connecticut River and along the early road that led from Boston, Massachusetts, to Lower Canada.

An initial reaction to this great volume and variety of stenciling could be that numerous artists visited the state. But on closer inspection many of the stenciled buildings with multiple stenciled rooms share at least one design, making one think that a very prolific stencil artist, perhaps with a partner in possession of a vast portfolio of designs, produced this bounty of wall stenciling. Most Vermont stenciling falls under the very large umbrella of the Classical II group, with the "rose festoon" frieze found in many of the examples. The Classical I group, however, did not seem to cross the Connecticut River into Vermont.

A survey of a few known Vermont examples, courtesy of Polly Forcier, presents an intriguing picture. Starting in the northwestern part of the state, the Leavenworth house of Hinesburg and the Rich Hollow Tavern of North Montpelier, both along the early road to Lower Canada, feature many unfamiliar designs but include those seen before in the Dutton house (II.35), the Carlisle house of Walpole, New Hampshire (II.33), the Peck house of Wickford, Rhode Island (II.10), and the Dering house of Sag Harbor, New York (II.37). The south-to-north distribution of these designs suggests that the artist approached by river from the south before heading northwest on the road to Canada.

Farther south near the banks of the Connecticut River, the Quechee Inn in the town of the same name seems to be decorated by a different hand than the previous examples with the exception of one very insignificant vertical border, which seems also to be used in the Leavenworth house.

Continuing south to Chester, which is just south of Cavendish, stenciling found in the Wright farm bears a strong resemblance to that in the Dutton house, with a mostly borders-only layout used by the artist.

West of Chester, almost on the border with New York State, in the town of Dorset, stenciling very similar to that in the Quechee Inn once decorated the walls of the Barrows house. In the collection of Jessica Bond, the aforementioned stencil researcher from Dorset, are early stencils[26] that seem to include designs used in the Barrow house and the Quechee Inn, with a few also seen in the

"Rose festoon" border found in ballroom of Wright farmhouse, very similar to that in Wickford, Rhode Island. *Photo by Polly Forcier.*

Urn border used above chair rail in parlor of Rich Hollow Tavern, identical to that in Watkins Tavern (II.32). *Photo by Polly Forcier.*

Leavenworth house of Hinesburg. An inscription on the back seems to indicate that they belonged to a Henry Rogers, who was in Chelsea, Vermont, in 1814! It could be that Mr. Rogers was the artist responsible for the stencil decoration in at least the Barrows house of Dorset and the Quechee Inn.

Several probable reasons for the vast blending of designs found on Vermont walls come to mind. Perhaps the demand for wall stenciling in Vermont was such that numerous copyists were attracted to the area, or perhaps the span of its popularity was long enough to require the sprucing up of the early-nineteenth-century work by a second stencil artist working the area some twenty or so years later. The best parlors and front halls at least would have been restenciled if there were an artist available. Often the lesser back rooms would be left with their original early decoration intact. Thereby stenciling by two different artists working twenty years apart could be found in the same house. We have already seen walls in New Hampshire (II.26) and Maine (II.24) with two layers of early-nineteenth-century decorative painting.

Whatever the reason, wall stenciling in Vermont flourished during the first quarter of the nineteenth century, fueled by an influx of artistic talent both from the coastal areas to the east as well as from the south by way of New England's historic waterway, the Connecticut River.

Conclusion to the Classical Group in New England

The neoclassical influence on American wall stenciling produced a body of work of infinite beauty and variety, which uniquely complemented the decorative arts and politics of urban Federal America. Smaller in proportion as well as volume, the style was adopted by fewer artisans than the folk genre, seldom traveling beyond the western New England border with only a few examples recorded thus far outside that area.

In general, Classical Group stenciling seems to date to a slightly earlier period than the Folk Group, since it is found in a great proportion of houses constructed prior to 1790, an indication that it could have developed before that date; and it seems to die out in the 1830s, well before the demise of the Folk Group in the 1840s.

A study of the designs and styles used suggests that perhaps as many as six artists were working in the classical genre. Unfortunately no written documentation or signed walls have been found thus far, making definite attributions all but impossible. Several names have come to the fore; however, the author's research has not produced enough proof to list them as probable or even possible wall stencilers.

The team of Daniel Bartling and Sylvester Hall, who advertised in New Haven, Connecticut, in 1804, seemed very promising. But upon a careful rereading of their newspaper advertisement, it appears more likely that they were offering to apply a protective coat of varnish to previously painted walls, rather than to ornament the walls themselves. Varnishing walls previously painted with aqueous distemper painting was a common practice around 1800. (For more information see appendix A on paint materials.)

The text of their ad appears below:

Connecticut Herald, New Haven,
February 28, March 6, and March 13, 1804
VARNISHING & POLISHING, in a new and elegant manner D. BARTLING & S. HALL
Respectfully inform the Ladies and Gentlemen of New Haven, that they will execute on Mahogany Furniture of every description, either old or new, that beautiful CHINESE MODE OF VARNISHING and POLISHING, in a manner that will last for years and always retain a pleasing and beautiful gloss, without the old and laborious method of rubbing and brushing, which not only takes a great deal of the time of the servant, but destroys and racks the strength of the furniture, and defaces the natural color of that beautiful wood.

Also, that truly elegant FRENCH MODE of VARNISHING on plain or stamped Paper Hangings, when fixed in rooms, which will secure the colors from fading, cause them to appear brighter, effectually prevent bugs and vermin from collecting in them and bear washing without injury to the color or gloss. Likewise . . . that much admired imitation of stamped paper, done on the walls of rooms, far superior to the manner commonly practiced in this state.

Even if their ad did mean that they were actually decorating walls, it is not clear if they stenciled or did freehand decoration or even murals. Both Margaret Coffin[27] and Nina Fletcher Little[28] suggested that they were freehand wall painters. Bartling's earlier ad in a Boston newspaper and later in Providence said nothing about painting walls, but it did place him in Rhode Island about the time the classical stenciling was executed in Wickford. Hall, on the other hand, did apprentice in some sort of craft, is credited with painting a scenic overmantel in Connecticut, and removed from Connecticut to Burke, Vermont, an area of great stencil activity. Nonetheless, as satisfying as it would be to credit Bartling and/or Hall with a portion of the stenciled houses in New England, the evidence is far from conclusive.

Another promising name was Braverter Gray, who has been mentioned as the artist responsible for stenciling in the Hillsborough, New Hampshire, area. After studying the available documentation, it was very disappointing to conclude that there is no definite information to support that theory; in fact it is just as likely that he was a carriage maker/painter.

Before publishing her book on American wall painting in 1954, Nina Fletcher Little acquired a collection of ephemera belonging to a Braverter Gray. Information contained in this collection states that Gray, who was born in Hillsborough in 1785, apprenticed with a Jonathan Webster from 1800 to 1804, at which time he returned home to Hillsborough. Unfortunately Webster's field of expertise is not known. In addition, if Little, after studying all this material in her personal collection, had considered Gray or Webster, his teacher, to be wall decorators of some sort, their names would have been listed under her "Biographical List of Painters" on page 15 in the aforementioned book. They were not.

Sotheby's auctioned the Gray collection in 1994. The auction catalogue describes the material as a "fascinating collection of information about paints, painting, japanning and decorating woods and stone" and goes on to say, "account book lists various jobs in Hillsborough, Salem and Boston, sales and repairs of sleighs, trunks, etc., and the purchases and sales he made to the people of those towns." There is no mention of decorating interiors.

Little uses the Gray collection in the first chapter of her aforementioned book under the heading "Interior Paint, 18th Century" as examples of homemade recipes for eighteenth-century oil-based paint traditionally used on wooden interiors, furniture, sleighs, trunks, and so on. The recipe for distemper paint made by mixing pigment with boiled glue and whiting, the paint of choice by nineteenth-century wall decorators, is not included.

Braverter Gray was in the right place at the right time, but there is too little evidence to proclaim him a wall stenciler, as yet.

Thus the artists responsible for the large and impressive body of classical stenciling in Federal New England remain in complete anonymity—for now!

D. Bartling ad, which appeared in a July 1799 Providence newspaper. *Courtesy The Rhode Island Historical Society.*

Chapter 11

The State of New York and the Niagara Peninsula

By 1810 New York City had not only recuperated from the vigors of the Revolutionary War but had firmly established itself as the leading seaport, financial center, and artistic capital of the country. City directories of 1811 and 1812 contained numerous ads for artists engaged in practicing and teaching a vast array of decorative painting techniques. Nearly eighty of the studios of the advertising artists were located below Fourth Street in lower Manhattan.[1]

The author's reaction to these facts was a strong sense that there must have been nineteenth-century wall stenciling in New York City, especially since between 1790 and 1820 hundreds, if not thousands, of Federal-style town houses were said to have been constructed for the mushrooming numbers of prosperous master craftsmen, small merchants, and upwardly moving professionals in the area.[2] These town houses would seem to provide perfect commissions for wall-stenciling artisans, probably working in the classical genre.

Unfortunately, the same rapid development that attracted wall painters to an area seems to be responsible for the demise of most of their work. Putnam's 1853 series, "New York Daguerreotyped," stated that the cities' rate of change had "utterly obliterated everything that is old and venerable, — leaving not a single land-mark — of the dwellingplaces of out ancestors."[3]

This "rapid, feverish, itching for change"[4] most likely accounts for the lack of extant wall stenciling in New York City as well as neighboring metropolitan areas of eastern New Jersey and western Long Island, areas that most assuredly had a goodly number of Federa-period paint-decorated walls, including numerous examples of mid-Atlantic–style wall stenciling.

Stenciled roundel found on ceiling of second-floor ballroom of Bristol Tavern in southeastern New York State. About 4 feet in diameter, it is one of two originally on the ceiling of the twin-fireplace meeting room.

II.37. Henry Dering house, 1750 and 1789
Sag Harbor, Long Island, New York
Artist: Classical II, circa 1800

THE "HARBOR OF SAG" emerged as an important coastal port early in the eighteenth century. Its extreme easterly position on the tip of Long Island's southern fork made it a more desirable colonial port than that of New York City to the west. Settled in the mid–seventeenth century by English emigrants and later populated by English from New England, mainly Connecticut, it had social and commercial ties to New England rather than to the Dutch western part of Long Island—much to the exasperation of the colonial Dutch and later English governors.

During British occupation throughout the Revolutionary War, many residents fled to their origins in Connecticut. In 1777 a number of these patriotic refugees crossed Long Island Sound in whaling boats and raided the British troops, burning twelve British vessels at anchor in the Harbor of Sag.

After the war a cosmopolitan community quickly developed, which was sophisticated enough to support Long Island's first newspaper, the *Long Island Herald*, first published in 1791. A search of early issues of this paper for advertisements placed by artists revealed many articles originating in Walpole, New Hampshire. David Frothingham, editor of the *Herald*, obviously subscribed to a Walpole newspaper. He was in good company since it is said that President George Washington himself subscribed to the *Farmer's Weekly Museum*, Walpole's renowned newspaper.

Also discovered in the Sag Harbor paper were several ads placed by artists seeking work in this cultured community. They were general in the services offered and not specifically seeking wall-stenciling commissions. The most interesting is one placed by an experienced artist from Hartford, Connecticut, who was about to set up shop in Sag Harbor, seeking to take advantage of the artistic and financial vitality of the area.

At least one wall stencil artist visited eastern Long Island, as demonstrated by the fragments of wall stenciling found in a museum house called the Custom House. This house is composed of two sections; one a 1750s half house that was joined to a late-eighteenth-century house to create this large Federal house with a cornice board decorated with a carved-rope motif. This was the home of Henry Dering, first custom master and postmaster of Sag Harbor. It is not clear if the custom and post offices were actually housed in his residence or at one of the many other properties owned by the Dering family in the vicinity of the harbor.

This house narrowly escaped demolishing in the 1940s

Dering house. *Courtesy of the Society for the Preservation of Long Island Antiquities.*

before being purchased and moved to its new location by Charles Edison, former governor of New Jersey. It is now a revered museum under the care of the Society for the Preservation of Long Island Antiquities.

The stenciling found in the two second-floor chambers is a small and understated version of that seen before in Rhode Island, Connecticut, and New Hampshire. Its second-floor location could partially explain its subdued appearance, since the more visible first-floor rooms usually received the artist's most ambitious work. The narrow borders-only layout and blue/green on yellow color scheme strongly suggest early work of the Classical II type as seen along Main Street in Wickford, Rhode Island (II.8 and II.9).

Work by this artist in the Carlisle house in Walpole, New Hampshire (II.33), is an example of his development into a very flamboyant decorator indeed. The same design used as a frieze in the Dering house has been downgraded to a vertical corner filler in the Carlisle house. Recent photographs of the same design found under wallpaper in both houses show them both to be strikingly similar in technique and coloration. Both suggest original colorations of dark blue/green stenciling on medium yellow ocher ground, which aged or faded to light blue stenciling on an off-white ground. The same transient quality of the yellow ocher pigment is also apparent in the Wick-

ford houses, with only faint traces of the yellow ground still visible.

One gets the feeling that the work in the Dering house is an example of very early work by the Classical II artist, who developed his skill, portfolio, and confidence as he worked his way up the Connecticut River Valley, stopping first to decorate a group of pre-Revolutionary houses on the west side of Rhode Island's Narragansett Bay. Or perhaps he formed a partnership with a more experienced and flamboyant artisan.

Other decorative painting was discovered in the Dering house. The front chamber, in addition to stenciled borders, had some sort of faux paneling in the dado area, and most of the doors in the house were grained in faux red or yellow cedar finish, much of which has been nicely re-created. One can't help but wonder what painted decoration, if any, was on the walls of the first-floor parlors.

Finding this work in an early eastern Long Island seaport, positioned prominently on the route traveled routinely by packet ships connecting early seaport cities, provokes many questions about the artist's travel route. He seems to have been on his way north, but from where? Was he recently arrived from the Continent? Did he sail out of Philadelphia? Or did he depart from a southern port, leaving a trail of familiarly stenciled walls in southern and mid-Atlantic coastal cities and towns?

Detail of two extant borders in a second-floor back chamber, both seen in the Carlisle House (II.33) Walpole, New Hampshire.

THE SECOND EXAMPLE of classical-genre stenciling in New York State is quite atypical of that seen thus far in the six states that make up New England. Its excellent design and execution suggest an artist well trained and possessing considerable artistic talent, perhaps originating from a different area than the previous artists.

The Amos Bristol Tavern is located in Delaware County, New York, where the headwaters of several important rivers, the Delaware for which it is named and the Susquehanna, originate.

Several historic references to the use of these aqueous travel routes have been noted. In 1723 the first wave of Germans to settle in the Schoharie and Mohawk Valleys, around 1710, tired of the extremely harsh conditions in New York State, fled the area. They made their way to the headwaters of the Susquehanna and floated down that river to the mouth of the Swatara Creek and on to Tulpohocken, Pennsylvania.[5] French's 1860 *Gazetteer of New York* states that lumber was rafted in large quantities from Delaware County, New York, to Philadelphia, Pennsylvania, on the Delaware River.[6]

Perhaps the most important access to the Treadwell area was the Susquehanna-Catskill Turnpike, which was chartered in 1800 and opened before 1804. It ran from the town of Catskill on the Hudson River (the primary route connecting New York City to Upstate New York) to Unadilla on the Susquehanna, passing directly in front of the Bristol Tavern. A western extension was constructed shortly after, making it a major route from metropolis to the western frontier. This route was in its prime before the Erie Canal opened in 1825. Traffic was so heavy that at times there was a continuous line of teams passing an average of one hotel per mile, most or all of which filled to capacity every night.

Bristol Tavern and the four others in Treadwell were certainly well situated. Settlers as well as artisans would have stayed there on their way to western New York, northern Pennsylvania, and on to Ohio. A 1958 article in the Binghamton, New York, *Sunday Press* described the Bristol Inn as one of the most delightful and best known on the highway, which was ornamented throughout with "beautiful stenciling in color!" Unfortunately most of this decoration was sacrificed in the 1950s in order to save the house after an extended period of neglect.

Only two areas of extant stenciling are still visible in a second-floor ballroom, one panel on the upper side of an inside wall and a roundel in the center of the ceiling,

Early (1939) photograph of early-nineteenth-century stenciling in Bristol Tavern ballroom and Masonic meeting room. *Courtesy Theodore McDowell.*

which includes the Masonic "square and compass" motif in the center. This room was used as a meeting place for the Aurora Lodge No. 227 between 1813 and 1834. The Masonic emblem was probably not original to the stenciling, being added at a later time. This also occurred in the Temperance Tavern of Gilmanton, New Hampshire (II.26).

An early (1939) photo of this room shows numerous stenciled motifs on all wall surfaces. A surviving wallpaper fragment shows a stencil motif from below the dado area in reverse on the back. The in situ stenciling on these walls seems to be impervious to water; however, the stenciling found on the back of that wallpaper fragment is easily removed by gently rubbing with a moistened Q-Tip, perhaps indicating that the stenciling was treated with an application of a sealer at some point in its history (see appendix A on paint materials).

Two small Polaroid pictures from the 1960s show a ceiling roundel and an overmantel that seem to be from another second-floor chamber. The ceiling decoration is now painted over, but the mantel as well as the rest of the wall area are papered over.

It is interesting to note that the two ceiling roundels in the Bristol Tavern bear a resemblance to those in two houses in Loudon, New Hampshire (II.27 and II.29). While not identical, they are very similar in coloration, style, and proportion. One wonders if the papered-over stenciling in the rest of the tavern might provide more similarities, somehow joining the three houses.

The walls of most of the remaining first-floor rooms, the hallway, and the remaining second-floor rooms are also covered with wallpaper, seemingly all dating to the same period. This presents a possibility of retrieving more of this fine stenciling someday. All the ceilings are painted, of course, presenting slim hope of retrieving additional stenciled ceiling medallions.

For now we must be content with enjoying the limited but choice extant examples of this craftsman's artistry, taking heart in the thought that a future stencil enthusiast might someday uncover more of his work!

Detail of intricate stenciled swag frieze. *Courtesy Theodore McDowell.*

II.39. Stephen Bates house, 1808
Canandaigua, New York
Artist: Unknown, 1810–1815

THE FINAL NEW YORK example of classical-style wall stenciling is very similar to, but not identical to, that seen thus far in New England. It was found in a house built by the eldest son of a local publican by the name of Phineas Bates, who came to Canandaigua in 1791 from Durham, Connecticut.[7]

In 1808 his son, Stephen, purchased 233 acres of farmland just outside Canandaigua. He married the daughter of a local deacon and added this house onto a much smaller one already on his property.

Border stenciling found in a first-floor parlor is described as being in red and black on a white ground, surrounding walls center-painted "salmon pink," a color combination very typical of New England stenciling of the same genre.

The stenciling, which probably dates to 1810–15, was painted over in the 1970s. Fortunately Philip Parr recorded the stenciling prior to its demise.

Facsimile of stenciling in a first-floor parlor of Bates house. *From tracings by Lois Tribe and Philip Parr.*

Shadwick house.

II.40. Thomas Shadwick house, 1835
Winona, Ontario, moved to St. Catharines
Artist: Unknown, 1835–1840

Re-created stenciling in parlor of Shadwick house. Also depicts faux rosewood paneling retained in this parlor. *Photo by Nick Traynor.*

ARTISTS WORKING IN the classical style of wall stenciling also visited the Niagara Peninsula of Ontario during the first half of the nineteenth century.

The first example of their work is the Thomas Shadwick house, originally located close to Winona, Ontario, but moved in the 1970s by Nick Treanor, a previous owner, to save it from being demolished to make way for the development of a gravel quarry. It now sits high on a hill, just a short distance down Pelham Road from the Loyalist Brown house (I.44), with its fine Georgian portico displayed at full advantage.

Built by Shadwick, a lumber mill owner who is said to have been a Loyalist from New Jersey, it was completed in 1835, according to an inscription still visible over a front parlor doorway that reads, "T. S. Clinton 1835." The initials obviously stand for Thomas Shadwick, the owner and probably commissioner of the stencil work and faux wood graining in the house; "Clinton" is the township where the house originally stood, and 1835 establishes the date for the completion of the house and possibly the wood graining and stenciling.

The skillfully executed faux bois that embellishes the elaborate woodwork is still in fine condition. It was described by Jeanne Minhinnick as "reddish figure graining, with mahoganizing or more probably rosewood, picked out in light yellow striping to imitate inlay." [8] This

yellow "stringing" was probably accomplished by the removal technique, which involved using an appropriate tool to remove the wet glaze to expose the yellow ground coat. It is quite possible that the woodwork was grained before being installed, since the woodwork is applied directly to the lath with the plaster walls applied after.

Unfortunately the handsome border stenciling in shades of rose, green, blue, and black that once decorated the walls of two front parlors has been painted over.

The stenciling and graining in the Shadwick house could have been executed by the same hand; however, quite often the painting of the wooden elements of a room was the specialty of a different artist using a different paint medium, namely oil-based paint, rather than the water-based paint preferred by decorators of plaster wall surfaces. Since Thomas Shadwick's trade was the milling of lumber, it has been suggested that the elaborate woodwork with its impressive painted finish was a sort of sample of his product. Perhaps, in addition to finely milled lumber, he supplied a skilled woodworker and a staff artist to finish the woodwork in the homeowner's choice of painted finish such as oak, cedar, mahogany, or walnut. Or perhaps this skilled carpenter was also talented with a paintbrush.

The Shadwick house, a fine example of Loyalist architecture, is in fine condition, presenting the possibility that someday its stenciling, which was meticulously re-created in the 1980s, can be retrieved from under its late-twentieth-century covering of paint.

Another Niagara Peninsula house, located not far from the Shadwick house, is said to have had similar graining and stenciling, and perhaps woodwork fashioned by the same wood artist as the Shadwick house. It is the Beamer Tavern, located in Pelham. This nineteenth-century tavern has been nicely restored, but its badly deteriorated stenciling and graining are now under paper and paint, with no picture surviving to record their existence.

II.41. Mary Gage farmhouse, 1796
Stoney Creek, Ontario
Artist: Unknown, circa 1820 and 1860

Courtesy of the Battlefield House Museum, Stoney Creek, Ontario, Canada.

MARY JONES GAGE and her two children, James and Elizabeth, moved to Canada from Orange County, New York, in 1787, making them some of the earliest settlers of the Niagara Peninsula. Her husband, a wealthy farmer, was fatally wounded while fighting for the Americans during the Revolution. Her brother, Augustus Jones, was a surveyor for the British government in Upper Canada, which probably accounts for Mary receiving a land grant from the British Crown. Mary and her family cleared the land, commenced farming, and by 1796 completed a one-and-a-half-story farmhouse. As the years progressed, her growing family prospered both in farming and in the merchant trade.

In 1812, however, all they had accomplished was threatened by the outbreak of war between America and Britain for the second time in three decades. This time, many of the battlefields were located in the Niagara area of Upper Canada.

In the spring of 1813, a pivotal battle known as the Battle of Stoney Creek occurred on the cleared fields surrounding the Gage farmhouse. The vastly outnumbered English managed to rout the Yanks by staging a surprise predawn attack while their opponents were still sleeping. This battle changed the momentum of the war in favor of the English, thereby preventing the annexation of the Niagara Peninsula and perhaps all of Upper Canada by the United States.

After the battle, many casualties, English and Americans alike, were treated by English doctors at a makeshift hospital set up at the aforementioned farmhouse.

During a 1970s restoration of this historic site, not one but two layers of nineteenth-century wall stenciling were discovered beneath subsequent layers of paint in the front hall.

Jeanne Minhinnick, who oversaw the re-creation of the old paint of the Gage house in the early 1970s, describes the first layer of stenciling as "much earlier and finer" with "imaginative delicacy and professional style" and goes on to say that the re-creation of the second stenciling only "roughly followed the (earlier) design beneath."[9]

The first, dating possibly to the 1820s, was very frag-mented and faint. Only one small sample could be retained. The second application, very simplistic and of a much later period, was re-created on wall board and placed over the original to protect both treatments. One original section of the later period can be seen framed under glass just inside the front door.

Perhaps with new technology for retrieving stenciled decoration from under later paint layers, someday more of the earlier stenciling can be retrieved from under the 1860s work, making the stenciling displayed on the walls of the Gage house more consistent with 1830s tastes in Upper Canada, which are so skillfully reflected in the room interiors and furnishings depicted consistently throughout the house.

Currently called the Battlefield House, this historic site is now beautifully restored and operated as a fine museum by the Niagara Parks Commission.

Late-nineteenth-century stenciling in the front hall of the Gage house. *Courtesy of the Battlefield House Museum, Stoney Creek, Ontario, Canada.*

Chapter 12

The States Below the Mason-Dixon Line

A scant five examples of classical-genre wall stenciling have come to light in the states south of the Pennsylvania border. They are vastly different in style and degree of sophistication, clearly demonstrating the vast contrast between the affluent urban coastal areas and the rural areas of the Federal-period South.

The two "tidewater" examples represent the work of formally trained artists commissioned by wealthy elitists very much influenced by English taste, politics, and customs.

The trio of "backwater" examples, all from Virginia's Shenandoah Valley, were commissioned and executed by those who lived outside the shadow of English taste, being more influenced by their area's infinite variety of ethnic and cultural backgrounds. These differences readily amalgamated in the atmosphere of untethered optimism that prevailed during the post-Revolution years to create a style of wall stenciling that can be considered purely American.

The trail of Classical Group wall stenciling, which seems to have originated in southeastern New England, ends in the southern section of the Shenandoah Valley, seemingly never crossing into the southern or northern frontier states.

Detail of original stenciled frieze found in two Shenandoah Valley homes. This image of faux red-velvet swag with intricate stenciled black and gold fringe was recorded when wallpaper was stripped from best parlor of Andrew Johnston house (II.46) in the 1990s. *Courtesy Giles County Historical Society.*

George Reed house. *Courtesy Historical Society of Delaware.*

II.42. *George Read II house, 1804*
New Castle, Delaware
Artist: Unknown, 1800 and 1824

Detail of re-created "Greek key" stenciled frieze seen in two areas of front stair hall, vibrant yellow in front section and mint green in back section. *Courtesy Historical Society of Delaware.*

WHILE GEORGE READ II was never able to attain the political prominence achieved by his famous father, George Read I,[1] he did succeed in building a most interesting mansion, utilizing the best Philadelphia craftsmen and materials. The family made all architectural design decisions without the help of a professional architect, and the house evolved as a blend of Georgian and the newest Federal styles.

George II's house featured a basic Georgian rectangular layout ornamented in the height of Federal decorative style with extremely high ceilings, ornate "punch and gouge" carved woodwork, and rooms painted in bright Pompeiian colors and filled with the latest Philadelphia furniture.

Throughout the house, the early-nineteenth-century popularity of decorative painting was evident. The many furnishings included "fancy chairs" with gilded or bronze-powder stenciled decoration, and gilded looking glasses with eglomise and reverse-painted tablets, all from the best chair and mirror manufacturers.

Most important, at least three first-floor areas originally featured stenciled frieze designs just below the cornice moldings. The center hall, which was painted a vibrant yellow in the front and mint green in the back section, was embellished with a large Greek-key stenciled border. This decoration was discovered under wallpaper and a layer of smoke and soot acquired during an 1826 fire that destroyed much of the New Castle waterfront, miraculously stopping at the border of the Read estate. The stencil work is believed to be original to the house, dating to 1804.

The two parlors to the left of the hall received stenciled frieze borders slightly later, around 1824, possibly when George Read III was living in the house with his family. The design in the front parlor, a room used by the family, is a large leaf with red ocher and medium blue-green accents on a dark gray leaf. The coloration is striking against walls painted peach or a tint of red ocher.

The back parlor, which was reserved for entertaining guests, is painted a medium blue-green or a tint of Prussian blue. (The "best room" of George Washington's Mount Vernon was also painted in Prussian blue pigment.) This room's frieze, which was too fragmented to be re-created with the others during a restoration in 1978, is said to have been a grape motif. This also may have been stenciled in red ocher and Prussian blue on a dark gray undercoat, thereby assuring that the two parlors would be color-coordinated when they were combined to accommodate large numbers of guests. The leaf motif and probably the grape motif were more of the later Empire style than the Greek key, which was Federal style.

These brightly colored walls and stenciling were darkened by the 1826 fire and most likely papered over for the first time shortly after Read's death in 1836. Having always lived well beyond his means, Read left his family in enormous debt, which forced them to auction off the contents of the house soon afterward. At this time it is also likely that they freshened the smoke-darkened walls with new wallpaper, to increase the house's sales appeal. In 1846 the house was purchased by James Couper, whose family owned it until 1920.

In 1920 the house was purchased by Philip Laird. In 1974 his wife bequeathed it to the Delaware Historical Society, which restored it to a fine museum house exemplifying the period of the Read family ownership (1797–1846). The stenciled cornice borders by two different stencil artists (both probably from Philadelphia) were re-created it the late 1970s.[2]

A famous Philadelphia tastemaker, Benjamin Henry Latrobe (1764–1820),[3] an English-born architect, interior designer, and furniture designer in the neoclassical mode, considered the Read house to be old-fashioned and in bad taste. Time has proven Benjamin Latrobe to have been wrong. Time also has vindicated George Read II. While never as prominent as his father, nor a financial or political success, he did realize his ambition to build an impressive mansion, which some now call the grandest in the state of Delaware.

Interior view of restored front parlor of Reed house, showing well-executed leaf-motif frieze plus elaborate woodwork and relief plasterwork on ceiling. *Courtesy of the Historical Society of Delaware.*

II.43. Nathaniel Russell house, 1808
Charleston, South Carolina
Artist: Samuel O'Hara, 1808

Russell house, in a photo taken circa 1880. *Courtesy of Historic Charleston Foundation.*

Detail of tromp l'oeil molded plaster cornice found in a third-floor chamber. *Courtesy Historic Charleston Foundation.*

A LARGE, IMPRESSIVE, Adam-style brick house was built in Charleston by Nathaniel Russell, who was born in 1738 in Bristol, Rhode Island. Russell's vast mercantile empire included trade with American cities, the British Isles, Europe, West Africa, Asia, West India, and South America. Most profits were from exports of rice and indigo, and imports of a vast array of goods, plus participation in the slave trade before and after the Revolution.

In the spring of 1808, Russell, his wife, their two teenage daughters, and approximately eighteen slaves moved into their splendid new mansion house.

Its neoclassical interior featured painted decoration by a Samuel O'Hara, who advertised in a Charleston newspaper in May of 1808 that samples of his work could be viewed at the new Russell house.

O'Hara, probably trained in Ireland, picked a classical palette of colors for the walls and woodwork, grained the interior doors in "Charleston high-style" mahogany with satinwood inlaid stringing, and polychromed and gilded the superb molded plaster cornices in numerous rooms.

But of primary importance to this study are the tromp l'oeil molded plaster cornices found in the front stair hall, which features a grand three-story free-flying staircase, and in a third-floor chamber.

The third-floor faux cornice is executed in three tones of raw umber: medium, dark for the shadows, and light for the highlights. The basic shape apparently was established with the aid of a stencil in the medium tone, and the shadow and highlights were applied freehand. The cornice was worked in oil-based paint on a distemper wall in a coloration described as robin's egg blue, probably a tint of Prussian blue.

John Canning, Connecticut master decorative painter, re-created the faux bois doors, using traditional techniques and materials. Paint analysis was performed by Susan Buck of Boston, Massachusetts.

This house, owned by the Historic Charleston Foundation, is undergoing continuous conservation and restoration, ensuring that the property will be an important educational resource for future generations.

II.44. John Burner house, 1820
Luray, Virgina
Artist: Unknown, circa 1830

THE USE OF THE painted swag to decorate the cornice area of interior walls started in eighteenth-century colonial America, as seen in the Sproat-Ward house (p. 9) of Lakeville, Massachusetts (colonial example 5, chapter 1). It is next seen used by the Classical I artist in the East Bay area of Rhode Island (II.7) and by the same artist in Walpole, New Hampshire (II.33). Another version almost exactly like its wallpaper twin was found in western Massachusetts (II.15). In Treadwell, New York (II.38), a swag with intricate stenciled fringe and tassels very similar to the Virginia version shown here was executed by yet another artist. This persistent use of the faux textile swag, probably introduced to America in eighteenth-century English portraiture, continued its popularity well into the nineteenth century.

This northern Shenandoah Valley work features a luxurious deep red, probably faux velvet swag, formed by the use of a large curved stencil and filled in freehand, which is bordered with intricate stenciled gold-colored knotted

View of Burner house parlor with original stenciling, faux painted paneling below chair rail, and superb grained woodwork. *Courtesy Virginia Historic Landmarks Commission, Richmond, Virginia.*

fringe and miniature tassels with two larger tassels between the swags. A stenciled flower-and-leaf-vine border accents all the architectural elements. Below the chair rail on the plaster dado is a painted version of wooden paneling with indented corners,[4] which was also used in the Middlebrook Tavern (I.58) located just south of Luray.

The Burner house decoration was probably painted soon after the completion of this fine spacious two-story brick house, named Massanutton Heights[5] by the Burner family, who have inhabited it for over 180 years. It could be the work of a local craftsman, since numerous artisans such as limners, fraktur artists, and furniture decorators resided locally.[6] In fact Johannes Spitler (1774–1837), well-known furniture painter, was said to be related to the Burners and lived in the same county. In addition Spitler was neighbor and relative of fraktur artist and Mennonite preacher Jacob Strickly[7] (1770–1842), who is said to have lived on an adjacent farm.

The inspiration for the red swag or drapery could also have been of a local nature. Charles Peale Polk (1767–1822) was a nephew of Charles Willson Peale and trained with his famous uncle, but he never achieved the status of fine artist; he is more often considered to be among the ranks of folk artists. Early in his career, in May of 1787, he advertised in a Philadelphia newspaper that he "Intends Carrying on, House, Ship and Sign Painting and Glazing."[8] He must have advanced to portraiture, since around 1799 he painted several portraits of prominent northern Shenandoah Valley residents[9] such as Major and Mrs. Isaac Hite (she was James Madison's sister), who resided at Belle Grove Plantation. Both featured red satin draperies with fringe and tassels. Around the same time Polk painted Judge and Mrs. Robert White of nearby Frederick County, also with impressive red swags in the background. This use of swags as background for the area's gentry could have impressed the wall stencil artist as being a sign of gentility and very appropriate decoration for the best parlor of an upwardly moving wealthy farmer.

This perhaps local artist traveled at least as far as Pearisburg, Virginia, located in the southern part of the Shenandoah Valley, where he left traces of his work in at least five rooms of example II.46.

II.45. *Spengler Hall, 1820*
Strasburg, Virginia
Artist: Unknown, 1825

THE HANDSOME, twelve-room Federal-style brick residence called Spengler Hall, complete with two massive solid brick columns flanking the front entrance, was built in 1820 by Captain Anthony Spengler. Here the captain and his wife raised ten sons and two daughters, whose descendants have occupied the house continuously to the present time. Spengler Hall's spacious front lawn borders on an early road, which was to become the main turnpike running through the Shenandoah Valley.

Of architectural interest is the front stair hall, which features a stairwell rising three floors without central support. Originally, classical-genre stenciling featuring an urn, starflowers, and connecting chain ran above the dado molding from the impressive first-floor entrance hall to the third floor. There, a four-foot-long by eight-inch-high section of original stencil work still remains. It is possible that a classical stenciled frieze of swag or festoon design is hiding under the existing wallpaper, covered over so long ago that it is forgotten by the current family member—the fifth generation to reside in Spengler Hall.

The surviving stenciled section, executed in red and yellow ocher, is very similar to the classical borders used above the chair rail or baseboard moldings in New Eng-

Spengler Hall.

land houses (II.23). It was not done by the same hand as the New England work, but it definitely was inspired by the same designs evident in the work of numerous craftsmen who worked in many different disciplines during the Federal period.

In 1862, during the Civil War, the house and nearby mill were occupied by Union troops. The Yankee general is said to have departed in such haste that he left his favorite chair sitting on the front porch, where it has remained for almost 140 years. In 1864 Confederate troops built tents on the lawn and pastures surrounding the Spengler house.

It is hoped that the remainder of the classical stenciling in this house was not lost to the rigors of war, but rather to a postwar desire to upgrade the decor with the newest fashions in wall hangings.

(Top) Original stenciled urn border extant on third level of front stair hall. *(Bottom)* Similar urn-and-shield border from front left chamber of Musterfield farm (II.23), Parsonsfield, Maine.

Andrew Johnston house. *Courtesy Giles County Historical Society.*

II.46. Andrew Johnston house, 1829–32
Pearisburg, Virginia
Artist: Unknown, 1835

THE BUILDER OF THIS handsome brick house in Pearisburg, Andrew Johnston, was descended from a Saxon clan with origins in Annadal, Scotland. Early on, due to political and religious persecution, many members of the clan migrated to Ireland. The builder's father, David, born 1726 in Ireland, upon the death of his father and subsequent inheritance of the family estate by his older brother at age ten, set sail for America as a cabin boy, landing at Norfolk, Virginia. Not much is known about the years before he married and settled in Culpepper, Virginia, in 1751, but it is quite possible that he apprenticed in a craft such as tanning soon after his arrival in Virginia.

Two of David's eight children, Andrew and David Jr., were among the earliest settlers of Pearisburg, where they jointly owned over 1,600 acres of land, were prominent civic leaders, and engaged in a thriving mercantile and tanning business.

Andrew's first house was described in his will as his "River Plantation"; his second, his "town house," was built between 1829 and 1832. It was an impressive L-shaped brick house with late Federal and early Greek Revival elements. A handsome front porch with two square and two fluted ionic columns was added at a later time.

Shortly after completion of this "town house," the same decorative painter who decorated a house in Page County, Virginia, located a short distance north on the Great Wagon Road, visited the Johnston house. Working in the classical borders-only style, he painted the same faux red-velvet frieze with intricate stenciled fringe in the best parlor. The secondary border, which outlines all architectural elements, was a very simple undulating vine with a single berry placed at regular intervals, in light and dark yellow, probably raw sienna pigment, and black-green. Only the berry is definitely stenciled, but the very regular repeat of the vine suggests some mechanical aid to establish the pattern, namely a stencil plate. The window and door frames and chair rail were found to be pink (which also could be the base color for faux rosewood graining), the ceiling was a tint of artificial ultramarine, and the plaster dado was paint-decorated with faux wood paneling in shades of now soft red over soft yellow. Only a small sample of the dado work was retained.

The rest of the decorative painting was restored in 1998 by Olin Conservation, Inc., of Great Falls, Virginia, conserving over 50 percent of the original decoration and re-creating the rest.

The decoration in the parlor was known to the Johnston family, who had lived in the house continuously until 1985, but additional painted rooms that were found during the restoration had been covered so long that they had been completely forgotten.

It was discovered that the present dining room, located in the ell section, had faux graining on the dado in colorations similar to those in the parlor but of a different configuration. A small section of the original was retained.

Under a thick covering of paper and paint, original decoration in a bedchamber was revealed, including a simple dark green frieze with the same vine-with-berry border as the parlor and a new interesting border flanking the windows. It was a very wavy vine with thistlelike leaves and a large centered fruitlike motif placed at regular intervals. The fruit could be either a pinecone, pineapple, or a naively executed thistle. Considering the family's Scottish ancestry, the thistle seems to be the correct choice. The original woodwork color proved to be yellow, and the dado area had faux graining in colors similar to the

previous two rooms but in yet another grained configuration. This room was re-created (except for the dado, where just a small sample of the original was retained) by Brushworks Decorative Painting, Meadowview, Virginia, in the late 1990s.

Paint analysis by Matthew Mosca of Baltimore indicated that the walls were covered with oil-bound paint and the ceilings with distemper paint.

In 1985 the house and land were given to the newly formed Giles County Historical Society by the Johnston family, to be used as a house museum and research center and subsequently placed on the Virginia Landmarks Register and the National Register of Historic Places in 1993.

This important example of work by an artist who visited at least two houses along a major travel route to the southern frontier, working in yet another variation of classical-genre wall stenciling, is now well preserved in an accessible museum setting for the enjoyment and enlightenment of decorative arts and material-history enthusiasts.

View of re-created stencil decoration in Johnston house parlor, with panels of original faux bois graining on plaster below the chair rail. *Courtesy Giles County Historical Society.*

Conclusion

The trail of Classical-style wall stenciling ends with this example in Pearisburg, Virginia, at the southernmost part of the Great Wagon Road. Perhaps the influence of this book will bring to light (literally and figuratively) many new examples of wall stenciling from the American Federal period, both in traditional eastern areas and in areas of the country where stenciling is thought to be almost nonexistent and therefore tends to be under researched. The study of American wall stenciling executed during the period from 1790 to 1840 provides invaluable insight into the founding and development of the United States. The work is, in a real sense, "a stenciled image of a new nation."

APPENDIX A

Early Paint Materials

Paint can be described as a dispersion of small solid particles in a liquid medium, which, when applied to a surface and allowed to dry, becomes a solid, protective film. It also enhances the surface visually by adding color and sheen, making the use of paint a way to beautify as well as protect the interior and exterior surfaces of early architecture.

Three types of paint were used predominantly during America's Federal period: oil-based, distemper, and casein (often called milk paint). Distemper was the paint of choice for most wall decorators, both stencil and freehand, who worked on walls covered with a ground of whitewash often tinted. Oil paint was most often used on the wooden elements of the interior and exterior. Casein was often used on furniture and occasionally on interior and exterior woodwork.

Paint is made up of three elements: pigment, binder, and vehicle. There are two types of pigment, both of which usually come in powdered form. Whiting (chalk), slaked lime, and white lead are known as "hiding" pigments since they make the paint an opaque white. Whiting and lime are suitable additives for making distemper and whitewash; however, lead is only compatible with oil-based paint. Colored pigments are known as "tinting" pigments since they turn the white paint to colored paint.

The binder is the medium used to bind the pigment particles together. A natural glue, often rabbit skin, dissolved in hot water is the binder for distemper; milk for casein; and oil, most often linseed, for oil-based paints.

The vehicle is the thinning liquid, which helps to carry the particles of pigment. For distemper, water is the vehicle; for oil paint, a volatile thinner such as turpentine is used. Quite often oil was added to casein paint, making it sturdy enough for exterior surfaces. The author, however, has found very little evidence of the use of casein paint by wall decorators.

Early pigments most often used by wall stencilers are (a) minium, French for red lead, a bright, medium red, naturally occurring lead oxide; (b) Venetian red, a cheap, plentiful earth pigment, which provided the "barn red" so popular for exteriors; (c) yellow ocher, the most common iron oxide, a vibrant yellow tinged with brown or orange; (d) Prussian blue, invented about 1740, the first synthetic pigment, an expensive pigment with a slight green tinge though less expensive versions show a faint reddish tinge; (e) indigo, one of a few colorants that come in semipaste or liquid form, made from indigo leaves and stems, used primarily as a dye for textiles but also to tint water- or oil-based paint. Whiting and bone black were the noncolor pigments used to tone distemper. White lead and the common lampblack mixed well with oil but were not compatible with water-based paints. Most green pigments of the period, such as terre verte and verdigris, were too transparent or unstable to be used by wall decorators; thus green was usually made by mixing one of the blues with yellow ocher or the later chrome yellow.

The identification of early stencil paint can be difficult due to the thinness of its application and because its obvious fragile qualities have often been disguised due to the widespread practice of varnishing over distemper wall stenciling in order to make it washable and durable. This greatly alters the appearance and characteristics of distemper paint, which tends to absorb the characteristics of its varnish covering.

For more information on early American paint materials, the following publications are recommended: *Preservation Brief #28*, U.S. Department of the Interior, National Park Service, 1849 C Street NW, Washington, DC 20240; and *Paint in America*, National Trust for Historic Preservation, 1785 Massachusetts Ave. NW, Washington, DC 20036.

APPENDIX B

Who's Who of American Wall Stenciling

Edward B. Allen. Authored one of the earliest books on American wall painting, which included several examples of wall stenciling. It was published by Yale University Press in 1926. His research material is in the collections of the Society for the Preservation of New England Antiquities (SPNEA), Boston, Massachusetts.

S. E. Betts and L. W. Langdon. Early nineteenth-century stencil artists whose signatures were found stenciled over the mantel in the Gibbs house, Blandford, Massachusetts. S. E. Betts was also seen on the wall of another Gibbs house in Blandford just before the house was demolished.

Jessica Bond (1908–2001). Resident of Dorset, Vermont, charter member and master craftsman of the Historical Society of Early American Decoration (HSEAD). Researcher and recorder of wall stenciling in the New England area, with great concentration on her home state of Vermont. Her findings were published in the *Decorator*, biannual publication of HSEAD, fall 1997–fall 2000.

Christine Edwards Borkan. In 1990 completed a study of wall stenciling in the Western Reserve section of Ohio as her master's thesis at the University of Delaware.

Esther Stevens Brazer (1891–1945). Early researcher and teacher of early American decorative painting techniques, in whose honor HSEAD was founded in 1946. Wrote extensively on the subject with a major book, *Early American Decoration*, published in 1940. Her research material is in the HSEAD collections at the American Folk Art Museum,[1] New York City.

Susan Buck. Paint analysis and conservation, Newton, Massachusetts.

Jeduthan Bullin. Early nineteenth-century decorative painter from Keene, New Hampshire. Is said to have taught his nephew Jothan Stearns, who decorated the Grimes house in Keene, New Hampshire.

John Canning. Twentieth-century master decorative painter, classically trained in the United Kingdom using traditional techniques and materials. Located in Connecticut.

Stephen Clark (1810–1900). Eighteen-year-old student from western New York who wrote in his diary that he stenciled walls during the summer of 1828. It is not known if he worked as an apprentice or if he stenciled walls at other times during his life.

Linda Croxson and Philip Ward. Locustville, Virginia, contemporary restoration artists who re-created stenciling and faux finishes in the Clover Hill Tavern, Virginia, and the Read house, Delaware.

Moses Eaton, Sr. (1753–1833). Born in Dedham, Massachusetts; moved to Hancock, New Hampshire, in 1793. Fifth-generation Eaton in America, Revolutionary War veteran, farmer, and documented stencil artist.

Moses Eaton, Jr. (1796–1886). Well-documented early-nineteenth-century stencil artist. His paint box, found by Janet Waring in his attic around 1937, is now in the collections of SPNEA.

Margaret Fabian. Along with her husband, conducted a seven-year survey of 460 homes and taverns in New England during the early 1980s. Results including photographs, slides, tracings, facsimiles, and data sheets are housed in the special collections of the New Hampshire Historical Society, Concord, New Hampshire.

Polly Forcier. Quechee, Vermont, resident, current researcher, and artist specializing in authentic American wall-stenciling designs. Owner of MB Historic Décor, Norwich, Vermont.

Erastus Gates. Nineteenth-century stencil artist, credited with stenciling the Coolidge House in Plymouth, Vermont, and numerous other houses in southern Vermont. An ancestor of President Calvin Coolidge.

J. Gleason. Early-nineteenth-century stencil artist whose name was found stenciled on a wall in Foster, Rhode Island. Thought to be member of the Gleason family that settled in Massachusetts in the seventeenth century.

Kenneth Jewett. Formerly of Peterborough, New Hampshire, twentieth-century stencil researcher. Published *Early New England Wall Stencils, a Workbook*, in 1979.

L. W. Langdon. Nineteenth-century stencil artist whose name was found stenciled on a wall in East Granby, Connecticut.

Kris Lemmon. Twentieth-century restoration artist from Cincinnati, Ohio. Worked on the Coleman house, Cynthiana, Kentucky.

Leroy. Early-nineteenth-century stencil artist who signed several walls in western New York State.

Nina Fletcher Little (1903–1993). Preeminent researcher and writer on American folk art, with great knowledge of painted folk art. Published *American Decorative Wall Painting* in 1952 with subsequent enlarged edition in 1973. Research material in the collections of SPNEA, Boston.

Gina Martin. HSEAD master teacher and craftsman, twentieth-century researcher on early American decorative painting techniques including wall stenciling. Her research material is part of the HSEAD collection at the American Folk Art Museum, New York City.

Jeanne Minhinnick. Twentieth-century researcher on decorative wall painting in Ontario, Canada. Her book *At Home in Upper Canada*, published in 1970, contains examples of Ontario wall stenciling similar to that found in America.

Matthew J. Mosca. Historic paint research, Baltimore, Maryland.

Paine. A student of Rufus Porter, primarily a nineteenth-century muralist but probably stenciled an occasional room.

Philip Parr. Contemporary stencil researcher from Caledonia, New York. Was guest curator for the 1985 exhibit titled *Wall Stenciling in Western New York, 1800–1840* at the Rochester Museum & Science Center. His tracings and room drawings are part of the collections at the Rochester Museum.

Rufus Porter. Well-known nineteenth-century muralist, scientist, and writer who used stencils to execute sections of his murals and an occasional stenciled border to frame his murals.

Henry Rogers. Name found on the back of nineteenth-century stencils indicating that he was an early American stencil artist working in the classical genre in Vermont around 1814.

Jothan Stearns (1791–1832). Said to have decorated the left front parlor of the Grimes house, Keene, New Hampshire. He apprenticed with his Uncle Jeduthan Bullin of Keene.

Stimp. Nineteenth-century stencil artist long attributed with stenciling houses in western Massachusetts, Connecticut, and eastern New York State.

Janet Waring (1879–1941). Twentieth-century American wall-stenciling researcher. Published book *Early American Stencils on Walls and Furniture* in 1937. Resided in Yonkers, New York, and summered in western Massachusetts. Had a major exhibit at the George Walter Vincent Smith Art Gallery, Springfield, Massachusetts, in 1939. Her research material is housed at SPNEA, Boston, Massachusetts, with copies at the Metropolitan Museum, New York City.

Frank Welsh. Paint analyst and conservator, Bryn Mawr, Pennsylvania.

David Wiggins. Twentieth-century neo-itinerant artist specializing in period decorative painting techniques. Formerly of Sanbornton, New Hampshire, now resides on the island of Nantucket, Massachusetts.

Lydia Eldredge Williams. Early-nineteenth-century artist who is said to have stenciled two rooms of her home in Ashfield, Massachusetts.

APPENDIX C

Resources

When initial discovery of what seems to be nineteenth-century wall stenciling has been made, it is important to proceed with care, observing several simple procedures: first, do not use excessive water in the removal of the rest of the wall-paper, since most nineteenth-century wall stenciling was executed in water-soluble paint; and second, keep removed paper, since very often an imprint of the stenciling is retained on the reverse of the paper.

Next, carefully record the stenciling no matter how fragmented. The fragments remaining may not be identifiable to you, but a knowledgeable stencil expert will be able to identify the design and fill in the missing sections. Record by taking color photographs or slides, taking tracings, and if possible executing facsimiles.

Register the house and its decorative painting with your state branch of the National Historic Preservation Commission. This commission is responsible for placing houses on the National Register of Historic Properties, but whether or not you wish your house to be on the Register, it is important to have your newly discovered wall stenciling on file with this national agency. If they are not yet taking colored pictures, supply them with colored digital images if at all possible.

Once you have carefully uncovered and recorded, it is time to decide to either conserve, re-create, or perhaps cover the stenciling with suitable cover to preserve it for future generations of caretakers. If you choose to cover, it is important to keep pictures, tracings, and facsimiles with the house records for the next owners.

The following organizations will be helpful:

United States Department of the Interior, National Park Service, Cultural Resources, 1849 C Street NW, Washington, DC 20240. Their booklet, titled *Standards for Rehabilitation and Guidelines for Rehabilitating Historic Buildings*, will be very useful.

Historical Society for Early American Decoration, formed in 1946 to preserve early American painting techniques. Membership includes numerous artists knowledgeable in the field of nineteenth-century American wall stenciling (including the author) who would be able to accurately interpret, trace, and execute facsimiles of original stenciling. Their web page address: *http://members.aol.com/HSEADBG*. The society also maintains a liaison member who can be reached through the American Folk Art Museum, New York City, where the society's collections are housed.

The Association for Preservation Technology International (APT), an association of professional persons directly involved in preservation activities, maintains a list of professional craftsmen and services related to historic preservation including paint conservators. Fax: 888–723–4242. Web address: *www.apti.org*.

AIC, the American Institute for Conservation, provides lists of accredited conservators by area. The address is 1717 K Street NW, Suite 301, Washington, DC 20006. Web address: *http://aic.stanford.edu*.

Glossary

antebellum. Before the American Civil War.

base coat. The layer(s) of undiluted opaque paint applied directly preceding the decoration.

dado. In this book refers to the area, either plaster or wood, between the chair rail and the baseboard.

dogtrot. A breezeway or open space between rooms, often called pens, of a log house, sometimes enclosed. Log houses with this feature are known as "dogtrot" houses.

fanlight. A lunette, a half-round or half-elliptical opening filled with glass to admit light, often capping a doorway.

faux. An imitation of a natural material created with paint, either fanciful or realistic.

faux bois. To imitate wood with a painting technique.

faux marbre. To imitate marble with a painting technique.

Flemish bond. The pattern of bricks laid alternately with ends or sides exposed, whether horizontally or vertically.

fluting. Decoration by means of parallel grooves sunk in columns or pilasters or horizontal borders.

gilding. The application of a thin metal leaf to a surface to create the effect of solid metal, usually gold.

glaze. A paint, more or less strongly colored, that is sufficiently transparent for the paint layer beneath to show through.

grain. Arrangement of the fibers in natural wood.

layout. The basic plan or arrangement of an ornamented surface. In wall stenciling the placement of the various elements such as horizontal borders at the ceiling, chair rail, and baseboard, vertical borders to divide the wall into panels, and filler motifs alternated in the vertical panels.

lintel. Horizontal architectural member supporting the weight above an opening such as a door or fireplace.

pilaster. An upright form, resembling a flattened column, projecting from a wall.

reeding. Decoration by means of parallel lines of raised wood, usually placed in rows upon friezes, legs, and other plain spaces or in rows encircling columns. Said to resemble a bunch of reeds tied together. Reeding is the reverse of fluting.

stencil. A thin plate in which letters or figures are cut in such a way that a color applied to the surface marks the characters on a surface beneath.

trompe l'oeil. From the French for "fool the eye." The use of paint to create very realistic copy of marble or wood. Similar to faux but never fanciful, always realistic.

Notes

1. COLONIAL PAINTED DECORATION
(pages 1–9)

1. Hamilton, *Introduction to Wallpaper*, p. 7.
2. Bridenbaugh, *Vexed and Troubled Englishmen*, p. 76.
3. Bremer, *Puritan Experiment*, p. 63.
4. Ibid., p. 47.
5. The guilds of painter-stainers combined two crafts, those who painted wood, plaster, and other surfaces and those who stained hangings, usually referred to in sixteenth century as painted cloths, a cheaper substitute for woven tapestries. Ayres, *Home in Britain*, p. 161.
6. Bridenbaugh, *Vexed and Troubled Englishmen*, p. 81.
7. The production of industrial hemp was made illegal in the United States in the 1930s due to its THC content (the psychoactive ingredient in marijuana), though it is less than one percent. See *New York Times*, February 17, 1997.
8. Russell, *Farming in New Hanover*, p. 141.
9. Indigo was primarily a dye for textiles; a less common use was as the earliest blue pigment used in water-based paint. Its popularity dwindled after Prussian blue became available around 1704.
10. Nina Fletcher Little, "Dating New England Houses," part 1, *Antiques*, March 1945.
11. Founded perhaps as early as the twelfth century on the medieval concept of high-quality art and craft. Formally abolished in 1835.
12. James Ayres, "The Vernacular Art of the Artisan in England," *Antiques*, February 1997.
13. Nina Fletcher Little, *American Decorative Wall Painting*, p. 3.
14. Prime, *Arts and Crafts in Philadelphia*, p. 300.
15. Ayres, *Home in Britain*, p. 161.
16. Ibid.
17. Prime, *Arts and Crafts in Philadelphia*, p. 42.
18. Parkes, "The History and Technology of Floorcloths," *APT Bulletin*, vol. 21, nos. 3–4, 1989.
19. Prime, *Arts and Crafts in Philadelphia*, p. 302.
20. Dow, *Arts and Crafts in New England*, p. 211.
21. Nina Fletcher Little, *American Decorative Wall Painting*, p. 3.
22. Frank S. Welsh, "Peter Wentz Farmstead," *APT Bulletin*, vol. 7, no. 2, 1975, p. 124. Also see *Antiques*, October 1982, p. 788.
23. Since paint analysis is not available, it is impossible to know if this is an example of graining with transparent oil glazes or an earlier graining technique using opaque paint.
24. For more information on the Hunter house and colonial decoration in Rhode Island, see Downing, *Early Homes of Rhode Island*.
25. Weston, *History of Middleboro*, p. 431.
26. "Tulipomania" started in Holland in the early 1630s, spread through much of Europe, and was brought to America's shores by immigrants of various nationalities, especially the Dutch, who settled in New York in the seventeenth century.

2. WALL STENCILING IN FEDERAL AMERICA
(pages 10–14)

1. Cummins and White, *The Federal Period*, p. 64.
2. In 1790 the ten largest urban centers and their populations were Philadelphia, 44,000; New York, 33,000; Boston, 18,000; Charleston, 16,000; Baltimore, 14,000; Salem, 8,000; Newport, 6,700; Providence, 6,400; Marblehead, 5,700; and Gloucester, 5,300.
3. Dumas, *Hero's Reward*, p. 9.
4. Prime, *The Arts and Crafts of Philadelphia*, p. 215.
5. Leigh Rehner Jones, "Wall Painting in Central New York," p. 7.
6. Prime, *The Arts and Crafts of Philadelphia*, p. 305.

PART I: THE FOLK GROUP (page 15)

1. See information on early paint materials in appendix A.
2. See list in appendix B.

3. THE SOUTHERN NEW ENGLAND STATES
(pages 16–53)

1. Lynch, *Foster, Rhode Island*, p. 20.
2. The Rhode Island Preservation Commission report gives the date as 1790–1810; also, a will made by Daniel's father in 1792 states that Daniel was then living in the area where this house is located.
3. John Barber White, *Genealogy*, p. 244.
4. Ibid., p. 245.
5. Ibid., p. 246.

6. Elisha A. Steere (1783–1849) married Esther Appleby (1792–1867), the daughter of Thomas and Waite (Smith) Appleby and sister to John Smith Appleby.

7. Fragments of original stenciling have been preserved in each room; the rest was recreated by the author in 1997–98.

8. John Barber White, *Genealogy*, p. 246.

9. Waring, *Early American Stencils*, p. 68.

10. Thomas Paine sold the tavern to George Mowry in 1830.

11. Waring, *Early American Stencils*, p. 68.

12. The pink color could also have been caused by wallpaper glue residue. The only picture available of the original stenciling is a small photograph in which it is impossible to tell whether the ground color is indeed pink or not. This would be the only record of Gleason using light red as a wall color. Owners have promised to alert the author if wallpaper is planned.

13. Perhaps a later generation of the Gleason clan.

14. According to a previous owner of this house, Artemis was an accomplished carver who carved the Turk's head that for many years ornamented a building at the junction of Westminster and Weybosset Streets in downtown Providence, across from the Providence Market Place. Described as "a huge thing of hideous appearance and painted in the most exaggerated colors," this carving was reproduced in stone on the Turks Head Building built on the same location in 1912, which still stands. Artemis may have been responsible for some of the fine Federal woodwork added to his house during the 1823–27 restoration, as well as the carved woodwork on the other houses in the area.

15. This design is illustrated twice in Janet Waring's book, *Early American Stencils*, first on p. 11, as a fifteenth-century stencil design from a church in Chatelroy, France, and again in fig. 24 (following p. 32), as stenciling dating from 1791 in a bedroom of the Peter Jayne house, Marblehead, Massachusetts.

16. Allen, *Early American Wall Paintings*, 1926.

17. Waring, *Early American Stencils*, 1937.

18. Brazer, *Early American Decoration*, 1940.

19. For lists of societies and organizations having collections of wall and floor designs or other information pertaining to Federal-period wall stenciling, see appendix B.

20. Brown, *Salt Pork*, p. 78.

21. Mrs. Greenwood was a cousin of Bertram K. Little. She was credited by Nina Fletcher Little, Bertram's wife, with being the inspiration for their lifelong interest in collecting New England country arts. It is interesting to note that when they were first married in 1925, the Littles spent weekends in an unrestored 1825 cottage in Hudson. They later purchased and restored two houses in Massachusetts, one in Brookline and the other in Essex County.

22. Greenwood befriended Dow while he was curator of the SPNEA between 1919 and 1936. He was a respected historian who, during his tenure as secretary of the Essex Institute in Salem from 1898 to 1919, published a long list of books and articles on early New England history. House restoration was apparently only a sideline for him; his brother Eugene did the actual restoration work.

23. The Greenwood collection of early American decorative arts was given to the Smithsonian Institution, Washington, D.C.

24. Abner Goodale's daughter Lucy married Asa Thurston, one of the first missionaries to the Sandwich Islands (Hawaii), in 1819 under unusual circumstances. Asa, a bachelor fresh out of Andover Theological Seminary, was selected to go to the islands as one of a pioneer group of missionaries, with the stipulation that he marry and take his wife with him. This was in September, and the departure date was late October. Lucy's cousin, William Goodell, a fellow student of Asa's, suggested Lucy as a suitable candidate. After a very hurried courtship, Lucy agreed to marry Asa and leave home, family, and friends for a distant and "heathen" land. Asa Thurston Twigg-Smith, the present owner, descends from this most interesting union.

25. Wall, "Time Stone Farm," pp. 41 and 51. Wall was president of the New York Historical Society at the time.

26. Grady et al., *Goodale Farm*, pp. 36–37.

27. During this period the farm grew from a subsistence farm, which produced enough for the family, to a business operation that supplied at least half the family's income.

28. Nylander, *Wall Papers*, p. 99.

29. The 1790 census for Marlborough lists a John Gleason, John Gleason, Jr., and a Joseph Gleason all as heads of families living in Marlborough. The mother-in-law of Johnathan Gleason, b. 1772, Worcester, Massachusetts, was Elizabeth Goodale Smith. See John Barber White, *Genealogy*, p. 205. Also, Thomas Goodale married Sarah Gleason, May 3, 1770; see *Vital Records of Marlborough*, 1908, p. 406.

30. Sumner Wood, *Taverns and Turnpikes*, p. 293.

31. Sumner Wood, *Ulster Scots*, p. 188.

32. Gina Martin's photographs and sample boards are in the collection of the Historical Society of Early American Decoration in the library of the Museum of American Folk Art, New York City.

33. Bond, "A Treasury," in *The Decorator*, spring 1998, p. 6.

34. For information on freehand-painted walls, see Coffin, *Borders and Scrolls*.

35. *The Great River: Art and Society of the Connecticut Valley*, Wadsworth Atheneum, 1985, p. 89.

36. Hard, *The Connecticut*, p. 163.

37. Frederick Wood, *Turnpikes of New England*, p. 396.

38. It is quite possible that this house had other stenciled rooms, which totally disappeared before the present owners began their meticulous restoration in the 1970s.

39. Waring, *Early American Stencils*, p. 33.

40. *Early American Homes*, October 1997, p. 30.

41. John Barber White, *Genealogy*, p. 145.

42. In the collections of the Gunn Museum.

43. Waring, *Early American Stencils*, p. 44.

44. Ibid.

45. Ibid.

46. Edward B. Allen, *Early American Wall Paintings*, p. 73.

47. Curtis, "Lives of a 1719 Saltbox," p. 30.

48. Bond, "A Treasury," in *The Decorator*, S 99, p. 18.

4. THE NORTHERN NEW ENGLAND STATES
(pages 54–72)

1. Of the 1,080 soldiers to depart from Cambridge, Massachusetts, in September 1775, only 675 arrived fifty-one days later in Canada. Nearly 40 percent had either died or deserted due to extremely harsh conditions such as bitter cold, lack of food and clothing, and poor equipment. Randall, *Benedict Arnold*, pp. 148–87.

2. Eaton, *Eaton Family*, pp. 9 and 52.

3. For more information on Porter, refer to Jean Lipman's *Rufus Porter Rediscovered*.

4. See Rufus Porter ad on p. 141.

5. Tarbox, "Fanciful Graining," 34–37.

6. Ian Bristow, *Paint in America*, p. 53 (edited by Roger Moss).

7. Fales, *American Painted Furniture*, p. 216.

8. Daboll, *New England Almanack*, p. 15, article by A. A. (Antoine Alexis).

9. Waring, *Early American Stencils*, p. 67.

10. Horsman, *Frontier*, p. 22.

11. Blackmer, Green, and Taylor, *Pictorial History*, p. 3.

12. Polly Forcier, *Historic Homes and Properties*, April 1998, p. 3.

13. Captain John built his log cabin on the military road that led from Charlestown, New Hampshire, on the Connecticut River to Crown Point, New York.

14. Waring, *Early American Stencils*, p. 73.

15. Part of a speech given by President Calvin Coolidge in Bennington, Vermont, on September 21, 1928.

5. NEW YORK AND NEIGHBORING CANADA
(pages 73–97)

1. Most German settlers in the Hudson and Mohawk River Valleys prior to the Revolutionary War came from the lower Palatinate region of Germany. Many fled from war, famine, and religious persecution, first to Holland and later to England, whose Queen Anne settled four thousand in New York during 1709–10. The first arrivals are known as the "first wave" of German immigration to America.

2. O'Callahan, *Documentary History*, p. 542.

3. Leigh Rehner Jones, "Wall Painting in Central New York," p. 9.

4. Brown, *Salt Pork*, p. 74.

5. Coffin, *Borders and Scrolls*, p. 24.

6. French, *Gazetteer*, p. 679.

7. Wood, *Ulster Scots*, p. 22.

8. The author has long felt that the stenciling in the first and second floors of the Sage house is atypical in style and design of Stimp's work. The work in the attic, however, is executed entirely with attributed Stimp motifs.

9. Devoe, *Decorative Arts*, p. 150.

10. Waring, *Early American Stencils*, p. 44.

11. French, *Gazetteer*, p. 335.

12. Ibid., p. 335.

13. Devoe, *Decorative Arts*, p. 150.

14. When Electra Havemeyer married J. Watson Webb in 1919, she became the mistress of an eighteenth-century brick farmhouse on Lake Champlain, a wonderful place to display her growing collection of Americana. A very young Henry F. Du Pont, founder of the Winterthur Museum in Delaware, visited in 1923 and was greatly impressed with Electra's collections, in particular a set of pink Staffordshire china artistically displayed on a pine dresser at the top of a stairway. After Electra and her husband died in 1960, their five children presented the same pink china and dresser to Winterthur, which opened in 1951, just one year before Shelburne Museum. Lord, *Du Pont and Winterthur*, pp. 127 and 257.

15. *Palatine Settlement Society Newsletter*, summer 1988, p. 2.

16. Nelli-Nelles, *Immigrants from the Palatinate, 1710*, 1:5.

17. It is interesting to note that when English sympathizers, called Loyalists, moved to Canada during the Revolutionary War, they named one area in Ontario where they settled St. Catharines; also Christina Nellis's younger sister's name was Catharine.

18. Cooperstown, *Nellis Tavern, a Preliminary Report*, p. 14.

19. Annabelle J. Schwab, "Another New York State Stenciled Wall," *The Decorator*, fall 1965, p. 17.

20. Parr and Wass, *Wall Stenciling in Western New York*, p. 50.

21. Ibid., p. 56.

22. Ibid., p. 44.

23. Ibid, p. 63.

24. O'Callaghan, *Documentary History*, II:1153.

25. Huling, *Rhode Island Emigration*, p. 89.

26. Burrows and Wallace, *Gotham*, p. 258.

27. Minhinnick, "Paint in Early Ontario," p. 21.

28. Greenaway, *Interior Decorative Painting*, p. 15.

29. The Brown family seems to have been among the first-wave Palatinate Germans who settled Schoharie, New York, in 1711. French, *Gazetteer*, p. 601.

30. Burrows and Wallace, *Gotham*, p. 219.

31. John Butler, an able Tory leader in the Revolution, was born in Connecticut and died at Niagara in 1794. In 1776 he organized a band of marauders, white men and Indians, who raided settlements mostly in central New York. After the war he removed to Canada and was rewarded by the British government with land and a pension.

32. Minhinnick, *At Home in Upper Canada*, p. 136.

33. Minhinnick, "Paint in Early Ontario," p. 25.

34. Ibid., p. 31.

6. THE MIDDLE STATES (pages 98–118)

1. Henry Antes was among the great master builders of the early colonial period and an important religious/political leader in the middle colonies in the eighteenth century.

2. Photos of original stenciling taken by George Eisenman in January 1963 are in the collections of the Philadelphia Athenaeum. Copies of the originals are in the collections of the

Philadelphia Preservation Commission and the Independence National Historical Park.

3. Frank Welsh, "Report on Early Wall Stenciling in Philadelphia," *APT Bulletin*, 5, 2, 1973, p. 55.

4. 1790 Pennsylvania Census, p. 463.

5. Ayres, *British Folk Art*, p. 108.

6. Pottstown developed in 1735 when John Penn sold 14,600 acres to Scotch emigrants from Glasgow. Faris, *Old Trails*, p. 64.

7. The disputed boundary between Pennsylvania and the states of Maryland and Virginia (the borderline between the free and slave states) was finally fixed by Charles Mason and Jeremiah Dixon, English mathematicians and surveyors, between 1762 and 1767. It is known as the "Mason and Dixon line."

8. Many of these buildings have been restored, and the area is now operated as a museum by the Maryland and Pennsylvania Railroad Preservation Society.

9. Kilbourne, *History of Stewartstown*, pp. 1–2.

10. In the eighteenth and nineteenth centuries "mechanic" was synonymous with craftsman or artisan. The town was named Mechanicsburg to encourage craftsmen, artisans, and workmen to settle in the village.

11. Ayres, *British Folk Art*, pp. 108, 109, and 112.

12. Wenger, "Samuel Rex's Country Store," vol. 2, p. 6.

13. Many early walls that seem to be painted with gray paint were originally blue. Prussian blue pigment tends to turn gray with age.

7. THE SOUTHERN STATES (pages 119–128)

1. Morison, *History of the American People*, p. 86.

2. Ibid., p. 89.

3. Hatch, *Byrds of Virginia*, p. 6.

4. National Register of Historic Places Inventory Nomination Form, 7-606, Clover Mount, December 1979.

8. THE FRONTIER STATES (pages 129–156)

1. Dumas, *Hero's Reward*, p. 13.

2. Ibid.

3. Named for the Society of the Cincinnati, which was a fraternal society formed after the Revolution by officers of the Continental Army to ensure continued brotherhood and benevolent aid to its members—also to ensure that their troops received the land grants given to them as payment for military service. The society is perpetuated through the eldest living male descendant of original members.

4. Lossing, *Cyclopaedia of United States History*, p. 1024.

5. Borkan, "Ohio Choices," p. 20.

6. Dorothy and Richard Pratt, *A Guide to Early American Homes*, p. 197.

7. Bond, "A Treasury of Old Stencil Walls," *The Decorator*, fall 1999, p. 30.

8. Borkan, "Ohio Choices," p. 108.

9. Letter from Keegan to Gina Martin, January 1972.

10. Editorial Note, *Antiques Magazine*, September 1945.

11. *Education Services Institute Welcomes You to the Ferris House*, brochure by the Education Services Institute, 1989, Cincinnati, Ohio.

12. Letter from Charles J. Livingood to Mary Donley, November 1930, collection of the Mariemont Preservation Foundation.

13. Ginny Hunter, "Historic Mariemont House," *Cincinnati Post*, November 18, 1986.

14. Dumas, *Hero's Reward*, p. 11.

15. Roger G. Kennedy, *Orders from France*, p. 28.

16. Lancaster, *Antebellum Architecture of Kentucky*, p. 112.

17. Clay Lancaster, "Primitive Mural Painter of Kentucky," *American Collector*, December 1948, p. 7.

18. Ibid., p. 8.

19. Perhaps named for Minerva in Roman mythology, who was the goddess of wisdom, invention, and handicraft.

20. A visit to this site in January 2001 sadly revealed that house and stenciling had vanished!

21. Patrick, *Architecture in Tennessee*, p. 3.

22. Getty, *Carroll's Heritage*, p. 86.

23. Hutchison, "Domestic Architecture in Middle Tennessee," p. 404.

24. Letter from Mrs. Bert Prueher, General Winchester's great-granddaughter, to the author, April 1997.

25. Allen, *Cragfont*, p. 16.

26. McAlester and McAlester, *Field Guide to American Houses*, p. 82.

27. Geibner and Hulan, "Stencil House," *Historic American Building Survey*, TN-190, p. 2.

28. Fleming, "Folk Artist Jacob Maentel," p. 98.

29. In late 1774, before war with England was officially declared, the Provincial Congress of Massachusetts authorized the enrollment of twelve thousand men who should be prepared to take up arms at a minute's warning, thus the name "minutemen." There were similar organizations in other colonies, especially Virginia and Pennsylvania.

30. In 1801 a five-day interfaith revival meeting took place in Bourbon County, Kentucky. Many of the several thousand people in attendance, including Jaquess and his extended family, experienced the spiritual cleansing of the "Second Great Awakening."

31. Borkan, "Ohio Choices," p. 108.

32. Black, *Simplicity*.

33. The New Harmony State Historic Site is the location of two of America's earliest utopian communities. The Harmony Society, a German religious group led by George Rapp, existed there from 1814 to 1824, after which time it was purchased by Robert Owen, a British industrialist and social theorist who sought to create a more perfect society through free education and the abolition of social classes and personal wealth. This history is interpreted through a collection of properties owned and maintained by the society.

PART II: THE CLASSICAL GROUP (page 157)

1. Coffin, *Borders and Scrolls*, forward by Philip Parr, p. vii.
2. Nylander, Redmond, and Sander, *Wallpaper in New England*, p. 13.
3. Ibid., p. 91.
4. Prime, *Arts and Crafts in Philadelphia*, part II, p. 305.
5. Morison, *Maritime History of Massachusetts*, p. 25.

9. THE SOUTHERN NEW ENGLAND STATES
(pages 159–186)

1. Daniels, *Dissent and Conformity on Narragansett Bay*, p. 52.
2. Field, *State of Rhode Island*, II:505.
3. Waring, *Early American Stencils*, p. 19.
4. Channing, *Early Recollections of Newport*, p. 149.
5. Nylander, *Wall Papers*, p. 74.
6. Ibid., p. 24. For more information on Thomas Webb, see Field, *State of Rhode Island*, III:502.
7. Daniels, *Dissent and Conformity on Narragansett Bay*, p. 43.
8. The portico, probably added circa 1820 but missing when the house was purchased in 1981, was re-created from an 1870 photograph.
9. In 1790, after Rhode Island had reluctantly endorsed the federal Constitution, the state was divided into two customs districts, Newport and Providence. There were also six surveyors for the seven ports of delivery, one of which, Pawtuxet, was in the Providence district while the other six—North Kingstown, Wickford, East Greenwich, Westerly, Bristol, Warren, and Barrington—were in the Newport district. Field, *State of Rhode Island*, I:273.
10. Ibid., II:478.
11. Brown, *Salt Pork*, p. 1.
12. Kennedy, *Lincoln, Rhode Island*, p. 16.
13. Arnold, *Arnold Memorial*, p. 36.
14. The Ballou family owned land in Lincoln as early as the seventeenth century.
15. Nina Fletcher Little, *American Decorative Wall Painting*, p. 101.
16. Ibid., p. 143.
17. Robert O. Jones, *Warwick, Rhode Island*, p. 70.
18. Arnold, *Arnold Memorial*, p. 121.
19. Possibly executed by Rufus Porter, nineteenth-century artist, journalist, and scientist, who advertised his services as an ornamental painter in the *Providence Patriot* in November 1822 (p. 141).
20. A design similar to that seen in the Jacob Maentel painting at the beginning of part II.
21. Waring, *Early American Stencils*, p. 52.
22. Handler, "Temperance Tavern," p. 50.
23. Martin, *Authentic Stenciled Wall Designs*, design no. B13.
24. Benjamin Franklin came to Rhode Island in October 1775 to visit his "friends in the little colony on Narragansett Bay." He was on his way back to Philadelphia from Cambridge, Massachusetts, where he had met a young blacksmith-turned-

soldier from Rhode Island named Nathaniel Greene, who went on to become one of the most famous Revolutionary War generals. Keyes, *Ben Franklin*, p. 215.
25. Waring, *Early American Stencils*, p. 55.
26. Owen Jones, *Grammar of Ornament*, p. 39.
27. "Living with Antiques: The East Haddam Home of Frederic Palmer," *Antiques Magazine*, p. 56.
28. The design was recorded by Walpole artists Dutchie Peron and Norma Koson in 1979. The house was destroyed by fire in 1997.
29. Polly Forcier, *Border Wall Stencils from Vermont and New Hampshire*, p. 4.
30. Hard, *Rivers of America*, p. 166.
31. Pettit, *Printed and Painted Fabrics*, p. 89.
32. Ibid., p. 90.
33. Ibid., p. 159.
34. Ibid., p. 139.
35. Brazer, *27 Articles*, p. 12.
36. Morison, *Maritime History of Massachusetts*, p. 13.
37. Ibid., p. 23.
38. Ibid., p. 24.
39. Thomas Gage, commander in chief of the British army in America and governor-general of Massachusetts, after being forced to retreat from both Concord and Lexington in the first open hostilities between Britain and its recalcitrant Massachusetts colonists in April 1775, was reduced from governor to commander of forces occupying the city of Boston. He resigned in October 1775 and was succeeded by General William Howe as chief of the British forces in America.
40. Known as the Lindens, this fine colonial house, built by Robert Hooper shortly before the beginning of the Revolution, was purchased by George M. Morris in 1936 and moved to Washington, D.C. It contained five painted or stenciled floors, some of which were uncovered after the building was moved.
41. The frieze in this back room was included in Janet Waring's 1937 book between pages 56 and 57. This design is very similar to one in the Carr house (II.9) in Wickford, Rhode Island. The secondary border around the doorway is similar to one found in the Arnold house (II.7) in Apponaug, Rhode Island.
42. Alfred F. Shurrocks, "Fuller's Tavern," *Old Time England*, April 1928, p. 147.
43. Lafayette, valued officer of the Continental Army and close friend of General George Washington during the Revolution, was invited by President Monroe in 1824 to visit America as a guest of the Republic. He visited all twenty-four states and was received everywhere with demonstrations of love and respect. He departed with his spirits and his finances greatly elevated. In consideration of his important services and financial support to the Revolutionary cause, Congress voted to reward him with $200,000 in cash and a township of land.
44. Since before 1720, ferry service was available at the port of Bristol connecting the east and west sides of Narragansett Bay. Wood, *Turnpikes of New England*, p. 298.
45. Hepplewhite, *Cabinet-Maker and Upholsterer's Guide*, introduction by Joseph Aronson, p. v.

46. Nylander, Redmond, and Sander, *Wallpaper in New England*, p. 76.

47. Waring, *Early American Stencils*, p. 32.

48. Ibid., p. 55.

49. Margaret Coffin reports that the scroll painter also scribed lines into the plaster to aid the layout of decoration, *Borders and Scrolls*, p. 5.

50. Innerwick was demolished in the 1970s.

51. It sported a sign dated 1765 hanging at its door depicting a post rider carrying the English flag—an interesting sign for a tavern whose keeper (Caleb Grosvenor) was said to be a loyal patriot with two sons serving during the Revolution!

52. The Boston Turnpike Company was incorporated by the Connecticut legislature in October 1797 to build a road from Hartford through the towns of East Hartford, Bolton, Coventry, Mansfield, Ashford, Pomfret, and Thompson to the Massachusetts line.

53. Brown, *Salt Pork*, p. 60.

54. Sandra relates that the house was vacant except for a large family of bees who strongly objected to her presence, making the job rather challenging.

10. THE NORTHERN NEW ENGLAND STATES (pages 187–223)

1. Cummings and Candee, in Roger Moss, ed., *Paint in America*, p. 13.

2. Little and Little, *Collection Catalogue*, part II, item #1054.

3. Patricia Johnston, "William Matthew Prior," *Early American Life*, June 1979, p. 20.

4. It is interesting to note that Reverend Foxcroft reportedly remained loyal to the king of England during the Revolutionary War, as did at least 20 percent of the population. The reverend, then, would hardly have been a suitable client for the nephew of Paul Revere!

5. Antoine-Alexis Cadet-de-Vaux, "Memoir on a Method of Painting with Milk," *The Repertory of Arts and Manufactures*, London, 1801, p. 411.

6. Lipman, *Rufus Porter*, p. 180.

7. Ibid.

8. Fabian Collection, Special Collections, New Hampshire Historical Society, Concord, New Hampshire.

9. It bears some resemblance to the ruffed grouse, a popular subject of early artists and textile designers. See example 41 in John Audubon's *Birds of America*.

10. Hurd, *History*, p. 496.

11. Nina Fletcher Little, *Little by Little* (Boston: Society for the Preservation of New England, distrib. by University Press of New England, 1998), p. 96.

12. Hurd, *History*, p. 485.

13. Ayres, *British Folk Art*, p. 110.

14. Moore, "Academy at New Hampton," p. 8.

15. Clark, *Eastern Frontier*, p. 337.

16. Martha McDanolds Frizzell, *A History of Walpole* (Walpole, N.H.: Walpole Historical Society, 1963), p. 14.

17. Ibid., p. 192.

18. Hurd, *History*, p. 496.

19. Waring, *Early American Stencils*, p. 50.

20. Ibid., p. 52.

21. Marjorie Whalen Smith, *Historic Homes of Cheshire County*, II:63.

22. Clark, *Eastern Frontier*, p. 227.

23. Bond, "A Treasury of Old Stenciled Walls," fall 1999, p. 18.

24. Ibid., p. 28.

25. Ibid., p. 32.

26. Ibid., fall 1997, p. 32.

27. Coffin, *Borders and Scrolls*, p. 10.

28. Nina Fletcher Little, *The Connecticut Antiquarian*, December 1953, p. 24.

11. STATE OF NEW YORK AND THE NIAGARA PENINSULA (pages 224–232)

1. Evans, *American Furniture*, p. 100.

2. Burrows and Wallace, *Gotham*, p. 375.

3. Ibid., p. 695.

4. Ibid., Walt Whitman quote, p. 706.

5. Kuhns, *German and Swiss Settlements*, p. 50.

6. French, *Gazetteer*, p. 257.

7. Parr and Wass, *Wall Stenciling in Western New York*, p. 14.

8. Minhinnick, "Paint in Early Ontario," p. 24.

9. Ibid., p. 22.

12. STATES BELOW THE MASON-DIXON LINE (pages 233–242)

1. George Reed I became the most prominent political figure in Delaware during the eighteenth century, signing both the Declaration of Independence and the Constitution of the United States. He held many public offices, including acting president of the State of Delaware, U.S. senator for Delaware, and chief justice and attorney general for Delaware.

2. The Read house stenciling was re-created by Linda Croxson and Philip Ward of Locustville, Virginia.

3. In 1799 Latrobe became America's first professional architect when he designed the Bank of Pennsylvania in Philadelphia. After the burning of Washington, D.C., in 1814, Latrobe reconstructed the nation's capital in a combination of classical Greek, Roman, and Egyptian motifs, thus introducing America to a classical interpretation of architecture and furniture.

4. Virginia Historic Landmarks Commission, National Register of Historic Places Inventory—Nomination Form, Massanutton Heights, 1975.

5. Massanutten Mountain, Page County, Virginia, was home to a separatist Swiss-German religious community.

6. *Folk and Decorative Art of the Shenandoah Valley* (Bridgewater, Va.: Shenandoah Valley Folklore Society, 1993), p. 5.

7. Schaffer and Klein, *American Painted Furniture*, p. 162.

8. Prime, *Arts and Crafts in Philadelphia*, II:29.
9. *Folk and Decorative Art* (see note 6 above), p. 7.

APPENDIX B: WALL STENCILING WHO'S WHO
(pages 245–246)

1. The museum previously known as the Museum of American Folk Art changed its name to American Folk Art Museum in 2002.

Bibliography

Allen, Edward B. *Early American Wall Paintings, 1710–1850.* New Haven: Yale University Press, 1926

Allen, Ward. "Cragfont: Grandeur on the Tennessee Frontier." *Tennessee Historical Quarterly,* vol. 23, no. 2, June 1964.

Arnold, Elisha Stephen. *The Arnold Memorial: William Arnold of Providence and Pawtuxet, 1587–1675.* Rutland, Vt.: Tuttle Publishing Co., 1935.

Audubon, John James. *The Birds of America.* London: Published by the author, 1827–30.

Ayres, James. *British Folk Art.* Woodstock, N.Y.: Overlook Press, 1977.

———. *Building the Georgian City.* New Haven: Yale University Press, 1998.

———. *The Shell Book of the Home in Britain.* London: Faber & Faber, 1981.

Black, Mary. *Simplicity, a Grace: Jacob Maentel in Indiana.* Evansville, Ind.: Evansville Museum of Arts & Science, 1989.

Blackmer, Ramone, Barbara Green, and Gloria Taylor; *A Pictorial History of Stockbridge and Gaysville, 1761–1976.* Bethel, Vt.: Spaulding Press, 1986.

Bond, Jessica Hill. "A Treasury of Old Stenciled Walls, 1810–1840." 6 installments in *The Decorator,* biannual publication of the Historical Society of Early American Decoration, fall 1997 to fall 2000.

Borkan, Christine Edwards. "Ohio Choices: Wall Stenciling in the Western Reserve before 1860." Master's thesis, University of Delaware Early American Culture Program, 1990.

Brazer, Esther Stevens. *Early American Decoration.* Springfield, Mass.: The Pond-Ekberg Co., 1940.

———. *27 Articles by Esther Stevens Brazer.* Reprinted from *Antiques Magazine.* Uxbridge, Mass.: Taft Printing Co., 1947.

Bremer, Francis. *The Puritan Experiment,* rev. ed. Hanover, N.H.: University Press of New England, 1995.

Bridenbaugh, Carl. *Vexed and Troubled Englishmen, 1590–1642.* New York: Oxford University Press, 1968.

Brown, Henry A. L. *Salt Pork and Poor Bread and Whiskey.* Bowie, Md.: Heritage Books, 1997.

Burrows, Edwin G., and Mike Wallace. *Gotham: A History of New York City to 1898.* New York: Oxford University Press, 1999.

Cady, John Hutchins. *The Civic and Architectural Development of Providence.* Providence: Aderman Standard Press, 1957.

Channing, George G. *Early Recollections of Newport, Rhode Island.* Newport, R.I.: Nichols & Noyes, 1868.

Clark, Charles E. *The Eastern Frontier.* New York: Alfred A. Knopf, 1970.

Coffin, Margaret. *Borders and Scrolls: Early American Brush Stroke Wall Painting, 1790–1820.* Albany, N.Y.: Albany Institute of History and Art, 1986.

Crawford, Mary Caroline. *Little Pilgrimages: Old New England Inns.* Boston: L. C. Page & Co., 1924.

Cummins and White. *The Federal Period: New York.* New York: Benziger, 1972.

Curtis, John Obed. "The Lives of a 1719 Saltbox." *Early American Homes,* October 1997.

Daboll, Nathan. *The New England Almanack and Gentlemen and Ladies Diary.* New London, Conn., 1803.

Daniels, Bruce C. *Dissent and Conformity on Narragansett Bay.* Middletown, Conn.: Wesleyan University Press, 1983.

De Dampierre, Florence. *The Best of Painted Furniture.* New York: Rizzoli, 1987.

Delaney, Edmund. *The Connecticut River, New England's Historic Waterway.* Chester, Conn.: Globe Pequot Press, 1983.

Devoe, Shirley Spaulding. *Decorative Arts: 18th and 19th Century Research and Writing of Shirley Spaulding Devoe.* Compiled and edited by Shirley S. Baer and M. Jeanne Gearin. Historical Society of Early American Decoration, 1999.

Digan, Anne, and Mary Catherine Smith. *Nellis Tavern: A Preliminary Report.* Cooperstown, N.Y.: Cooperstown Graduate Program, 1983.

Doerflinger, Thomas M. *A Vigorous Spirit of Enterprise: Merchants and Economic Development in Revolutionary Philadelphia.* Chapel Hill, N.C.: University of North Carolina Press, 1986.

Dow, George Francis. *The Arts and Crafts in New England, 1704–1775.* New York: DaCapo Press, 1967.

Downing, Antoinette F. *Early Homes of Rhode Island,* Richmond, Va.: Garrett & Massie, 1937.

Downing, Antoinette F., and Vincent J. Scully, Jr. *The Architectural Heritage of Newport, Rhode Island, 1640–1915.* New York: American Legacy Press, 1982.

Dumas, David C. *Hero's Reward: Military Land Grants and the Opening of the West.* Providence: Charles G. Cowan, 1988.

Durham, Walter T. *James Winchester, Tennessee Pioneer.* Nashville, Tenn.: Parthenon Press, 1979.

Eaton, Daniel C. *Eaton Family from 1635 to the Fifth Generation.* New Haven, Conn.: Tuttle, Norehouse & Taylor, 1884.

Editors of the Early American Society. *Early Homes of Rhode Island*. New York: Arno Press, 1977.

Evans, Nancy Goyne. "The Christina M. Nestell Drawing Book." *American Furniture*. Milwaukee: Chipstone Foundation, distrib. by University Press of New England, 1998.

Ewbank, Thomas. *Report of the Commissioner of Patents for the Year 1849*. Washington, D.C.: Office of Printers to the Senate, 1850.

Fales, Dean A., Jr. *American Painted Furniture, 1660–1880*. New York: E. P. Dutton, 1979.

Faris, John T. *Old Trails and Roads in Penn's Land*. Philadelphia: J. B. Lippincott Co., 1927.

Federal Writers' Project of the Works Progress Administration for the State of Connecticut. *A Guide to Its Roads, Lore and People*. Boston: Houghton Mifflin Co., 1938.

Field, Edward. *State of Rhode Island and Providence Plantations at the End of the Century: A History*. Vols. I and II. Boston: The Mason Publishing Co., 1902.

Fleming, Mary Lou Robson. "Folk Artist Jacob Maentel of Pennsylvania and Indiana." *Pennsylvania Folklife*, vol. 37, no. 3, spring 1988.

———. "Jacob Maentel: A Second Look." *Pennsylvania Folklife*, autumn 1991.

Fletcher, Margaret. *Wall Stencils in Rhode Island*. Report of the Consultant Bureau of the Providence Preservation Society, 1973.

Foley, Edwin. *The Book of Decorative Furniture: Its Form, Colour, and History*. London: T. C. & E. C. Jack, 1911.

Forcier, Polly. *Floor Stencils of New England*. Norwich, Vt., 1990. Catalogue.

Fowler, Daryl J. "Consolidation of a Medieval Dairy: Cogges Farm Museum." *APT Bulletin, The Journal of Preservation Technology*, vol. 20, no. 1, 1988.

Freeman, Robert Eliot. *Cranston, Rhode Island*. Statewide Historical Preservation Report, P-C-1, 1980.

French, J. H. *Gazetteer of the State of New York*. Syracuse, N.Y.: R. Pearsall Smith, 1860.

Gamon, Albert T. "The Peter Wentz Farmstead." *Antiques*, vol. 122, no. 4, October 1982.

Getty, Joe. *Carroll's Heritage*. Westminster, Md.: Johnson Graphics, 1987.

Giebner, Robert C., and Richard H. Hulan. *Historic American Buildings Survey*, TN-190. Written in 1972, transmitted to the Library of Congress in 1985.

Grady, Anne A., Lucinda A. Brockway, Chris L. Eaton, and Brian Powell. *The Goodale Farm, Historic Structure Report*. Boston: Society for the Preservation of New England Antiquities (SPNEA), 1990.

Greenaway, Cara. *Interior Decorative Painting in Nova Scotia*. Art Gallery of Nova Scotia, 1986.

Guehan, Yannick, and Roger Le Puil. *The Handbook of Painted Decoration*. New York: W. W. Norton & Co., 1996.

Hamilton, Jean. *An Introduction to Wallpaper*. London: Her Majesty's Stationary Office, 1983.

Handler, Mimi. "The Temperance Tavern at Gilmanton Four Corners." *Early American Life*, August 1993.

Hard, Walter. *The Rivers of America—the Connecticut*. New York: Rinehart & Co., 1947.

Hatch, Alden. *Byrds of Virginia*. New York: Holt, Rinehart and Winston.

Hepplewhite, George. *The Cabinet-Maker and Upholsterer's Guide*, 3d ed. of 1794. New York: Dover Publications, 1969.

Horsman, Reginald. *The Frontier in the Formative Years*. New York: Holt, Rinehart & Winston, 1970.

Hughes, Helen. "The Reclamation of Lost Architectural Paint Finishes." *Traditional Paint News* vol. 1, no. 1 (Edinburgh, 1995).

Hulling, Ray Greene. "The Rhode Island Emigration to Nova Scotia." *The Narragansett Historical Register*, vol. 7, no. 2, April 1889.

Hultgren, William O., Kevinetta O'Brien, David Orrell, and Allen H. Reid. *The Way We Were: A Charlton Photographic History*. Charlton, Mass.: Charlton Historical Society, 1992.

Hurd, D. Hamilton. *History of Merrimack and Belknap Counties, New Hampshire*. Philadelphia: J. D. Lewis and Co., 1885.

Hutchinson, Albert W., Jr. "Domestic Architecture in Middle Tennessee." *Antiques Magazine*, September 1971.

Jones, Leigh Rehner. "Nineteenth Century Interior Decorative Wall Painting in Central New York." Master's thesis, New York State Historical Association, Cooperstown, New York, 1979.

Jones, Owen. *The Grammar of Ornament*. England, 1856. Reprint, New York: Portland House, 1986.

Jones, Robert O. *Warwick, Rhode Island*. Statewide Historical Preservation Report K-W-1, 1981.

Kennedy, Hazel Wade. *A Guide to Historic Pawtuxet*. Providence: Oxford Press, 1972.

Kennedy, Pamela A. *Lincoln, Rhode Island*. Statewide Historical Preservation Report P-L-1, 1982.

Kennedy, Roger G. *Orders from France: The Americans and the French in a Revolutionary World, 1780–1820*. New York: Alfred A. Knopf, 1989.

Kenney, John Tarrant. *The Hitchcock Chair*. New York: Clarkson N. Potter, 1971.

Keyes, Nelson Beecher. *Ben Franklin: An Affectionate Portrait*. Surrey, Eng. World's Work, 1956.

Kilbourne, John D. *History of the Borough of Stewartstown*. Compiled 1951.

Kuhns, Oscar. *The German and Swiss Settlements of Colonial Pennsylvania*. New York: Henry Holt and Co., 1901.

Lancaster, Clay. *Antebellum Architecture of Kentucky*. Lexington, Ky.: University of Kentucky Press, 1991.

Lindsey, Jack L. *Worldly Goods: The Arts of Early Pennsylvania, 1689–1758*. Philadelphia: Philadelphia Museum of Art, 1999.

Lipman, Jean. *Rufus Porter Rediscovered*. New York: Clarkson N. Potter, 1968.

———. *Techniques in American Folk Decoration*. 1951. Reprint, New York: Dover Publications 1972.

Little, Bertram K., and Nina Fletcher Little. *Collection Catalogue*. Parts I and II. New York: Sotheby's, 1994

Little, Nina Fletcher. *American Decorative Wall Painting, 1799–1850*. 1952. Reprint, New York: E. P. Dutton & Co., 1973.

———. *Floor Coverings in New England Before 1850*. Sturbridge, Mass.: Old Sturbridge Village, 1967.

———. *Neat and Tidy*. Boston: Society for the Preservation of New England Antiquities, distrib. by University Press of New England, 2001.

Lockwood, Ernest L. *Episodes in Warwick History*. Providence: Snow & Frenham, 1937.

Lord, Ruth. *Henry F. Du Pont and Winterthur: A Daughter's Portrait*. New Haven: Yale University Press, 1999.

Lossing, Benson J. *Harpers' Popular Cyclopaedia of United States History*. New York: Harper & Brothers, 1893.

Lynch, Ancelin V. *Foster, Rhode Island: Statewide Historical Preservation Report*, P-F-1, 1982.

Magnuson, Rosalind. *An Architectural Walking Tour of Kennebunk's National Register Historic District*. Kennebunk, Maine: The Brick Store Museum, 1993.

Marlowe, George Francis. *Coaching Roads of Old New England*. New York: Macmillan Co., 1945.

Martin, Gina. *Authentic Stenciled Wall Designs*. Catalogue with line drawings, 1970s.

McAlester, Virginia, and Lee McAlester. *A Field Guide to American Houses*. New York: Alfred A. Knopf, 1995.

McLaughlin, Kathleen, editor. *Nellis-Nelles: Immigrants from the Palatinate, 1710*. Vol. I. Herkimer County Historical Society, 1997.

McGrath, Robert L. *Early Vermont Wall Paintings, 1790–1850*. Hanover, N.H.: University Press of New England, 1972.

McPartland, Martha R. *The History of East Greenwich, R.I.* East Greenwich Free Library Association, 1960.

Middleton, Alicia Hopton, compiler. *Life in Carolina and New England*. Bristol, R.I.: Privately printed, 1929.

Minhinnick, Jeanne. *At Home in Upper Canada*. Erin, Ont.: Boston Mills Press, 1994.

———. "Paint in Early Ontario." *APT Bulletin*, vol. 7, no. 2, 1970.

Moore, Norma Jean. "An Academy at New Hampton." *The Hamptonia Magazine*, New Hampton School, fall 1996.

Morison, Samuel Eliot. *The Maritime History of Massachusetts, 1783–1869*. Boston: Northeastern University Press, 1979.

———. *The Oxford History of the American People*. New York: Oxford University Press, 1965.

Morrison, Hugh. *Early American Architecture*. New York: Dover Publications, 1987.

Moss, Robert W., editor. *Paint in America*. Washington, D.C.: Preservation Press, 1994.

Nebiker, Walter A. *Historic and Architectural Resources of Glocester, Rhode Island*. Preliminary report. Providence: Rhode Island Preservation Commission, 1980.

———. *Historic and Architectural Resources of Smithfield, Rhode Island*. Providence: Rhode Island Preservation Commission, 1992.

Nylander, Richard C. *Wall Papers for Historic Buildings*, 2d ed. Washington, D.C.: Preservation Press, 1992.

Nylander, Richard C., Elizabeth Redmond, and Penny J. Sander. *Wallpaper in New England*. Boston: Society for the Preservation of New England Antiquities (SPNEA), 1986.

O'Callaghan, M. D. *Documentary History of the State of New York*. 3 vols. Albany, N.Y.: Wee, Parsons & Co., 1850.

Parkes, Bonnie Wehle. "The History and Technology of Floorcloths." *APT Bulletin*, vol. 21, nos. 3–4, 1989.

Parr, Philip, and Janice Tauer Wass. *Wall Stenciling in Western New York, 1800–1840*. Rochester, N.Y.: Rochester Museum & Science Center, 1985.

Patrick, James. *Architecture in Tennessee, 1768–1898*. Knoxville, Tenn.: University of Tennessee Press, 1981.

Pease, John C., and John M. Niles. *A Gazetteer of the State of Connecticut and Rhode Island*. Hartford, Conn.: William S. March, 1819.

Pettit, Florence H. *America's Printed and Painted Fabrics, 1600–1900*. New York: Hastings House, 1970.

Prime, Alfred Coxe. *The Arts and Crafts in Philadelphia, Maryland and South Carolina, 1721–1785*. Parts I and II. New York: DaCapo Press, 1969.

Randall, Willard Sterne. *Benedict Arnold, Patriot and Traitor*. New York: Quill/William Morrow, 1990.

Rogers, L. E., editor. *The Biographical Cyclopedia of Representative Men of Rhode Island*. Providence: National Biographical Publishing Co., 1881.

Russell, Howard S. *A Long, Deep Furrow: Three Centuries of Farming in New Hanover, New Hampshire*. Hanover, N.H.: University Press of New England, 1967.

Sayer, Robert. *The Ladies Amusement or Whole Art of Japanning Made Easy*. Bath, Eng.: Harding and Curtis, 1966. Facsimile reprint.

Schaffner, Cynthia V. A., and Susan Klein. *American Painted Furniture, 1790–1880*. New York: Clarkson Potter, 1997.

Shuway, Floyd, and Richard Hegel, editors. *New Haven: An Illustrated History*. Woodland Hills, Calif.: Windsor Publications, 1981.

Smith, Marjorie Whalen. *Historic Homes of Cheshire County, New Hampshire*. Vols. I, II and III. Brattleboro, Vt.: Griswold Offset Printing, 1971.

Smith, Robert E., editor. *Palatine Settlement Society Newsletter* (St. Johnsville, N.Y.), summer 1988.

Tarbox, Sandra. "Fanciful Graining—Tools of the Trade." *Clarion Magazine* (New York), fall 1981.

Wall, Alexander J. "Time Stone Farm." *New York Historical Society Quarterly Bulletin*, April 1936.

Waring, Janet. *Early American Stencils on Walls and Furniture*. New York: William R. Scott, 1937.

Warren, Elizabeth Sargent. *Historic and Architectural Resources of Bristol, Rhode Island*. Providence: Rhode Island Preservation Commission, 1990.

———. *Historic and Architectural Resources of Pawtuxet Village, Cranston and Warwick*. Report P-K-1. Providence: Rhode Island Preservation Commission, 1972.

———. *Historic and Architectural Resources of Warren, Rhode Island*. Report B-W-1. Providence: Rhode Island Preservation Commission, 1975.

Weiss, Ellen. *North Kingstown, Rhode Island.* Statewide Historical Preservation Report, K-W-1. Providence: Rhode Island Preservation Commission, 1979

Wenger, Diane. "Samuel Rex's Country Store." In *Historic Schaefferstown.* Lebanon, Pa.: Historic Schaefferstown, Inc., 1996.

Weston, Thomas. *History of Middleboro, Massachusetts.*

White, Colonel Hunter C. *Wickford and Its Old Houses.* Rhode Island: The Main Street Association, 1960.

White, John Barber. *Genealogy of the Descendants of Thomas Gleason of Watertown, Massachusetts, 1607–1909.* Bowie, Md.: Heritage Books, 1992. Facsimile reprint.

Wood, Frederick J. *The Turnpikes of New England.* Boston: Marshall Jones Co., 1919.

Wood, Sumner Gilbert. *The Taverns and Turnpikes of Blandford, 1733–1833.* Blandford, Mass.: Published by author, 1908.

———. *Ulster Scots and Blandford Scouts.* Blandford, Mass.: Published by author, 1928.

Wright, Louis B. *American Heritage History of the Thirteen Colonies.* New York: Simon & Schuster, 1967.

Young, E. H. *History of Pittsfield, N.H.,* 1953.

Zahn, Guillaume. *Beaux Ornemens et les Tableaux les plus Remarquables de Pompeii.* Berlin, 1828.

Zea, Philip, and Suszanne L. Flynt. *Hadley Chests.* Deerfield, Mass.: Pocumtuck Valley Memorial Association, 1992.

Zeinert, Karen. *The Amistad Slave Revolt.* North Haven, Conn.: Linnet Books, 1997.'

Index

Abbey Aldrich Rockefeller Folk Art Center, 154

Acorn border (stenciled), 51 fig.

Adamesque (style), 157, 170, 189, 236

Adams, John (president), 57

Age of Classicisms, 157

Airville, Pa., 104, 106

Albany, N.Y., 74

Allen, Edward B., 190, 245

Allen, Ethan, 86

American Folk Art Museum (AFAM), 56, 79, 184

American Institute for Conservation (AIC), 247

American Museum in Britain, Bath, England, 48

Amherst College, Mass., 89

Anderson-Lucas (house), 124

Angell, Daniel (tavern), 165, 166 & fig.

Annabal, Norma, 85

Anne (queen of England), 73, 83

Antebellum, 249

Antes, Henry (house), 99

Antietam Hall, 115

Antiquarian and Landmarks Society, Connecticut, 50

Appalachin Mountains, 151

Appomattox Court House, Va., 121–123

Apponaug, R.I., 168

Apprentice system, 2

Apron, stenciled, 69 fig.

Arch and candle motif (frieze), 18 fig., 25 fig., 51 fig., 63 fig., 89 fig.

Argyle, N.Y., 76

Arnold, Benedict (colonel), 55

Arnold, Thomas (house), 168 & figs.

Arter, Solomen (house), 114 & fig.

Arts and Crafts in Philadelphia, Maryland and South Carolina, 99

Ashland, N.Y., 78

Association for Preservation Technology (APT), 247

Augusta County, Va., 126

Aurora, Ohio, 132

Badger, Daniel, 119

Ballou, Nathan (house), 167 & fig.

Ballroom(s), stenciled, xi, 100 fig., 116 fig., 165 fig., 177 fig.

Barge (flatboat), 44, 152, 171

Barrington, R.I., 161

Barrows (house), 221

Barry, Edith Cleaves, 59, 189

Barry, William F., 59

Bartling, Daniel, 222, 223 fig.

Base coat, 249

Baseboard(s), painted, 5, 22, 110 fig., 111 fig., 122, 128 fig.

Batchelder, Captain Abraham (house), 203 & fig., 204 & figs.

Bates, Stephen (house), 229 & fig.

Bath, England, 48

Battey-Barden (house), 28 & figs.

Battlefield House, 232

Beamer Tavern, 231

Bell-and-swag motif, 21 fig., 24 fig., 26 fig., 34 fig., 37 fig., 43 fig., 45 fig., 53 fig.

Belle Grove Plantation, 238

Bellows, Benjamin, 211

Bellows, Colonel Caleb (house), 211 & fig.

Berkshire Mountains, 41, 50, 132, 179

Bernham, Thatch, 195

Berry, Major William (house), 62 & fig., 63 & figs.

Bethany, N.Y., 90

Betts and Langdon, 40 fig., 245

Bidwell Tavern, 148

Binder, for making paint, 243

Binghamton Sunday Press, 227

"Bird Man of Loudon, The," 203

Bishop, Adele, 76

Black, Mary B., 154

Blackstone River, 167

Blackstone, William, 167

Blandford Historical Society, 40

Blandford, Mass., 40

Bledsoe Creek, Tenn., 144

Bleecher Building, Hermanus, 79

Bond, Jessica Hill, 42, 131, 217, 220, 245

Boone, Daniel (Wilderness Trail), 140

"Border Group," 157

"Borderman," 62

Borkan, Christine Edwards, 125, 130, 131, 245

Boston News Letter, 172

Boston, Mass., 172

Bourbon County, Ky., 137

Bradley, S.C., 127

Brazer, Esther Stevens, x, 39, 79, 183, 190, 245

Brick Store Museum, 59, 189

Bridgeman, Marion, 137

Bristol, Amos (tavern), 224 fig., 227 & fig., 228 & fig.

Brockville, Ont., Canada, 97

Brown, John (abolitionist), 134

Brown, John (house), 94 & fig., 95

Brown, Owen, 134

Brown, Susanne R. L., 63

Brownsburg, Va., 124

Broz, Rose A., 154

Brushworks Decorative Painting Co., 241

Buck, Susan, 236, 245

Buffalo Trace, 138

Bullin, Jeduthan, 245

Bump Tavern, 78 & fig., 79 & fig.

Bunch of Grapes Tavern, Boston, 129

Burner, John (house), 237 & fig.

Burnett, Carter, 78

Busbequius (Austrian ambassador), 74

Butler's Rangers, 94

Cabbage Rose motif, 85, 95, 131

Cadet-de-Vaux, Antoine-Alexis, 194

Cady (house), 72

Calico printer(s), 172

Campbell, Laughlin, 76

Canada, 91; Lower (Quebec), 93, 220; Upper (Ontario), 93

Canals, 44, 74

Canandaigua, N.Y., 229

Canning, John, 47, 52, 53, 236, 245

Captain General's Cavaliers, 26

Carli, Othman, 102

Carlisle, John (house), 213 & fig., 214 & figs.

Carr (house), 52

Carr, Samuel (house), 170 & fig., 171 figs.

Carroll County, Md., 144

Carter, Robert ("King"), 4

Casein (paint), 243

DATE DUE